'FIFTIES FLASHBACK

by
Albert Drake

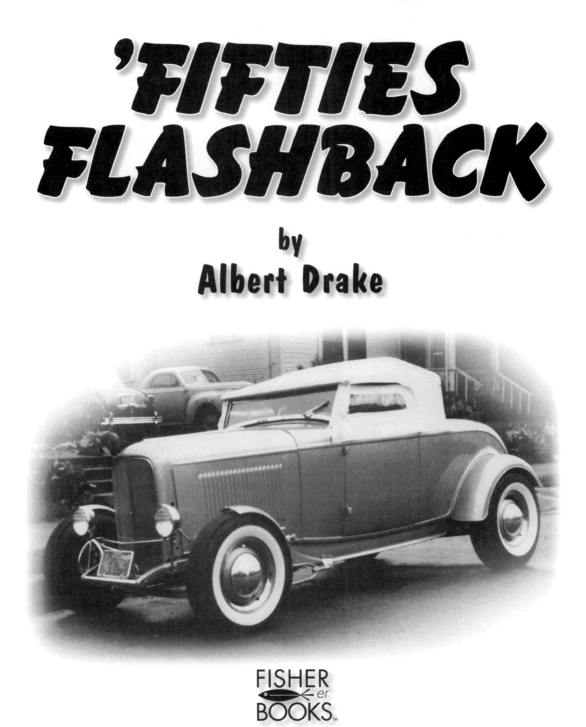

FISHER
BOOKS

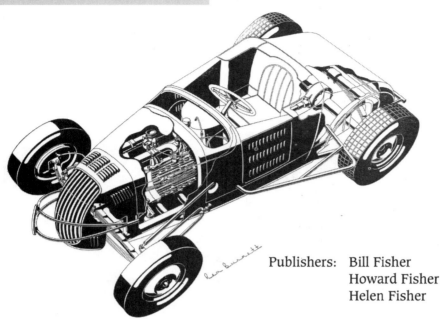

Publishers: Bill Fisher
              Howard Fisher
              Helen Fisher

Managing Editor: Sarah Trotta

Editor: Bill Fisher

Cover Art,
Interior Design
and Production: Gary D. Smith, Performance Design

Photography
from the
collections of: Al Drake, Bill Fisher, Gary D. Smith

©1998 Albert Drake

Published by Fisher Books
4239 W. Ina Rd., Suite 101
Tucson, AZ 85741
520-744-6110
www.FISHERBOOKS.com

ISBN 1-55561-161-3

Printed in U.S.A.

Printing 10 9 8 7 6 5 4 3 2 1

Contents

Acknowledgments

The following essays first appeared in *Rod Action* as the "'Fifties Flashbacks" column. My thanks to editors Brian Brennan, Steve Anderson, Eric Pierce, Jon Gobetti and Rex Reese.

Back Row Specials
A Hot Rodder's Wish Book
Hubcaps
Rappin' Pipes
Why There Were Hot Rods at
    Mid-Century
The Lost Pix
Clubs
Street *Was* Fun in '51
Not-So-Hot Rods
Top Rods
Gettin' Down
Traditional vs. Non-traditional
'29 A-Willys Roadster
Study Hall Mechanix
Street Racing
The Day They Broke 100 MPH at
    Scappoose
1953: The Year of the Dragster
What We Read: Books
What We Read: The Clymer
    Books
The Good Old Bad Days
Gook Wagon
1953 Oakland Roadster Show
The Cherry
The Beast

We Never Called Them Kemps
Bonneville 1955
Biker!
I Remember the Day James Dean
    Died Like It Was Yesterday
Things I Don't Remember
Update on Blue Dots, Dice and
    Flamers
The Service Station
Memento Mori

The following essays first appeared in *Street Rodding Illustrated* as the "Nifty 'Fifties" column." My thanks to editors Jerry Dexter, Phillipe Dahn and Tom Vogele.

Track Roadsters
What We Read: Magazines
What We Read: *Hot Rod Comics*
What We Read: Henry Gregor
    Felsen's Novels

The following essays first appeared in *Rodder's Digest* as the "Textures of the 'Fifties" column. My thanks to editor Gerry Burger.

Textures of the 'Fifties
The Mild Custom
The Mild Custom II

The above essays are reprinted with permission.

The remaining essays were written especially for this book.

Thanks once again to my son, Moss Drake, for being my riding mechanic on the computer: we won!

Photos from the collections of:
Al Drake
Bill Fisher
Gary D. Smith

About the Author

Albert Drake has been a hot rodder since 1951, when he built a '29 A-V8 roadster and joined the old Road Angels club. That same year he became a charter member of the Columbia Timing Association (CTA) and the National Hot Rod Association (NHRA) (membership #4054).

In addition to the *'Fifties Flashbacks* column that he has written for *Rod Action* for 16 years, he's published some 300 articles and features in *Street Rodder, Rodder's Digest, Rod Action, Popular Cars, Custom Car, American Rodder, Collector Car, Old Cars Weekly, Hot Rod & Custom* (England) and others.

His automotive books include *Street Was Fun in '51*, the first book on historical hot rodding; *Hot Rodder!*, the first history of hot rodding from the 'Twenties to the 'Nineties; and *Flat Out*, the history of So-Cal dry lake competition from 1930-50. Although his primary interest is rod and custom history, he has written two books on the Pontiac GTO: *The Big 'Little GTO' Book*, a definitive history, and *Herding Goats*, an oral history.

Author Al Drake beside 1934 Ford coupe. Photo by Dale Moreau, 1996.

One Saturday in 1954, the Road Angels held a reliability run from the parking lot at Franklin High. It was a huge success, with lots of cars and people. I believe this 1949 Mercury coupe belonged to Joe Beard.

Joe Bailon brought "Miss Elegance," his radically customized 1941 Chevrolet Coupe, from California for the 1952 car show at the Exposition Center in Portland. Wheel covers were made from plow discs, the grille from tubing, and the front fenders recall the Tucker car. Later the car was destroyed, but Bailon is planning a clone.

Introduction

It's essential to remember specific, concrete details about rodding in the 'Fifties.

This book is a collection of selected "'Fifties Flashbacks," a column I've been writing for *Rod Action* for the past 16 years. Although they were written without book publication in mind, I welcome this opportunity to peruse my files, selecting and organizing past columns, plus adding some new and unpublished material into a book which will, I feel, give the reader a good idea of what it was like to be a hot rodder during the Fabulous 'Fifties.

Actually, the column came about by accident. During the winter of 1982 I was working on a book, *Street Was Fun in '51*, the *first* book on historical hot rodding, and it occurred to me that I could develop some of the ideas touched on in the book. A couple of years earlier, in 1980, I'd published two essays in *Rod Action*, and so I wrote a letter to the then-editor, Brian Brennan,

suggesting a column about 'Fifties rodding. Brian simply returned my letter with a paragraph circled in red ink and the words "great idea" written beside it. I wrote four columns, mailed them, and had several more written by the time the first column appeared in August 1982. One thing that has always interested me about writing the column is the length—it's long enough to develop an idea without being overly long. Because I've enjoyed writing the column and because it's been well-received by readers and the next six editors of *Rod Action* I worked with, I've continued to explore the possibilities of that time period. I also wrote columns for two other magazines: "Nifty 'Fifties" appeared in the now-defunct *Street Rodding Illustrated* and "Textures of the 'Fifties" appeared in *Rodder's Digest*.

What is this preoccupation with the 'Fifties? people ask. Well, when I began writing the column in 1982 the 'Fifties seemed just around the corner, and the things we did back then were vivid in my memory. Besides, the 'Fifties was my decade. I got interested in hot rods in 1950, was busy with rods, customs and motorcycles for nearly ten years, and by 1959, when I left town for the university, I simply didn't have the time or money to do more with cars. So when I think about rods and customs I think of the 'Fifties, because it was a great time.

How to explain the 'Fifties to someone too young to remember those years? Metaphorically, I could say it was one long picnic, the basket filled with tuna-fish sandwiches, fried chicken, Jello salad and Cokes, purely

American food, and no ants or mosquitoes. It was like falling in love: intense, beautiful, bittersweet at times. It was a ten-year vacation in a super-large hardware store, floor after floor filled with stuff Made in America. Sometimes the entire decade is compressed into a single image of a teenager sitting on a naked front tire tinkering with an engine, the sun hovering in a cloudless sky. Oh, of course it rained occasionally, then as now, and to be accurate I want to include the bad weather too. But in memory it seems as though the sun was always present.

Innocence and enthusiasm

It was a time of innocence and enthusiasm. There were far fewer people and many more personal freedoms. We enjoyed the paradox of low expectations and impossible dreams. There was a general spirit of optimism. It helped, of course, that everybody was young, and perhaps that condition alone colors my view of the decade.

Lately, using hindsight, some commentators have been deconstructing the decade, emphasizing negatives such as communism, the cold war and McCarthyism. They emphasize the conservative politics of the Eisenhower-Nixon years, and the repression felt by various groups. They want you to believe that the decade was a cold, hard time when conformity of mind and spirit was valued. They deride the notion that the emerging television families, as seen on "Leave It to Beaver" and "Father Knows Best", had anything in common with real families who, they say, were largely dysfunctional.

Well, I've lived through several decades, and the 'Fifties seems the decade with the most stability. There was the Depression of the 'Thirties, WW II raged through half of the 'Forties and social unrest characterized the 'Sixties. The 'Fifties seem like a quiet island of time. Although I grew up in a small house in a lower-class neighborhood, my life, in most ways, did not seem unlike the lives of Beaver Cleaver or Ricky Nelson. Fathers were off to work, mothers took care of things at home and kids were always up to some kind of high-jinks, and although this arrangement may not seem ideal to everyone today, it worked pretty well back then.

I'm always questioning my view of the 'Fifties, and I try to remember it clearly, from a personal perspective, because it's always easy to romanticize the past. So many years have disappeared since the 'Fifties, and the world has changed so much that people who did not live during the decade have trouble understanding the context of the times. For example, it's necessary to understand personal economics, and to realize that a dollar then was worth much more than a dollar today. I'm sure that people then, as now, were exploited economically, but the fact is that most people did not earn much money. In 1951 I earned 50¢ an hour working in a theater, and from 1953 to 1955 I earned $1.00 an hour working full-time in a garage. I later complained to myself about the low pay, and then recently I called a slightly older fellow I'd worked with and asked what he had earned. He had been paid only $1.65 an hour, and he was an experienced mechanic with a wife and several children to provide for. A rodder six years older than I am remembers working in a different garage where he made $37.50 for a 44-hour week.

Although this reminiscence on economics may seem like a digression, it's important because it puts things in perspective. While one could buy a nice 1936 Ford in the early 'Fifties for around $75—that is, two weeks' pay—a dual intake manifold cost $35 and aluminum racing heads cost $75. Therefore, it was common to see a rod with dual carbs and stock (or milled) heads. The amazing thing, given the low wages, was that guys had money to spend on a fixed-up car, and that they were willing to do it. An economist might say that in those days wages reflected more "real" money, the money left after taxes and various deductions. I always had lousy jobs, but in 1955 I owned a '29 A-V8 roadster, a beautiful 1947 Ford mild custom and a 1951 BSA Gold Star factory racer. What more could one ask for?

A spirit of optimism

It was this spirit of optimism that characterized the 'Fifties—anything was possible—on both the personal and national levels. I know I felt the optimism in the air—whether it was a miracle cure like the Salk vaccine that wiped out the dreaded infantile paralysis, or the advent of CinemaScope, or "hi-fi"—something *marvelous* was always happening.

At the same time there was a sense of stability and well-being. I was curious whether my personal outlook had been distorted by the passage of years, so I checked on what a scholar had to say:

"Never before had the United States enjoyed such great economic growth as it did during the 'Fifties. Except for brief

recessions at the end of the Korean War and in 1957-58, the country experienced unrivaled prosperity. The Gross National Product, which is the total of all the nation's goods and services, climbed from $318,000,000,000 in 1950 to an astounding $503,000,000,000 in 1960. The number of job holders rose from 53 million in 1950 to over 70 million by 1960. Moreover, the average family income climbed steadily during the decade. Stock market prices reached a record high. Basic industries, such as steel and oil, operated at near capacity. There were also some major new industries, such as computers and electronics."

I was unaware of all that during the 'Fifties, but it must have filtered into my consciousness to give me that feeling of optimism. My daily life was touched in smaller but equally amazing ways. In 1954 the first fast-food place opened near where I worked, and it served 19¢ hamburgers. One could get a hamburger, milkshake and French fries for only 45¢! I could see a new 3-D movie for a quarter. In 1955 I tasted pizza for the first time when a Shakey's opened in Portland. Our city had had television since 1948, but we didn't get a set until 1954. Although I spent most of my free time in the garage or cruising around, I loved to watch TV before going to bed, when the couple channels available showed old movies. It seemed like a minor miracle to be able to watch a movie in one's own front room.

50-million TV's

I've since read that in 1948 there were fewer than 17,000 TV sets in the entire United States, but by the end of the 'Fifties Americans owned roughly 50-million sets. Nearly 90% of all American families had television, and many had more than one set. What a dramatic change in how one spent one's leisure time. When *Hamlet* was shown on

Something marvelous was always happening.

"Mario Acquilino's Najinski-like flag waving leap starts a match race between a roadster and a chopped and channeled coupe" from Hot Rod Magazine, *December 1954.*

3

Frank "Ike" Iacono's GMC powered '33 Ford coupe turned the quarter at 121 mph. From December 1954 issue of Hot Rod Magazine.

television in 1953, more people watched it at home in one night than had seen it performed on stage in the 350 years since it was written! And don't forget the spin-offs, such as frozen TV dinners (introduced in 1954), and the TV trays to hold them.

Purely 'Fifties stuff!

The national car craze was born in the 'Fifties, and people really did love their cars. They needed them, as more people moved from the cities to the suburbs. The Federal Highway Act of 1956 provided billions of dollars to construct the modern interstate highway system that we enjoy today. Since it was no longer necessary to drive on the old two-lane roads, more people began taking long vacations by automobile. And what cars they were! Gorgeous, flashy and powerful. The horsepower race began in 1949 with the new Cadillac and Oldsmobile OHV V-8 engines. It accelerated considerably when Chrysler introduced its 180 hp V-8 in 1951. The fins of the 1948 Cadillac caught on, and by the mid-'Fifties almost every car had them. Yes, there were excesses: the fins got bigger, there was more chrome trim toward the end of the decade, but looking back, all the cars are

gorgeous—even some makes and models that weren't fully appreciated at the time.

So when I think about rods and customs I think of the 'Fifties because it was a great time. The economy was solid, people were working, the wheels of industry were constantly turning, Detroit was building terrific cars and America was the greatest country in the world.

The beginning of the 'Fifties was pretty much the beginning of rodding for most of the country, and everything was new. Hardly anyone had a chopped coupe or sedan. If you saw one, even on the pages of a magazine, it was exciting. Slightly modified cars were everywhere, and if you saw a car with even a couple changes, such as a nosed-and-decked job, you spent some time inspecting it. A friend of a friend bought a slightly used 1951 Mercury coupe and had the local garage install an Olds V-8 engine in it—talk about high tech! That seemed like the ultimate conversion, but it was really only the beginning of a major activity—engine swapping.

At the start of the decade the first car shows opened, and although they were small they were terribly exciting, permeated with the odors of lacquer thinner

and rubbing compound. And this was years before the advent of angel hair! Because it was the beginning there was nowhere to go but forward. At every drag race records were broken; it was a time of experimentation, and there was always a chance for the average guy to set a record. Drag strips began to open all over the country, the National Hot Rod Association (NHRA) was formed and by mid-decade, when the Drag Safari toured, drag racing had become a national activity.

Custom cars loomed large. By mid-decade anyone could afford an early 'Fifties Ford, Mercury or Chevrolet, and there was an abundance of chrome trim, taillights, grilles, etc., from new cars available for transplanting. As an indicator of the popularity of custom cars, by the late 'Fifties a half-dozen magazines were devoted to the lead sleds.

It's important to remember these things clearly. It's essential to remember specific, concrete details about rodding in the 'Fifties. As the year 2000 draws closer, the 'Fifties drop back, a time nearly a half-century past. In the middle of the 21st century, Hollywood, if it still exists, might want to make a movie about what kids did 100 years earlier. It can put a fenderless car before a drive-in facade and play a rock 'n roll sound track, but there might be some viewers who would leave the theater wondering what the 'Fifties were really like. My hope is that this book will inform them.

Back Row Specials

These were cars that were unattractive, undesirable or in some cases, not running.

The language of the classifieds was new to me. As I avidly read the automotive section ads I learned from my father that R&H meant radio and heater, something not all cars had, and that WSW meant white sidewall tires. The automotive ad section then was only a fraction of the size it is today in most papers, and the majority of the cars were new or fairly new, and too expensive for me. But every day there'd be a dozen or so cars within my price range, which was about $50. I'd draw a circle around a 1934 Chev coupe for $35, or a 1936 Ford sedan, R&H, for $45. Although I wanted a roadster or a '32 Ford coupe, for at least a day I'd dream about buying one of the budget-priced cars listed in the ads. I'd dream about adding duals, painting WSW on it, driving it to high school, imagine the looks of envy on the faces of my school chums, imagine girls asking if they could have a ride.

THE SUNDAY OREGONIAN, JUNE 27, 1948 ★ ★ ★ 15

For Sale—Used Cars

"Double Checked"
USED CARS
are
CITY TESTED
and
APPROVED
at
WINDOLPH MOTOR CO.
DRIVE
WITH THE KNOWLEDGE
YOU ARE SAFE.
NEW CAR WARRANTY
ON ALL
'46 AND '47 PONTIACS

'47 PONTIAC
8 sed. cpe., cream, R&H.
'46 PONTIAC
6 sed. cpe., maroon, R&H.
'47 PONTIAC
8 sed. cpe., gray, R&H.
'47 PONTIAC
8 Torp. sed., gray, R&H.
'47 PONTIAC
8 sed. cpe., black, R&H.
'47 PONTIAC
6 str. sed., gray, R&H.
'47 PONTIAC
str. sed., gray, R&H.
'47 PONTIAC
sed. cpe., black, R&H.
'46 PONTIAC
6 sed. cpe., maroon, R&H.
'47 PONTIAC
8 sed. cpe., two-tone gray. R&H.
'46 PONTIAC
6 Torp. sed., gray, R&H.
'46 PONTIAC
6 str. sed., blue, R&H.
'47 PONTIAC
8 sed. cpe., black, R&H.
'47 PONTIAC
8 str. sed. cpe., 2-tone gray, R&H.
'46 PONTIAC
6 Torp. sed., gray, R&H.
'47 PONTIAC
ced. cpe., gray. R&H.
'47 PONTIAC
8 sed. cpe., black, R&H.
'47 PONTIAC
2-dr., blue, R&H.

For Sale—Used Cars

Barnard Motors, Inc.
CADILLAC-OLDSMOBILE
TRADE-INS
MANY ARE ONE-OWNER
NO TRADE-INS REQUIRED
OUR GUARANTEE
YOUR PROTECTION

1947 LINCOLN Sedan. Beautiful tan finish. Radio, heater, overdrive. Excellent condition. Initial payment only $850, balance GMAC terms. Full price $2550.
1947 STUDEBAKER Land Cruiser. Radio, heater and overdrive. One owner; low mileage. Finished in very popular light grey color. Initial payment $865, bal. GMAC terms. Full price only $2595.
BARNARD MOTORS.
INC.
1946 OLDSMOBILE '76 Club Sedan. Beautiful dark blue finish and equipped with radio and heater. A very clean car. Initial payment $750, balance GMAC terms. Full price $2225.
CADILLAC-OLDSMOBILE
TRADE-INS
1946 OLDSMOBILE CONVERTIBLE coupe. This very popular model is equipped with radio, heater and hydramatic drive. Very low mileage and a one-owner car. Ideal for that vacation trip you are planning. Initial payment only $860, balance GMAC terms. Full price $2575.
BARNARD MOTORS
INC.
1947 BUICK CONVERTIBLE Coupe. Radio and heater. Light blue finish. Excellent condition throughout. Initial payment $925, balance GMAC terms. Full price $2725.
CADILLAC-OLDSMOBILE
TRADE-INS
1946 MERCURY CONVERTIBLE Coupe. Radio, heater and beautiful maroon finish. One-owner car with very low mileage. In-

For Sale—Used Cars

Braley & Graham
BUICK DISTRIBUTOR
FOR
OREGON

'41 PONTIAC 5-PASS COUPE. This popular body-type car features beautiful light blue duco, good rubber and is spotless, both inside and out and with radio and heater and only ---------- $1395
GMAC
TERMS
'39 DODGE COUPE—An economical car which is exceptionally clean, with the motor in A-1 shape. Heater, at ---------- 825
NO TRADES
REQUIRED
'39 PLYMOUTH 2-DOOR sedan. This car was owned by our senior mechanic and you can't find one in finer complete shape throughout. Radio and heater ---------- 895
GMAC
TERMS
'36 STUDEBAKER 4-DOOR sedan. Here is a lot of transportation for very little money. Plenty of worry-free miles ahead for only ---------- 345
NO TRADES
REQUIRED

Braley & Graham
BUICK DISTRIBUTORS
FOR
OREGON
W Burnside at 14th
AT 9251

TODAY
TOMORROW
EVERY DAY.
$25 TO $200 LESS

For Sale—Used Cars

LOGAN
SAVES
YOU MONEY
on
ALL USED CARS.
PRICED TO SELL
HIGHEST QUALITY
and
BETTER VALUES
at
LOGAN OLDSMOBILE.
EASY TERMS.
OLDSMOBILE
TRADE-INS

'46 OLDS "78"
4-door. R. and Htr. ----$2295
'40 OLDS "6"
4-Dr. Sdn. Heater ------$1050
'46 PONTIAC 6
Conv. Coupe. Radio and Heater. Very clean throughout ----$2295
EXCLUSIVELY
OLDSMOBILE
'42 PONTIAC "6"
4-door R. and Ht. ------$1495
'41 CHEVROLET
Special De Luxe 4-Dr. Sdn. Radio and Heater ------$1295
'41 CHEVROLET
4-Dr. Sdn. Radio. Heater --$1150
HIGHEST QUALITY
BETTER VALUES
'40 CHEVROLET
Sedan. Radio, Heater ----$1175
'40 CHEVROLET
2-Door Sedan. Heater ----$1075
'40 CHEVROLET
De Luxe 2-door. R. and Htr. $1095
OLDSMOBILE
TRADE-INS
'41 CHRYSLER
Coupe with radio and htr., $1075
'40 GMC PICKUP
Very clean throughout ----$795
'41 DE SOTO
Convertible Coupe. Radio

These ads are from the June 27, 1948 Oregonian, *a time when new cars were scarce. By 1951 the prices had dropped dramatically*

"A group of hot rods on the DuBont used car lot are checked over by two prospective customers" from Hot Rod Handbook *129, 1951.*

Transition period

It was a period of transition for myself and for the car industry. Because car production had ceased during WW II, cars of the 'Thirties were still being driven. But as post-war production caught up with demand, around 1950 the price of older cars was diminishing. I had friends who bought running Model A Fords for as little as $15. While these cars weren't advertised in the paper, they were out there, and I was determined to find one.

I came home from school one day and found a 1931 Chev coupe parked in front of my house; I ran the last block, excited with the thought that my father had bought it for me. The car had straight metal, original dark-blue paint and cream-colored wire wheels. It was sporty, and as I looked at it I saw

that it had possibilities of becoming a mild hot rod. But it turned out it was owned by a friend named Marvin, a kid a year older than me who lived next door to my house for years and now lived two miles toward town.

He'd bought the car the day before for $35 and was showing it off. We went for a ride, and what I remember was the cozy feeling in the coupe's small cockpit. That and the free-wheeling knob on the dash. When the car was going around 40 in high gear the driver pulled out that knob to disengage the driveline from the engine, and the car was coasting, which resulted in better gas mileage. The problem was that the car's engine wasn't under compression to help slow it, and the mechanical brakes weren't anything to brag about, so free-wheeling

became a liability. But driving around in that car, without a grown-up along, made me want a car of my own even more.

Just about every make was available

Every car lot had its back-row specials. These cars were unattractive, undesirable or in some cases not running. What they had in common was a cheap price tag. I'd walk past the glowing newer cars in the front rows and approach a scruffy older car, looking for possibilities. A lot on 82nd Avenue near my house had a sign saying "No Car Over $99." That was for me! The entire car lot was full of back row specials! They were cars from the 'Twenties and 'Thirties, and just about every make was available: Durant, Austin, Franklin, Ford, Maxwell,

Terraplane, Crosley, Essex—you name it. I don't doubt that this lot probably had some real classics from time to time, Auburns and Cords that had escaped the scrap drives of WW II, because those cars were dirt-cheap around 1950.

At Fred Meyers I bought a matching squirrel knob and gearshift knob in anticipation of owning my own car. When I wasn't haunting the back rows of car lots, I rode my bicycle around my neighborhood. I found a 1929 Model A sport coupe that had been sitting for years, and a 1933 Willys coupe with two flat tires. In those days no one seemed to care if you had an old car or two sitting in your yard or out front. My father always had one or two old cars around in addition to the 1941 Chev coupe he'd bought new before the war started, his only new car. Now he drove a 1942 Lincoln Zephyr

four-door with a Ford V-8 engine, and for some reason there were no old cars in our yard. If he hadn't sold the 1934 Terraplane coupe a few months before I developed a burning desire to own a car, I might have ended up with that. So I had to keep looking, a process I thoroughly enjoyed.

I lived on the edge of the city and many of the side streets were unpaved. I'd ride my bike over rutted roads filled with mud puddles, past empty fields, and when I came to a house I'd scan the yard. One house that sat alone among fields of Scotch Broom had a garage near the road. I stopped and peeked through a crack in the door and saw a coupe—a Chrysler, I think, circa 1930—covered with dust. In front of another house was a 1939 Crosley convertible; a diminutive two-door phaeton powered by a two-cylinder air-

cooled engine. The car was cute, and because I didn't have a driver's license it had a lot of appeal; I imagined I could drive it on the sidewalk if I had to.

I spent time looking for a car when I should've been doing my homework. Clothes were terribly important in high school, but I quit buying clothes to save money. I got a job at the Oregon Theater for 50¢ an hour and saved every cent I could. I pleaded with my father to let me buy something. Young men were being drafted to go to Korea, and every day at least one hot rod was for sale in the paper. He hesitated, and then, because he got his first car when he was 11, he gave in.

I looked even harder, but when I finally found *the* car, it wasn't from an ad in the paper or from the back row of a car lot. I paid a little more than I had planned, but it was a roadster after all. 🚗

The Ride

I kept pestering my father about it. Finally, he said, okay, I could buy it—but, I had to leave the fenders on.

Directly across the street from the Oregon Theater where I worked evenings and weekends was a tavern. One day a roadster was parked around the corner on the wide sidewalk beside the tavern, and because I was nuts about any old car I crossed the street to eyeball this one. It was a '29 Model A, silver-gray with a faded black top, and as I approached I could see the twin stubs of exhaust pipes that emerged just below the body. Otherwise it looked stock—from the rear anyway. It was full-fendered, with welled front fenders although the spares were gone. As I moved around to the front I saw a chrome-plated grille that resembled a 1933 Chrysler, and the solid hood side panels had three fluted cones to funnel back engine heat. There was a chrome step-plate on the running board, and when I peeked inside I saw a '39 Ford dashboard and the red leather seat, done with wide flat pleats. It was a hot rod! At some point I found that it had a stock 1936 Ford V-8 engine and transmission, with a Model A rear end and the original mechanical brakes.

I'm not sure how much I knew about the car then, and

June, 1951: Al Drake in his newly-finished '29 A-V8 roadster. It was red, with hopped-up 1949 Ford engine. Wheels are 16-inch General Jumbo. The famous squirrel knob is visible on steering wheel!

Illustration from Newhouse Automotive Industries ad for Speed and Power Handbook *in July 1949 issue of* Hot Rod Magazine.

how much I realized years later. For example, someone had added a valance or skirt to the lower edge of the front and rear fenders so they resembled 1934 Ford fenders. This was something that one would do in, say 1935 or 1936, to update the car. That treatment, plus the hand-made grille, suggests it was built in the mid-1930s. The title said the car originated in California, and I'd love to know who did the work.

I know the roadster sat beside the tavern for an extended period of time, because I kept telling my father about it. Somehow I must've found out that it was for sale, or my father inquired. I know I looked at the car many times, and I kept pestering my father about it. Finally he said, okay, I could buy it—*but*, I had to leave the fenders on.

On February 21, 1951—a day clearly etched in my memory—we drove to the tavern to buy the roadster but it was

gone! We did find the owner, Glenn Dowd and we did business. Then he rode with us to an abandoned old service station at 59th and Foster, a tiny place where my father had worked in 1937. There we found the roadster locked in the small shop. There's no way to describe my sustained excitement as Dowd fired up the engine and I climbed into the passenger seat. That '36 flathead was worn out, but it had enough power to make that car scoot. The drive to our house was brief, and the only thing I remember clearly was that at one point we saw a cop and Dowd quickly shifted into neutral, to quiet those noisy dual pipes.

Although my father was working full time, and I was in high school, somehow we worked on the roadster when we could and by June we'd made it into a real hot rod. My father traded a bulldozer blade for a

complete 1937 Ford coupe with a worn-out 1949 Ford engine. We pulled the engine and gave it a complete rebuild—bored 40 thousandths, all new parts, each part lovingly cleaned and the engine carefully assembled on the garage floor. We had a machine shop mill the heads and chop the flywheel. In early June my father took me to Coast Auto Supply where I bought a new Edmunds dual intake manifold, complete with gas lines and linkage, for $37.50—about half what I'd paid for the complete car.

Earlier, in March, I'd skipped a day of school and, against my father's orders, with quiet certitude, total ignorance and a cold chisel, I removed the front fenders, running boards and splash aprons. I'd love to have those fenders, that odd grille and hood today, but I threw them away—along with the running boards, step-plates, grab rails, taillights, spare-tire mounts, everything, even the '39 Ford dash, which we replaced with a '40 dash. The roadster came with General Jumbo aftermarket wheels, which I really disliked. It took me a while to get rid of them, but when I found a set of 1942 Mercury 16-inch wheels the old wheels went in the scrap heap. They're worth big bucks today, and while I still think they're unattractive I wouldn't toss them away. But I'd never seen a rod in *Hot Rod Magazine* with General Jumbo wheels, and this was going to be a real hot rod!

Goodbye fenders

But before all that, before I'd whacked off the fenders, before we did anything to the roadster, I took a ride. I'd had the car for a week or two, and whenever I could I'd sit in it in the driveway, fondling the oddly bent shift lever, gazing at the '39 gauges, holding the wheel in a way that suggested mobility. I'd sit and daydream for hours, thinking of what I wanted to do to the car, imagining it without fenders, painted red, the engine chrome-plated, imagined it featured in a magazine, the red-and-chrome roadster.

First joy ride

One evening, when my parents and sister were gone, I was sitting in the roadster and on impulse I flipped on the ignition, pumped the gas pedal and touched the starter button. I heard, felt, and, in some part of my brain, saw the Bendix drive engage the ring gear. It was a simple act, but a momentous one for me as I'd never really tried to start a car. And my heart pounded as I hit the button again, and a third time, holding it longer. After driving for 45 years I don't even think when I start my car, but that night, starting an engine for the first time, as fuel and spark met, a miracle happened. The engine fired, ran ragged, then roared, responding to my foot. The mufflers were old, and sound reverberated against the side of the house—a sound that terrified and excited me.

I didn't wait for the engine to warm up. By instinct, I slid the shift lever into reverse and slowly eased out the clutch. The driveway was grass, and even with the street level; there was no curb or cement apron to negotiate. The car rolled back into the narrow street and I braked, shifted into low, slowly rolling ahead. In those days my entire street lacked even an arc light; I felt like a fugitive, and debated about turning on the headlights. I gave the engine more gas, let up for the corner,

It was a simple act, but a momentous one for me as I'd never really tried to start a car.

Artwork from Bell Auto Parts' 1950 Catalog

then goosed it before slowing for the next corner. The simplest act, like steering, seemed unnatural. I groped in the dark for the light switch, and chased two dim pools of light to the next corner. The engine roared, and the sweet smell of exhaust came back through the holes in the firewall, filling the roadster's tiny cockpit. I eased the car through the fourth corner, down the section of the street filled with bumps and mud puddles, and as the lighted window in the front room of our house appeared on my right I swung the car into the driveway. I was back home and I hadn't even shifted out of low!

I killed the engine and lights in two quick gestures and sat in the darkness, breathing deeply of the exhaust fumes and the odor of raw gasoline, my heart pounding, feeling guilty, aware of wrongs I'd committed but also how *right* the quick ride felt. I gripped the steering wheel with both hands and stared through the windshield, hoping that all engine heat would have dissipated before my father came home.

What the inside of GM styling studios looked like in the mid '50s.

A Hot Rodder's Wish Book

Learning the name of anything is the first big step in becoming knowledgeable

I doubt that anyone ever read the L. L. Bean outdoor equipment catalog or the F. O. A. Schwartz toy catalog with the level of excitement I felt reading the ads in early rod magazines or a copy of the Eastern Auto catalog. Even today, 45 years later, I can experience a tinge of that old excitement when I peruse a thumb-worn copy of a 1948 *Hot Rod Magazine.*

First, it was all new to me. I didn't know anything about cars, and so I read the ads not to buy so much as to learn. I learned lots of little things, like the difference between a 1940 and a 1941 Ford dash, or a Stromberg and a Chandler-Groves carburetor. The ads couldn't teach me how to rebuild a carburetor, but they told me the names, and learning the name of anything is

"Coupes go fast, too!"

Yes, breath-taking performance is not limited to roadsters. Make your coupe or sedan go fast by following the information in California Bill's *New* HOT ROD MANUAL.

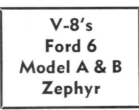

V-8's
Ford 6
Model A & B
Zephyr

128 colorfully bound pages, chock full of construction drawings, photos, and valuable, easy to read and understandable technical data. Complete info on how to build A-V8's, install hydraulic brakes on any Ford, and how to rework V-8, Merc, Ford 6, Lincoln and 4-barrel engines, for speed and power.

SENT POSTPAID FOR $2.00.   Mail your check or money order today

CALIFORNIA BILL
BOX L-6, EAGLE ROCK STATION, L. A. 41, CALIF.

California Bill's ad from the July 1949 issue of Hot Rod Magazine.

Hot stuff from the 1959 issue of the Almquist "Equipment of Champions" catalog.

the first big step in becoming knowledgeable. Primitive tribes believed that something didn't exist unless it had a name, and that if you knew its name you could call it into existence. Therefore, a hunter would invoke the name of the animal he hoped to kill so it would appear before him to be killed. That process was certainly true for me, a 15-year-old kid yearning and dreaming about cars and wanting more than anything to name one—to call it into existence.

Second, I had the feeling that not only was hot rodding new to me, it was new to most people. Rodding was thriving in Southern California, but just getting started in my area—or so I thought. At any rate, as a sport it wasn't established, the rules hadn't been written; it was like a baby taking its first steps, and that moment is terribly exciting.

Lead bullets

There was the freedom of the new, and yet almost from the start I felt that there were certain things that one did and did not do. For example, one did put solid side panels on a rod, but one did not mount chrome horns on the hood! How did I know? Well, from reading the same magazines that those ads appeared in. The feature stories showed me the desirable, the acceptable way to build a car and, by contrast, showed me what to avoid. If I saw a '38 Ford coupe with venetian blinds in the back window I'd ask myself whether I had ever seen that done to a car in a magazine. Of course I hadn't! Would Bob Pierson or Jack Calori run venetian blinds in their '36 Ford 3-window coupes? Heck no! That's like asking whether the Lone Ranger would use lead bullets!

Eastern Auto ad from the July, 1949 issue of Hot Rod Magazine.

Smith & Jones ad from the August, 1949 issue of Hot Rod Magazine.

Penguin Car Cooler ad from the 1953 Paramount Specialities Wholesale Catalog.

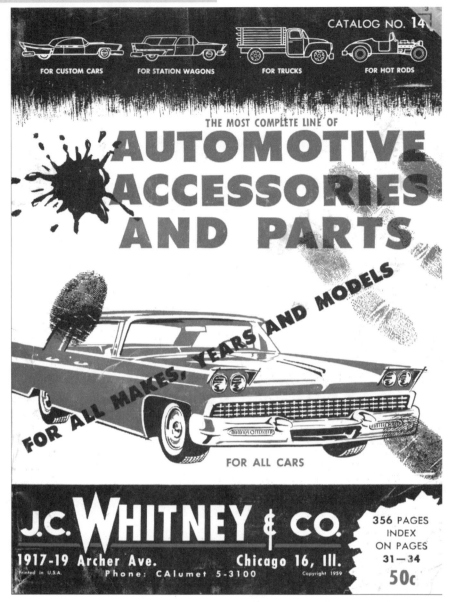

J. C. Whitney & Co. catalog from 1959.

Ads from August 1949 issue of Hot Rod Magazine.

Eastern California Custom Accessories Catalog cover from 1951.

Little by little I accumulated knowledge through the ads until I knew what I wanted: a '32 Ford grille, a pair of '39 Ford tail-lights, a cute little chrome license-plate light. The sport was new, but already certain things had established themselves as traditional.

Finally, I enjoyed reading the ads because I liked the shapes and textures of the items pictured. The chrome dash knobs, the sleek curve of an aluminum velocity stack, the beehive shape of a Mack Hellings air cleaner. I loved to study the cars in the ads and see what the company was selling: solid side panels, skirts, grille panels, spotlights. There were flowing exhaust headers, Edmunds cast-aluminum oil-bath air cleaners, lightweight flywheels, floating bar grilles sleek as flying wings, fiberglass-packed mufflers, and a full line of Stewart-Warner gauges. Lewie Shell often ran full-page ads packed with things I needed, from dropped axles to adjustable tappets to stroker kits. He also sold used parts and speed

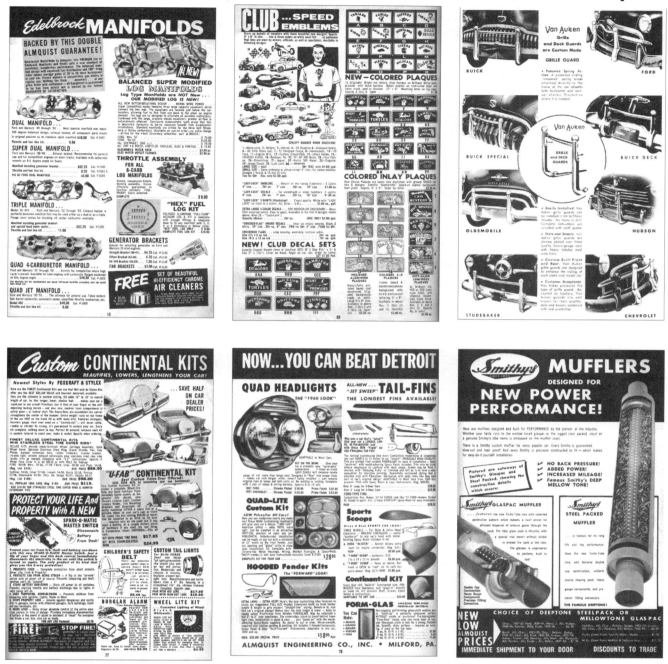

More "great" accessories from the 1959 issue of the Almquist "Equipment of Champions" catalog.

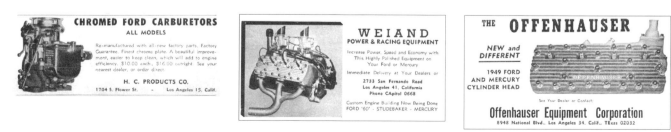

Ads from August 1949 issue of Hot Rod Magazine.

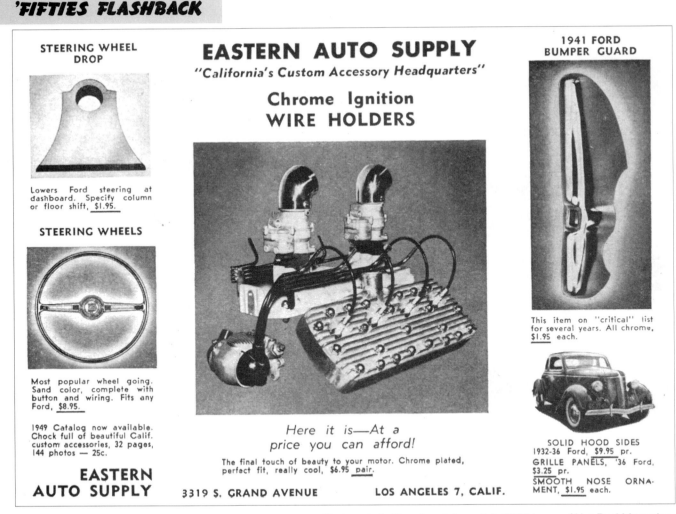

STEERING WHEEL DROP

Lowers Ford steering at dashboard. Specify column or floor shift. $1.95.

STEERING WHEELS

Most popular wheel going. Sand color, complete with button and wiring. Fits any Ford. $8.95.

1949 Catalog now available. Chock full of beautiful Calif. custom accessories, 32 pages, 144 photos — 25c.

EASTERN AUTO SUPPLY

EASTERN AUTO SUPPLY
"California's Custom Accessory Headquarters"

Chrome Ignition WIRE HOLDERS

Here it is—At a price you can afford!

The final touch of beauty to your motor. Chrome plated, perfect fit, really cool, $6.95 pair.

3319 S. GRAND AVENUE   LOS ANGELES 7, CALIF.

1941 FORD BUMPER GUARD

This item on "critical" list for several years. All chrome, $1.95 each.

SOLID HOOD SIDES 1932-36 Ford, $9.95 pr. GRILLE PANELS, '36 Ford, $3.25 pr. SMOOTH NOSE ORNAMENT, $1.95 each.

Eastern Auto Supply ad from July 1949 issue of Hot Rod Magazine.

equipment ranging from new '32 Ford center cross members to a '32 roadster body (only $50) to a complete two-port OHV engine (just $175).

Real chrome-plated brass

Looking back, I find the prices incredibly low. I put a 1940 Ford dash in my roadster so I bought a chrome-plated instrument panel to replace the plastic panel; it cost $6.50. From F. E. Zimmer I ordered 48 chrome head nuts—these were chrome-plated brass, not tinny slip-on covers—for only 10¢ each. Zimmer also sold complete column-shift-installation kits, which included everything but the transmission, for only $23.

Dropped axles were $15. A one-eighth stroker crankshaft was $15 exchange. I was working in a theater for only 50¢ an hour, but these prices did not seem excessive.

Our local auto supply stores had some of these items, but whenever possible I preferred to buy through the mail. Those sellers were in places like Los Angeles and Encino, and when I bought from them I felt as though I had my finger on the pulse of the hot rod industry. And I was a real sucker for their rhetoric: "Beautiful glistening chrome beauties of solid brass. Replace worn-out drab-looking plastic knobs on radio choke, throttle, etc." I looked at the dash

*Automotive Sales Company
Catalog from 1950.*

Ad in Hot Rod Magazine *for F. E. Zimmer Co.*

Cover from Honest Charlie's 1958 catalog.

Eastern Auto's April 1949 ad in Hot Rod Magazine.

knobs on my father's 1942 Lincoln Zephyr and was dissatisfied by their drabness. I looked at the photo of Jack Calori's '36 Ford coupe's interior and saw nothing drab there: the rich Cohyde rolled-and-pleated seats and doors, the six Stewart-Warner gauges, the white deluxe '49 Ford steering wheel, and the row of chrome-plated custom dash knobs, exactly like the ones shown in the ad! That was what my father's car needed, I thought, and what *he* needed to

spice up his drab life. Chrome knobs! I immediately sent for six (and I think I still have them).

I bought what I could afford, wished I could afford more, but never felt resentful that I couldn't. There was a great sense of pleasure in looking at the ads. Even the names had a power, and demanded to be chanted: Edelbrock, Navarro, Cyclone, Belond, Tattersfield, Appleton, Thickstun, Iskenderian, Sharp, Evans, Harman and Collins, Edmunds, Offenhauser, Weiand.

That's poetry! I'll try it one more time, naming the names, and perhaps I'll be able to invoke the actual, pulling back through time the equipment those names represent. Listen...

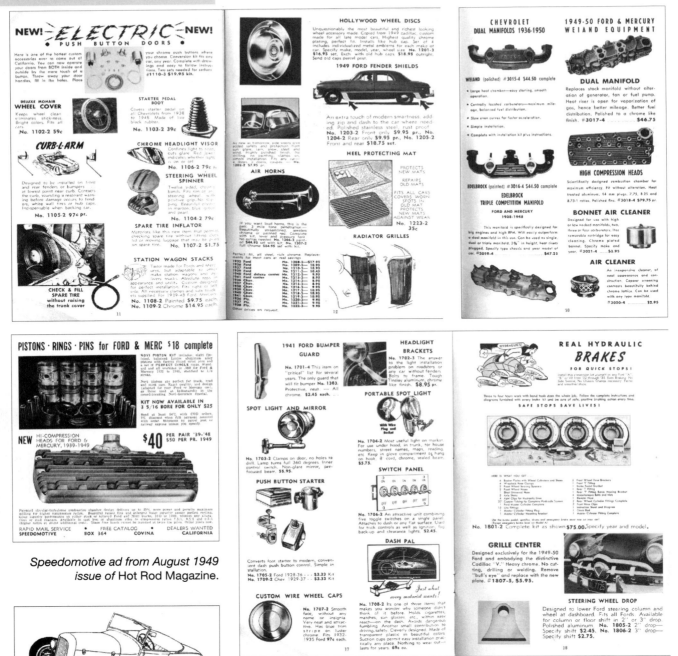

Speedomotive ad from August 1949 issue of Hot Rod Magazine.

A 1950s ROD & CUSTOM BUILDER'S WISH BOOK

Albert Drake

Al Drake's A 1950's Rod & Custom Builder's Wish Book *is a collection of ads.*

Pages from Eastern California Custom Accessories Catalog from 1951.

Ads from Motorlife, *September 1954.*

The invention of the wheel is one of man's greatest achievements, no doubt about it, but credit should also be given to the person who devised a cover for it. The wheel is functional but unattractive, and for the past 60 years car owners have been trying to cover it up or make it more presentable.

The first wheels were made of wooden spokes that connected the rim and the hub. When new they were varnished and often pin-striped, but after two or three years the varnish peeled, the paint wore away, and they looked dingy. Even worse, the wood dried out and the wheels creaked when the car was in motion; the noise could be very annoying. These wheels were really holdovers from the buggy

Hub Caps

Credit should be given to the person who devised a cover for the wheel.

1953 Oldsmobile hub cap.

Cadillac-type wheel disc has a gold emblem in center, fits all 15 and 16 inch wheels: $20 set.

Full-moon type wheel disc with center cross bar takes on spinner effect when rolling; $20 for four.

Ford and Merc full-moon type with center cross bar costs $18 for a set of four; note circular marking.

Universal design wheel discs were first designed for early Kurtis Kar ....$20 set.

Below, Cal-Nevar's wire wheel discs give a sports car look to a rod. Set cost is ....$109.00.

era and it wasn't until the late 'Twenties that several manufacturers introduced the disc wheel. With the advent of welded spokes, which did not require adjustment, wire-spoke wheels became popular during the 'Thirties.

One thing these very different types of wheels have in common is the use of a hub cap. The earliest hub caps, whether the screw-on or press-on type, were really dust covers to protect the bearings and retain grease. Small, they were made of brass or stainless steel and stamped with the manufacturer's name. By the 'Thirties the hub cap was making the transition from a functional to a decorative element of the car's design, and it was a good deal larger in size than the early dust covers.

Concealing the spokes

But by 1950 car enthusiasts were looking for something they could use to cover the wheels of the cars of the previous two decades. If you had a 1936 Ford or a 1930 Buick that you were fixing up, the first thing you wanted to do was to conceal the

vestigial stamped spokes. To do that you needed something that would cover the entire wheel.

Actually, the impulse to cover the wheel wasn't new in the 'Fifties. During the 'Thirties the wire wheel was considered by some people to be a styling liability as it recalled the image of the buggy. It wasn't streamlined, and besides, it was very difficult to keep clean. As early as 1932 Cadillac made a stainless-steel disc that fit under the screw-on hub cap and covered the spoked area. This was not an option, but a styling feature that Cadillac kept on most of its models until 1938, when Cadillac began using disc wheels. In 1934 Cadillac began offering a luxurious hubcap on its V-16 models. This cap featured a stainless-steel bar, slightly wider at the ends, that emphasized the sense of motion as the car was being driven. It might be considered the vestigial image of the old wooden-spoke wheel, but in fact it was a modern styling touch, and one that rodders and customizers would emulate 20 years later.

So the image of a full-wheel

cover conveyed a sense of luxury from the very beginning, and that image continues today. A plain-Jane model has tiny hub caps while the deluxe model has full hub caps. This explains part of the reason why hot rodders and custom car builders wanted a hub cap that would cover the entire wheel.

Eliminated wind noise

Not only was the hub cap easier to clean than the wire wheel, it eliminated the wind noise that emanated from the spokes. It was more streamlined. The Moon spun aluminum wheel covering wasn't invented during the 'Fifties. It was used by Bob Rufi, the first hot rodder to hit 140 mph at the lakes. That was in 1940, in a belly-tank type of machine, and what he used as wheel covers for streamlining were four wheel coverings from a WW I Jenny airplane.

By 1950, the trend of updating continued in two distinctly different ways. The builders of early model hot rods wanted to get rid of the old wire wheels and to replace them with 1940-48 Ford and Mercury disc wheels. If you look at photographs of hot rods of that period, 99% were running disc wheels with stock hub caps and beauty rings. Brand new 1940-48 Ford hub caps sold for only $1.65 each. Speed shops did a land office business selling wheel spacers that allowed the later model wheel to fit the early hub. You

You could install an interesting set of hub caps in a few minutes, and immediately transform a dull family car into an extraordinary machine.

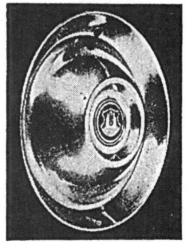

HOLLYWOOD DISCS

Ford, 1936-'39
$16.95 set.
Also for most
other cars.

A selection of Calnevar Deluxe Full Wheel Covers from the 1953 Paramount Specialties Wholesale Catalog.

weren't quite the answer. For one thing, the three-part unit was based on the stock hub cap with the manufacturer's name stamped in large letters. What was the point of building a mysterious custom car if any yokel could walk up to the car and read right on the hub cap that it was a Ford?

Hollywood hub cap

The first hub caps that aimed at the custom car market, such as it was in those early days, was the Hollywood hub cap designed by George DuVall, who also designed the famed DuVall windshield used on many So-Cal roadsters during the late 'Thirties. The first version was a large bowl-shaped cap with an S shape stamped in relief; when the wheel rotated the S shape spun around. A later version of this Hollywood hub cap had a chrome bar mounted on it—when the car was moving the spinning bar emphasized motion. Both models covered most of the wheel but

could also use the later hub and drum, of course, or, as someone discovered, a standard Model A piston ring as a shim. Chrome wheels were available, and at $10 each you'd think that they would have been on every sharp-looking rod but not so; I can recall seeing only two or three cars with chrome wheels before the early 'Sixties, when they suddenly became popular.

The person who was building a custom from a 1936-50 model could not be satisfied with the stock hub cap. He had to have a cap that was different, and that covered the wheel. In the 'Thirties it was found on Cadillacs and a few other cars, such as the Model 810 Cord, which made it desirable but very rare. Accessory manufacturers soon marketed a trim disc similar to that offered by Cadillac in 1932; it fit under the hub cap and against the beauty ring, and covered most of the wheel. These were used by many people who wanted to make the wheels on their cars more attractive, but for the custom car builder they

Wheelcovers from the 1959 issue of the Almquist "Equipment of Champions" catalog.

You could install an interesting set of hub caps in a few minutes, and immediately transform a dull family car into an extraordinary machine. Often that thin area of the rim that was left exposed was painted bright red. Those two small changes made a great difference, especially if you had a black car and wide whitewall tires.

By the early 'Fifties the custom car craze was booming and accessory manufacturers offered different types of hub caps. One was the ripple disk, with a corrugated pattern; it was originally designed for the Kurtis car (I liked the car but never liked the hub cap). Another type was the Flying Saucer, which resembled an earlier full-width hub cap but without the bar. There was also the full Moon cap, plain and slightly domed but didn't, despite its name, cover the entire wheel. Imitation wire-wheel hub caps were also on the market, but these didn't seem to catch on; perhaps that was because many car owners were trying to get away from the old-fashioned image that spoked wheels conveyed.

About this time Detroit began to call them *wheel covers* rather than *hub caps*; the latter covered the hub while the former covered the entire wheel. Most manufacturers offered a wheel cover of interest to the custom car builder: the 1950 Mercury cover was squared off, nameless, and had a wide trim ring; the 1951 Lincoln cover had a gentle curve, with a stylish no-name crest in the center; the 1953 Ford deluxe cover also featured a design in the center. All were very suitable for earlier model cars running 15-inch wheels.

still required a beauty ring. A later version made by other manufacturers mounted the bar on a full-width hub cap.

But the hub cap desired by owners of 1935-50 model cars was the late-model Cadillac hub cap. It was very heavy, nicely made, with high-quality chrome plating. One or two accessory companies marketed an imitation Cadillac hub cap, but it was much lighter and lacked the distinctive Cadillac emblem. Needless to say, real Cadillac hub caps were in demand, and an activity known as *hub capping* began to be practiced; if you had a Cadillac you didn't park it on a dark street overnight.

4B-56
4B-57

3B-56
3B-57

O-349—OS-14

STB-55

O-357A

O-346

STB-55-4B

O 357

B-15

8-C

59-69-79

NATIONAL WHEEL COVERS
Triple Chrome
CUSTOM FULL HUB CAPS
Give Wheel Size When Ordering

	LIST	NET	JOBBER
4B-56 15″ 4-Bar Starfire with checked back crown	$59.90	$39.00	$29.95
4B-57 14″ 4-Bar Starfire with checked back ground	59.90	39.00	29.95
3B-56 15″ Tri-Bar Starfire with checked back ground	57.90	37.70	28.95
3B-57 14″ Tri-Bar Starfire with checked back ground	57.90	37.70	28.95
O-349 15″ Olds Starfire	55.90	36.40	27.95
OS-14 14″ Olds Starfire	55.90	36.40	27.95
O-357A Tri-Bar 14″ only	55.90	36.40	27.95
STB-55 Tri-Bar Fiesta For 14″, 15″, or 16″ wheels	47.90	31.20	23.95
STB-55-4B Special 4 Bar 14″, 15″, or 16″	47.90	31.20	23.95
B-15 Bullet Checked For 14″ or 15″ wheels			
8-C 3 Dimensional Crest			
59 16″ Plain Moon with Spinner Bar	29.90	19.50	14.95
69—15″ Plain Moon with bar			
79—14″ Plain Moon with bar			
59A—16″ Plain Moon			
69M—15″ Plain Moon	27.90	18.20	13.95
79M—14″ Plain Moon			

69-M
79M
59A

F-57

M58

STOCK REPLACEMENT COVERS

	LIST	NET	JOBBER
B-28 Buick 55-56	31.90	20.80	15.85
C-57 Chevrolet 55			
C-58 Chevrolet 56			
C-59 Chevrolet 57			
F-55 Ford 55-56			
F-57 Ford 57			
O-346 Oldsmobile 54-55	29.90	19.50	14.95
O-357 Oldsmobile 57			
P-986 Plymouth 56			
P-987 Plymouth 57			
Also available in 15″			
S-77A Studebaker 53-55			
VW-15A Volkswagen and Other Foreign Cars 15″			

B-28

VW-15-A

P-987

NEW RADIATOR CAPS FOR ANCIENT CARS

		LIST	NET	JOBBER
729—"T" Model	Ea.	$2.50	$1.75	$1.50
724—32 Ford "B" or V8	Ea.	2.50	1.75	1.50
716—28-29 "A" Model	Ea.	2.50	1.75	1.50
718—30-31 "A" Model	Ea.	2.50	1.75	1.50
719—33 V8 Ford	Ea.	2.50	1.75	1.50
722—34 V8 Ford	Ea.	2.50	1.75	1.50

"A" GAS TANK CAPS

715—28-29 "A" Model	Ea.	2.50	1.75	1.50
710—30-31 "A" Model	Ea.	2.50	1.75	1.50

NEW HUB CAPS FOR ANCIENT CARS

725—"T" Model	Ea.	2.50	1.75	1.50
717—28-29 "A" Model	Ea.	2.50	1.75	1.50
711—30-31 "A" Model	Ea.	2.50	1.75	1.50
731—32-35 Ford	Ea.	4.00	2.75	2.50
755—Deluxe All Chrome 36-39 Ford, 39 Merc	Ea.	4.00	2.75	2.50

P-985

F-55

S-77A

BULLETS & SPINNERS
FOR FULL WHEEL COVER

CUSTOMIZING		LIST	NET	JOBBER
WS 310	Set of 4	$9.85	$7.40	$6.95
WS 320	Set of 4	14.50	10.85	9.95
WS 330	Set of 4	18.50	13.95	12.95
WS 340 (Fiesta)	Set of 4	3.95	3.00	2.75
WS 350 (Indented for Starfire)	Set of 4	4.50	3.75	3.45
WSB 300 FLIPPERS (Spinner) Blades	Set of 12	9.00	7.50	6.95

C-58

No. 729

No. 725

No. 710

No. 714

No. 715

No. 716

No. 711

C-57

No. 718

No. 731

No. 719

P-984

C-59

No. 755

No. 722

FIESTA — #WS 340
2¹⁵/₁₆″ dia.; 1⅝″ deep.
Packed 4 per set. Wt. 1 lb.

STARFIRE — #WS 350
2¹⁵/₁₆″ dia.; 1⅝″ deep.
Packed 4 per set. Wt. 1 lb.

#WS 310
4⅛″ dia.;
2⁵/₁₆″ deep.
Packed 4
per set.
Wt. 1¾ lbs.

#WS 320
4⅛″ dia.;
3⁵/₁₆″ deep.
Packed 4
per set.
Wt. 2 lbs.

#WS 330
8″ overall
width;
2⁵/₁₆″ deep.
Packed 4
per set.
Wt. 3½ lbs.

FLIPPER
BLADES
#WSB 300

A page from Honest Charley's Speed Shop Catalog entitled,
"10th Anniversary 1948-1958; Ten Honest Years of Speedy Progress."

Flipper hub caps

The most revolutionary cover was the Oldsmobile Fiesta, introduced in limited quantities in 1953, popularized in 1954, and continued through 1963. This full-width cover played on the idea of the much earlier Hollywood hub cap with the bar that spun when the car was moving; the Oldsmobile cover had a series of grooves, painted white, a crest in the center, and three "flippers" extending from the center. In 1956 Dodge Lancer hub caps were introduced; the bars were shorter but there were four of them, and the illusion of motion they generated when turning at slow speeds was heightened. I had a borrowed set of these covers on my roadster in the late 'Fifties; they were elegant, with heavy metal and high-quality chrome plating.

The "flippers" could be unbolted from the wheel cover, and customizers began to add extra "flippers," doubling the number on a Fiesta wheel cover. They were also bolted to other kinds of wheel covers. Soon accessory manufacturers began selling the "flippers," as well as spinners, bullets, and no-name wheel covers that incorporated these items. A customizer could take, for example, the plain but deluxe wheel cover from a 1955 Plymouth, drill a hole in the center, add a bullet, and, if he wished, bolt "flippers" to that. With so many beautiful stock hub caps to choose from, and so many ways to individualize them the sky was the limit. Around 1953 or 1954 custom hub caps began to appear not only on custom cars but also on hot rods, replacing the tradition of using original stock hub caps.

Trick paint jobs

Around 1955, as pin striping suddenly became popular, another trend got started: painting hub caps. A transparent paint that would stick to chrome was on the market, and customizers began to paint areas of their wheel covers, leaving other areas chrome-plated, and having a thin stripe painted as a dividing line. The paint was available in many colors, fairly durable, and transparent enough so the reflective surface below the paint could be seen. The star bursts and scallops painted on the hub caps were also painted on the dual spot lights, creating an interesting effect. Sometimes glitter was sprinkled on the painted surface. Occasionally an owner would mount one or two colored lights in the wheel well; the light would play off the rotating spinners and the shiny/painted surfaces at night. The effect was something else!

No caps = racer!

In the early days of drag racing you weren't required to remove your hub caps or skirts. A car drove to the drags, raced and came home, seemingly unchanged. Then, as hub caps began flying off accelerating machines, and cars were found to have wheels with cracks between the lugs, it became a rule that hub caps had to be removed before the car was safety inspected and during the race. Some owners simply took their hub caps off and left them off. That idea caught on with non-racers, and soon the image of a racer was a car without hub caps. For decoration an owner bought a set of chrome lug nuts and had the front dust covers chrome-plated. Eventually chrome wheels became popular,

Honest Charley "hisself."

and then chrome wheels with reversed rims. This led to the "mag" type wheels of the 'Sixties. Before that time the wheels manufactured by Ted Halibrand really were made of magnesium and were found on real race cars of the circle-track genre. Today their descendants are found on all types of vehicles.

If you had a custom car during the 'Fifties, or even a good-looking chair car with fancy hub caps, you had to buy a set of locks and a "key." The locks slipped over the valve stem, making it impossible to remove the hub cap; they turned freely so the hub cap couldn't be removed. If you had to add air to the tire or remove the hub cap you inserted your "key" and twisted. Such locks were the only insurance that you could go to a movie and come out and find your hub caps intact. Unfortunately, all the "keys" were identical! 🚗

Rappin' Pipes

The very presence of duals suggested speed, a hot engine, a race car.

DON'T LET THIS
HAPPEN TO YOU!

In the beginning, someone created dual exhausts. Today, with street rods running chromed XKE rear ends, disc brakes and supercharged engines, it's hard to realize how important a modification a dual exhaust system was in the late 'Forties and early 'Fifties. It made a car noticeable, different. A single tailpipe created an imbalance while dual tailpipes expressed symmetry. Perhaps that was the reason why people who did nothing else to a car, who in fact didn't seem to care about a car, wanted dual exhausts—they balanced things out.

There were other practical, psychological and aesthetic reasons. Dual exhausts—"dual pipes," "duals," "pipes"—gave a car a distinct sound; they also suggested a great deal. Before the advent of the 1953 Cadillac, the first car to have a factory-installed dual exhaust system, all cars drove off the showroom floor with a single, wispy-sounding tailpipe that usually emerged at an odd angle. The very presence of duals suggested speed, a hot engine, a race car. A machine with dual pipes *sounded*

DUALS

Gus Maanum

Artwork from Southern California Muffler Service Catalog.

Almquist ad from September 1954 issue of Motorlife.

fast, and never mind raising the hood to verify whether the engine had been modified.

Better gas mileage?

The practical reason for installing duals was that they reduced back pressure and allowed an engine to breathe, resulting in more power and better gas mileage. Statistics confirm this claim, but those who desired duals didn't need a reason for installing them; they knew the factory system was too quiet, too anemic. Dual pipes made a car sound peppy, and converted a Walter Mitty into a Tazio Nuvolari. The resultant noise was inevitable, for who would install *two* stock mufflers? The factory muffler was a constrictive labyrinth of baffles. If one was bad—two seemed to compound the problem.

Smithy's

I knew of one guy who punched holes in his new muffler to get some sound, but that was a poor method. Popular aftermarket mufflers were the Porter steel-pack—a long, heavy muffler painted blue—and the Smithy's—a muffler painted silver. A Ford or Merc equipped with Porter mufflers sounded like a motorboat—the soft blurb of exhausts exiting underwater—a desirable sound; equipped with Smithy's mufflers it was noisier, the exhaust note sharper. Both kinds of mufflers worked well but I thought that the Smithy's muffler was *too* loud. But the name Smithy's was synonymous with speed, noise. The first thing someone would ask was, "What're ya runnin', Smitties?"

For a real mean snarl there was the short-lived Rajax muffler, made in Portland. Other brands began to appear. Sandy

Belond was doing a land office business selling complete dual exhaust systems through the mail from his shop in Los Angeles, and nearby Dave Mitchell was experimenting with the first fiberglass mufflers. Howard Douglass was also well known for his exhaust systems. Few cars had headers, but ran the duals back from the stock exhaust manifold(s). As the demand for dual exhausts suddenly became evident, local shops sprang up to meet that need. And soon the streets were full of cars rapping pipes!

If you had a low dual-intake manifold without heat risers, or if you placed a penny over the heat riser in a stock manifold, the noise level was increased by 15 decibels. At a stoplight a Ford with blocked heat risers would bubble like a motorboat, then roar off in low, the noise gathering behind like a big, invisible cloud; the sound would fall forward as the driver let up on the gas, shifted, revved the engine, exhausts cracking, and then build again as he wound the engine out in second, the noise continuing to build even after the car was out of sight. What a thrill! It was a sound comparable only to that of an unmuffled motorcycle or a taxiing DC-3.

Social pressures

A set of pipes relieved engine back pressure, but tended to create social pressure. I spent my lunch hours during high school hanging out at The Doghouse, where we listened to each passing car's exhaust and judged the

I knew of one guy who punched holes in his new muffler to get some sound...

driver's "acceptable qualities." And we listened to the tonal pitches and subtle sound variations of dual pipes the way teenagers today listen to the subtle acoustics of a thousand-dollar stereo system. Some exhausts were too harsh, some too tinny, some too quiet. Mellow was the "correct" sound, and if there was a slight backing off, a crackling, when the driver shifted, that was a bonus. I enjoyed the flat hum of the duals on my A-V8 roadster, but felt frustrated because I couldn't really rap my pipes; by the time sound began to build up I was way beyond the speed limit.

Dual exhausts on a V-8 were natural, especially on the Ford flathead which had an inherent problem due to heat build-up between the center cylinders on each bank. But duals on a six-cylinder inline engine caused a reaction, a rebellion, as if this were something it didn't want or need but was subjected to because of youthful frivolity. First there was the problem of "splitting" the exhaust manifold, an operation akin to separating Siamese twins. Sometimes the split would be down the middle, three and three, but if the stock exhaust flange was in an inconvenient place, the division could be two and four. The result was the sound of anarchy!

MoPars were generally mellow at low rpm, but developed a sudden, lovely roar at around 3,000 rpm that continued to build to a thunderclap. Chevrolet and GMC sixes with dual exhausts were more violent. I recall riding in Roger Simonatti's 1938 Chev two-door with split manifold and steel-packs; he wound it out to 20 in low gear and the noise shook store windows. When I worked in a garage I took a friend's 1951 Ford six cylinder in to have a dual exhaust system built, an activity that we were performing on two or three cars each day. No commercial set-up was available for this car, so the dual system had to be handmade. To save a few bucks my friend wanted to leave the stock muffler on the car

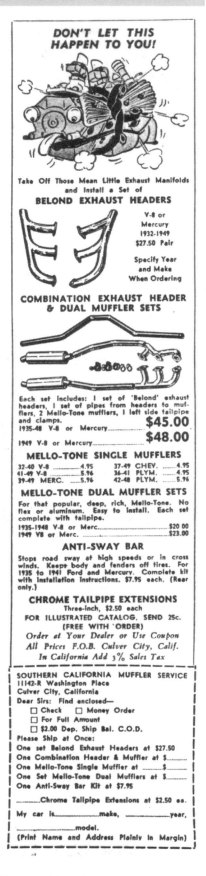
*How would you like to be able to fill out
this form and send it in today?*

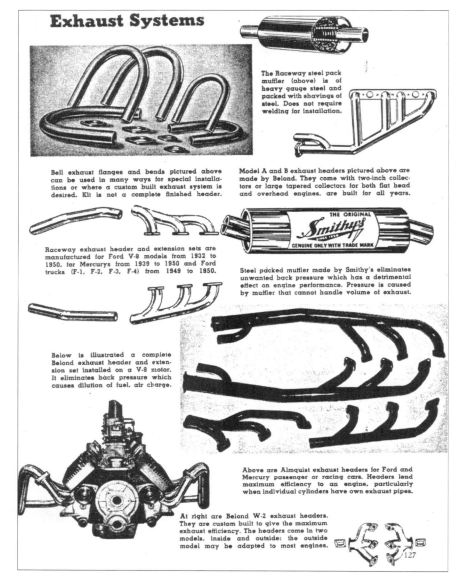

Exhaust Systems

The Raceway steel pack muffler (above) is of heavy gauge steel and packed with shavings of steel. Does not require welding for installation.

Bell exhaust flanges and bends pictured above can be used in many ways for special installations or where a custom built exhaust system is desired. Kit is not a complete finished header.

Model A and B exhaust headers pictured above are made by Belond. They come with two-inch collectors or large tapered collectors for both flat head and overhead engines, are built for all years.

Raceway exhaust header and extension sets are manufactured for Ford V-8 models from 1932 to 1950, for Mercurys from 1939 to 1950 and Ford trucks (F-1, F-2, F-3, F-4) from 1949 to 1950.

Steel packed muffler made by Smithy's eliminates unwanted back pressure which has a detrimental effect on engine performance. Pressure is caused by muffler that cannot handle volume of exhaust.

Below is illustrated a complete Belond exhaust header and extension set installed on a V-8 motor. It eliminates back pressure which causes dilution of fuel, air charge.

Above are Almquist exhaust headers for Ford and Mercury passenger or racing cars. Headers lend maximum efficiency to an engine, particularly when individual cylinders have own exhaust pipes.

At right are Belond W-2 exhaust headers. They are custom built to give the maximum exhaust efficiency. The headers come in two models, inside and outside: the outside model may be adapted to most engines.

127

and to install a used steel-pack on the dual side; it was an unusual combination that resulted in a particularly wicked sound. The car was quiet at low speeds, but as the engine wound out the exhaust note had the tonal qualities of gravel being shaken in a tin can. The owner was immensely pleased by the raucous sound his nearly new Ford made.

That mellow sound

Tonal qualities were difficult to predict. One method of obtaining that mellow sound was to pour oil in a new muffler and set it on fire, a break-in method called *burning it out*. Occasionally a car ran a "straight pipe," omitting the muffler. Sometimes a driver installed an exhaust cutout; this was an old idea, a valve that allowed exhaust gases to exit ahead of the muffler.

The correct sound was important, and all kinds of tricks were tried to achieve it. I remember a black guy who owned a Hollywood Graham running a Ford flathead; he achieved a distinctive sound by welding sections of brass bed pipe into the exhaust system. A couple of engine builders had a Ford shop truck that was one of the hottest rigs in town; it had an unusual exhaust system with a distinctive sound, achieved by crossing the header outlets from the center ports to the opposite side pipe.

Unacceptable Y pipes

There were exhaust sounds that were preferred, but the only exhaust set-up that was *unacceptable* was the imitation dual pipe that branched from the stock tailpipe ahead of the gas tank. It was simply a Y, a piece of flex pipe that looked like a second tailpipe. It was added by the owner (usually a jock or social-club type who drove a Hudson or Nash) because he felt the tremendous pressure that required that he have dual exhausts. The Y-pipe *looked* like

part of a real dual-exhaust system, unless one crawled under the car to investigate, but it sounded like a wet rag being dragged across the floor. The nerd who drove a car equipped with such a jury-rigged, pseudo-dual system was finally exposed on a cold morning when everyone could *see* the exhaust coming from only one side.

Chrome extensions

Chrome exhaust extensions were also important. Stock machines either lacked a chrome extension, or they had a flat, wide chrome deflector, usually with a red reflector imbedded in it. Few who were serious about their cars wanted a wimpy

deflector. We wanted first, a tailpipe that emerged straight back and level; second, tailpipes *exactly* equidistant from the ends of the bumper and the bumper guards. Some cars with in-line engines had a pair of tailpipes exiting on the same side, and some Chevrolets had the tailpipes close together in the center. But most drivers felt it was essential that the pipes be outside of the bumper guards. Only a nerd would have one pipe emerging from beside the guard, and the other emerging somewhere near the middle of the bumper, with both canted in different directions.

Chrome extensions were called *echo cans*; they were

Pages from a 1959 issue of Almquist Engineering catalog.

approximately 3-1/2 inches in diameter and up to 18 inches long (by 1954 the big extensions were passé, having been replaced by "pencil tips" no larger than the tailpipe itself). The positioning of these was important; they should not protrude farther than the width of the bumper guards. Some nerds would buy them longer than necessary and let them extend past the bumper by as much as a foot. There wasn't much vandalism in those days, but a guy I knew named Gary, who could have been the model for The Fonz, was terribly offended by this unstylish and ostentatious display, and liked to mete out his idea of justice by jumping on the protruding extensions. That was Gary's idea of rappin' pipes!

MUFFLERS

Burnished aluminum exhaust tip is of the economy type, sells for nominal 89c.

This large tail pipe tip has baffles built into the tip to produce a muffler sound effect. It sells in most shops for $3.50.

Stubby tail pipe tip is now available in various flange sizes for all makes, is $2.

Douglass split manifold for Chevrolet helps relieve pressure, sells for $6 to $8.

Hurricane by-pass, outlawed in some states, is still popular in many areas.

Belond header set, includes headers, extensions, tail pipes and mufflers, to $118.

Stubby exhaust tip, large size, comes in varying flange fittings for most cars.

Universal chromed tail pipe tip fits all makes, sells for a very reasonable $2.50.

Economy type straight through muffler sells from $4.70 to $7.50.

Right, silent tip tail pipe has baffles, cuts out much exhaust: $2.50.

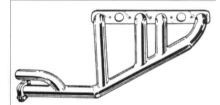

MODEL 'A' & 'B' EXHAUST HEADERS are made with 2 inch collectors or large tapered collectors for both flat head and overhead engines. When ordering, specify model desired. (Example: 2 inch flat head)

2 Inch Plain Finish	$30.00	Pr.
2 Inch Chrome Plated	42.00	Pr.
Large Plain Finish	37.50	Pr.
Tapers Chrome Plated	49.50	Pr.

From Bell Auto Parts 1950 catalog.

Cut Rate Auto Store ad from December 1954 issue of Hot Rod Magazine.

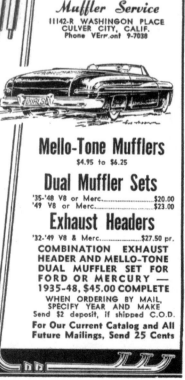

Vintage Tin

The car might not be worth much in terms of cold cash, but it was tangible wealth, something you could believe in.

Back in the good old days things seemed to stay in place a lot longer. Part of the reason was because people seemed to stay put. The mobile society began with WW II, but earned its label in the 'Sixties. When I was growing up during the 'Forties and 'Fifties, the same people lived year after year in the same houses in my neighborhood. Someone painted his house, another put up a picket fence, someone bought an almost-new car, but otherwise things went on pretty much the same day after day. Most people didn't even change jobs unless they were laid off. This steadfastness had its benefits, one being that you really did know your neighbors, and you could usually count on them in times of need.

Another result—not everyone would call it a *benefit*—was that

It was possible during the 'Fifties to find in abundance cars of the 'Twenties and 'Thirties. Model T and Model A Fords were everywhere.

people accumulated stuff; they filled up garages, basements and attics with the kinds of half-wanted goods that they would have thrown away if they had had to move. Kerosene lamps, an old quilt, a broken rifle, a box of used fishing lures, piles of old magazines, old toys and, of course, car parts. The spare-tire cover taken off a 1936 Ford when it was almost new, an air cleaner removed and never replaced, a radio kept when the car was traded in, a spare engine the owner always intended to rebuild. It piled up, got in the way and while something was going to be done with all that stuff nothing was. During the 'Fifties cars got much larger, far too large for garages designed to hold a Model A, so the car was parked in the driveway and the garage was filled with things which would, no doubt, someday be useful.

It was also common to park an entire car beside or behind the garage and leave it there for years. That's why it was possible during the 'Fifties to find in abundance cars of the 'Twenties and 'Thirties. Model T and Model A Fords were everywhere, and a would-be hot rodder could find his basic material by cruising through his neighborhood, or a short distance into the country. As I recall there was no pressure from local officials to remove an old car; no one seemed to complain about old cars being an eyesore.

This is quite different from the situation today, where people make a part-time occupation of complaining about their neighbors. In those days there was more room, fewer people and far less legislation. I've recently looked at aerial photos of my neighborhood taken 50 years ago, and there is so much empty land, far more than I remembered. Nearly every house had a vacant lot beside it. On some blocks there was only one house. If you have an empty lot or two as a buffer between your house and the next house you and your neighbors probably got along fine. And if one had an old car in his driveway, why would he complain about a neighbor who also had one?

Effects of the Depression

There seemed to be an *understanding* about the inherent potential value of an old car—an understanding that grew out of the lean years of the Depression. The car might not be worth much in terms of cold cash, but it was *tangible wealth*, something you could believe in, unlike paper money, and it could always supply parts for a second running car.

Nor was there any reason to dismantle the car or to haul it elsewhere. For example, there were no swap meets, no central place to which you could take the car or its component parts for resale. The price of scrap metal was low, so scrapping the old car was hardly worth one's time, although a certain number of old cars were scrapped. The impulse to scrap cars usually came from above, from the automobile manufacturers, to cut down on the glut of used cars, but in the years immediately following WW II there was no glut. As a result, old cars sat and sat, waiting to be resurrected by a rare restorer or, more likely, the hot rodder, who removed the fenders, bumpers, hood, spare tire and anything else that would come loose without too much effort. These unwanted parts were put up in

> **There seemed to be an *understanding* about the inherent potential value of an old car—an understanding that grew out of the lean years of the Depression.**

the rafters of the garage or in the woodshed, thinking that some-day he would do something with them. When swap meets became popular in the 'Sixties, this is the stuff that people hauled out of storage and traded for newer car stuff or sold—the big original 1932 Ford headlights, the 21-stud Ford V-8 block, the General Jumbo wheels, Graham-Paige taillights, etc.

I needed the money!

My father, who grew up during lean times, saved stuff. He had a large tin tobacco can into which he threw old roller bearings, brass petcocks, fittings, anything small he might some-day use. I have always been a saver too, although it turns out that I have not always saved what should have been saved. When building the '29 A-V8 roadster I threw away all kinds of things that I assumed I would never use, such as that interest-ing grille, those reworked front fenders, the entire hood, running boards with cast step-plates, taillights, the hardware and hinges for the rumble seat and much more. I can't believe that I got rid of all that stuff! And more—much more. Sometimes I'll recall a specific item, and wonder what happened to it; sometimes I can remember. For example, in late 1953 I bought a 1947 Ford coupe with a Thickstun dual intake manifold and the rare beehive air cleaner. Within a year I had replaced it with a Fenton dual intake, with the side-mount generator bracket, a pair of chrome air cleaners and a fuel block with neoprene hoses. Today I want that old Thickstun manifold back, and I wonder why I got rid of it. The two reasons I think of make a kind of sense. One, I

wanted to get modern, and while the Fenton set-up probably didn't make the car run any better, it looked so much nicer. Two, I sold the Thickstun set-up—manifold, two Stromberg carbs, that nutty air cleaner, lines and linkage—to a neighborhood kid, Bob Johnson, for $20. I can remember the guy who bought it and the amount, but not *why* I sold it. I have to remind myself that $20 was half a week's salary in 1954. I flat needed the money! If I'd had a better job that manifold might still be mine.

I also kept a lot of what most people then would have consid-ered junk. Only now it's spelled "junque." Because an increasing number of people are interested in things from the past, junk has now attained a level of respect-ability. I kept junk when it was in fact junk, for reasons sometimes unclear even to me. I only wish I'd kept more, and had had better

stuff to keep. I wish I'd had a Duesenberg grille or a Bugatti steering wheel to hang on the wall. Or, more within my interest range, an Auburn dash panel, a Winfield carburetor, a pair of old Federal-Mogul heads. Had I had them, they might still be there. But, when I needed a few bucks in a hurry, when I was leaving town for the Oakland Roadster Show, for example, I'd haul a load of dead batteries and several perfectly good radiators, as well as some sheet metal and an old engine or two, to Schnitzer and Wolfe, the local scrapyard, and sell them for a fraction of their actual worth. A couple times I

These unwanted parts were put up in the rafters of the garage or in the woodshed, thinking that someday he would do something with them.

was more deliberate and I said I was going to get rid of anything I'd had around for five years. One thing that went was a pair of 1942 Mercury rear axles, and within weeks I needed one of them! That taught me the lesson I'd learned long before but disregarded: hang onto whatever you don't need because you very well might need it. A darn good lesson in today's throwaway society!

Vintage Tin for sale! Any takers?

Hot Rodding B.C.
(before camera)

The truth is I didn't have the money to take photos in quantity.

I bought my first camera at Sandy's Camera Shop on March 5, 1952. I'm not certain where I got the money, but I am certain of the date because it was the day before the "Speedorama" car show opened. I needed a camera to take photos at the show. The camera, I'm sure, was an Ansco, the type where you open a lid on the top and look down into the viewfinder. Complete with flash attachment it cost around $15. The previous summer I had taken my first car photos at the Eugene drags using my parents' Brownie box camera—an absurdly simple camera that actually took quality photos. I'm not sure what happened to that box camera, but my camera was being used by my mother 30 years later and about two months before she died, in 1985, she left it somewhere. I tried, but couldn't find it. I can find another one easily, but I want the same camera that I used in the beginning.

The amateur photographer's equipment in the late '40s through early '60s.

Imprinted by the experience of owning a camera

It interests me to think that I was imprinted by the experience of owning a camera early on to take photographs of cars at shows, the local drags, eventually at Oakland and Bonneville—and now, nearly a half-century later, I'm doing the same thing. The major difference is that during the 'Fifties if I went to an event and took a dozen photos I was apparently satisfied. I went clear to Bonneville, an odyssey in the 'Fifties, and took 20-some photos! The truth is I didn't have the money to take photos in quantity. How I wish I had taken five or six rolls instead of five or six photos!

So there was a period of time when I was nuts about cars but lacked a camera, and those times after I got the camera but did not have it along or didn't have money for film. Those are the times I wonder about, especially late at night. I can see a rod, or a partial view of a rod, in the background of a photo and wish I could see it I clearly. Or someone will mention a particular car and I'll try to visualize it, chasing it around the circuitry of memory. Sometimes, as a car becomes clearer in my mind, as it almost hovers before me—then disappears, I have to ask myself whether that car ever did exist or if it is just a figment of my imagination, something I wished into being.

Imaginary cars?

Did I imagine the 1934 Ford coupe that sat at the tire-recapping shop about a mile from my house? I seem to remember so clearly riding my bicycle there on more than one occasion in 1950 or 1951, probably en route to Johnson Ford Specialty, a wrecking yard full of early Fords. That was so early in my car career that I hardly knew what I was looking at, but the way I remember the car it was severely chopped, channeled, had a long hood and a race car nose. It reminded me of the Pierson brothers' coupe I had seen in *Hot Rod Magazine*. Did I appreciate the fact that there were almost no chopped coupes or sedans at that time? I remember it was finished in gray primer, I could see that, but how did I know it had a Chrysler straight-eight engine, as indicated in some early notes I took?

I remember standing beside it straddling my bicycle, on a rainy morning, probably a Saturday, looking at the low fenderless coupe with a mixture of fascination, longing and stupidity. I don't remember talking with anyone about the car at the time. Nor did I see the car again after that time. I've asked numerous people, most older than me, if they remember that coupe and I have not found anyone who does. Nor have I found a photo of the coupe! It was so distinctive it could not be forgotten or confused with some other coupe. How is it possible that I'm the only person to remember that car? Perhaps if I had a photo—proof that it did exist—others would say, "Oh sure, I remember that car."

I'd love to have a photo...

I would also love to have a photo of the 1934 Ford roadster I saw parked near my father's service station in Lake Oswego in the summer of 1951 or 1952. I believe I saw it only once; it must have been during the summer because the top was removed. 1933-34 Ford roadsters were extremely rare—I can recall only one or two others, plus a couple coupes with tops removed—so it was worth looking at for that reason alone. This one was full-fendered, maroon, with big and little whitewalls and very tidy. I think it had a stock flathead V-8. The only modification I remember was the *sectioned* body! The car appeared stock, but not quite. I'm certain the car had California plates, so the owner might have been passing through on vacation. If it had been purchased by one of the many rich kids in Lake Oswego I'm sure I would

There was a period of time when I was nuts about cars but lacked a camera, and those times after I got the camera but did not have it along or didn't have money for film.

A Kodak Brownie Flash Six-20 from about 1948.

A Kodak Baby Brownie.

have seen it again. Many years later a guy told me he remembered the car and thought it went to Idaho; but no, he didn't have a photo either. That second sighting ought to confirm that I did indeed see the car.

Studebaker with the top cut off

Elsewhere I mentioned Bud Sargent's 1942 Studebaker sedan with the top cut off—a car I saw once or twice—but 50 years later, I realize that the car might have belonged to someone else. During 1948-49 I had two *Oregonian* routes, and for most of that time the branch was located at S.E. 88th and Foster across the street from where the national U-Haul company began. At the other end of the block, in a Quonset hut that's still there, Bud Sargent had a small body shop. He was well-known in Portland, and in addition to doing body work Sargent was active in circle-track roadster racing in the late 'Forties and early 'Fifties. The car I clearly remember seeing, as it came around the corner, drove past the *Oregonian* branch and pulled into Sargent's shop, was a Studebaker sedan, probably a four-door, with the top whacked off. I know it was a 1942 model because I

remember the indentation on the rear fenders behind the wheel well. I believe all the body seams were leaded smooth, it had skirts, was lowered and painted gray primer. I also remember its duals ended in brass extensions. Since others who knew Sargent do not remember the car I have to assume that it belonged to someone else and was being worked on in Sargent's shop.

Early Chrysler V-8 transplant

Another car with brass tail-pipe extensions was the Hollywood Graham sedan owned by a black guy. I clearly remember this car. On one occasion I was riding a city bus, left side, window seat, and I looked down as the car passed. I heard it too! Somehow I learned that it had a Ford flathead V-8 and sections of the dual exhausts were made from brass bed railings! In the 'Eighties I was told that the car had been owned by Bill Abel, who must have been the only black rodder in Portland, and that it later had an early Chrysler V-8 transplant. Around 1986 the car was parked for an extended period of time outside Dee Wescott's shop, in poor condition, which was where I finally photographed it. I later heard that what remained of it was sold at auction in Sandy, Oregon.

Others remember the 1939 Pontiac convertible that sat for at least a couple years inside the Beard brothers' body shop on S.E. Powell, where it was being sectioned. No one, however, can tell me who owned the car or whether it was ever finished. I think it had an Edmunds dual-intake manifold on the original in-line engine. To section a car seemed a huge task, and while I saw a couple sectioned cars in

national magazines I don't recall seeing one in the Portland area (except for that 1933-34 roadster) until 1957, when Ron Courtney finished the X-51, a sectioned 1951 Ford coupe.

I learned that around 1940 rodders considered the Pontiac a hot car, and I've talked with several old timers who owned hopped up 1936-40 Pontiacs. But in 1952 I thought that 1939 Pontiac convertible was rare, not especially attractive and its flathead inline engine was obsolete. It seemed an odd car for a section job. If it ever was finished, I'd love to see a photo.

Durant roadster with a flathead

In 1951 or 1952 I was sitting in Merhar's Drive-In when a cute but non-traditional roadster cruised through. It was blue with the front fenders and running boards removed, and it had a flathead Ford V-8 engine. The body and perhaps the chassis, or parts of the chassis, was Durant. The car was built in the late 'Forties by Don "Duck" Redmond, a slightly older fellow in the Road Angels. When I met him he had already sold the Durant. I suspect that most of the work had been done by his father, who around 1953 got a service station at 84th and SE Powell, across the street from the Beard brothers' custom body shop; and several hot rods were built in that station. I would love to have a photo of that odd-ball Durant roadster, especially because it is the only hot rodded Durant I have ever heard of. However, about the same time, there was a circa 1930 Durant coupe, with the top whacked off, parked near Franklin High. It was for sale and I looked at it, daydreamed of what I would do with it and then, like so many cars I do not have a photo of, it disappeared.

Some cars I have been seeking photos of for over 40 years. A good example was the 1936 Ford 3-window coupe I saw only once, at the burger joint at 52nd and SE Foster. It was the first day of spring, the one day that indicates winter is over; it was a Saturday and those lucky guys who owned convertibles had the top down for the first time in months. It was a lazy, carefree, sunny day, the kind of day when driving is really fun. My roadster was not yet together, so I was riding the bus to my job at the Oregon Theater; on the bus, on a day like that, I longed to be behind the wheel of an open car.

The bus pulled to a stop at the light at 52nd and I saw the car parked across the street: a low, primer-gray 1936 Ford coupe. Without even thinking, I jumped up and got off the bus, even though I'd have to walk the rest of the way to work. I was learning about cars, and it took several minutes to figure out what I was looking at. The coupe had been channeled, the running boards removed and a 1939 deluxe or 1940 standard grille and front fenders adapted to the body. Because it lacked a hood, the car's engine was very visible. It was a late-model flathead V-8 with lots of chrome, aluminum heads and a manifold that mounted two 1950 Mercury carburetors. From that moment on I have loved that set-up! I was shy, but I remember talking with the owner and he told me that the engine was a new Mercury—right out of the crate! I was impressed. Now that was a high-buck car, a distinctive car—one that others should remember. But

I've asked people about it for years and no one has been able to recall it. Lacking a photo of the car, I might think that moment never happened, except that I clearly recall that rare intake set-up and the owner's comment about the engine arriving in a crate; those are too concrete and too clear.

Less-clear images...

Other cars—and other images—are less clear. I recall a body, a '27 Model T roadster body, mounted on what was probably a reworked Buick chassis, circa-1941 with a Buick straight-eight engine and a factory dual-intake manifold. I would love to have a photo of that machine because something tells me that it was not very pretty. But the only other thing I can remember about it was the engine-turned dash panel, which probably also came from that Buick.

And what about the fenderless 1929 Ford phaeton that sat around SE 49th and Flavel? It had a great deal of chrome, but it was an awkward car. I think it was built on a 1934 Ford chassis, but perhaps the tall top or the post-1935 Ford front suspension put the front wheels too far back, so the grille and radiator stuck out. I saw the car only two or three times. In the summer of 1951 my father and I stopped to look at it, and in 1954 it came into Costanzo's Garage when I worked there.

I would love to see a photo of the white full-fendered 1929 Ford roadster with the Willys engine and running gear that sat on a side street in Milwaukie, Oregon. I saw it only once when a friend, Larry Deyoe, showed it to me, and as I recall it was a cute car. No one seems to have a

photo of John Farlow's '34 Ford 5-window coupe, a car I had almost forgotten about until Gary Guthrie reminded me. However, I clearly remember Farlow's 1934 Ford tudor, because I bought it from him in 1953, and besides, I have a photo of that car. The '34 coupe, as I recall, was basically stock with a stock engine, but it was deeply channeled in one afternoon. Gary had a neat 1932 Ford 3-window coupe and he had the same guy channel it one Saturday; we both have regrets that no one took a photo of that car either.

Cars no one would think of photographing

There were legions of cars that no one would think of photographing, simply because they were so common: the nosed-and-decked Chevs and Mercs, the 1950 Fords with straight-bar grilles, the purple 1936 Pontiac 3-window coupe that sat near Grant High, the bittersweet '40 Ford tudor with the big rake, the many cars with imitation Cadillac fins or continental kits, et al. I'd love to see photos of them—to see exactly what kind of hub caps they were running in 1949, and how many were painted and how many cruised the streets in primer, whether any had blue-dot taillights, etc. I can check out old issues of *Hot Rod Magazine* and *Motor Trend* to see the magazine-quality rods and customs, but I want to see the daily drivers, the slightly modified machines—some beautiful, some bizarre— that cruised past on a Saturday afternoon of my youth and then disappeared forever.

Why There Were Hot Rods at Mid-Century

The very presence of duals suggested speed, a hot engine, a race car.

In looking backward, I sometimes wonder whether I tend to romanticize the past. Sure, gas was cheap and plentiful, old cars were cheap and plentiful, the roads were smooth, the local bodyman would nose and deck your car for a sawbuck, the drive-ins were flourishing and driving was a pleasure because often you had the road to yourself. Yep, the 'Fifties were fabulous times to be a hot rodder.

But even I forget how pleasant driving was, how uncrowded the roads were. That was brought back to me recently when an old friend showed me a series of aerial photographs of our neighborhood in Portland. The photos were dated March 11, 1948; that was a Wednesday, and by the shadows I'd say that

Looking north at S.E. 100th and Harold around noon. A single dark sedan approaches a side street; otherwise not a car is in sight.

they were taken a little after 1:00 p.m.

This area of Portland is close to the city limits. I can remember the open fields where I played in the late 'Forties, but I had forgotten there was so much open space. Every house seems to be flanked by one or two vacant lots. The second thing I noticed were the trails that cut across these open spaces; no one walked the streets when a more direct route was possible.

Then I began to notice how few cars were parked along the streets. Only in one photo, which shows the grade school I attended, are there several parked cars, owned no doubt by the teachers. In fact, there are no cars in driveways. I imagine a world in which the father has driven the car to work and the mother, a non-driver, is at home with the kids. Or perhaps the cars are in garages. Or perhaps fewer people owned cars.

Finally I noticed that there was essentially no traffic on the main roads. Nothing moving! These are roads that I can barely navigate today because the traffic is so thick; it sometimes takes five minutes before I can turn from a side road onto a main thoroughfare. But imagine what driving was like on that Wednesday, March 11, 1948. You could get on a smooth main street and crank it on without worrying too much about running into some turkey. I mentioned the photos to a hot rodder about six years older than I am and he said, sure, you could drag race down Holgate and hit a hundred, no trouble. Take the fenders off a '34 Ford, put on duals and you could go looking for trouble, never mind about the mechanical brakes, no insurance, whatever. That was some four years before legal drag racing was established at an airport in the Portland area and street racing was a popular way to settle an argument. No wonder! Look at those empty streets, and miles between stop signs! Talk about freedom! I'm sure the story was the same in Pasadena, Dallas, Lansing, Iowa City, San Jose and a hundred other places that are now megatropolises facing gridlock.

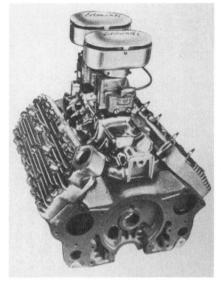

Photos from
Hot Rod Handbook *129, 1951.*

The Lost Pix

The roll had been kicking around undeveloped for decades.

When I asked my ex-father-in-law in 1981 to develop an old roll of film, I thought I knew what to expect. In 1957, a friend and I took a trip to Vancouver, British Columbia, and I assumed that this roll contained shots of that trip. I didn't expect much, however, as that roll had lain in a desk drawer for so many years. But when the film was developed, I was astonished to find that it went way back in time, and it retrieved images from a Sunday in July 1951, at the drag races in Eugene, Oregon. These were the first photos I'd taken at my first drag race!

The roll had been kicking around undeveloped for three decades, and only the first few frames had recognizable images; then the paper pulled off the emulsion, leaving only blackness. Damn! But rather than curse the darkness, I decided to celebrate the few images I could recognize.

I certainly remembered the trip. I had intended to drive to Eugene in my '29 A-V8 with my friend, Paul Downing, but my

Al Rogers' '28 A-V8 turned 88 mph. This is only shot I've seen of car with funny front bumper.

Primered, leaded '40 Ford deluxe coupe, with skirts and whitewalls, was typical of the period. It seemed like there were hundreds of them!

Kenny Austin's chopped and channeled '27 T coupe. That's probably Monte Rowland's new Merc in the background.

father squelched that idea. I didn't have my license yet, and he thought an adult should be in the passenger seat. So we gassed up Saturday night, made sandwiches and checked the roadster. At the last minute I threw in my parents' old 120 Kodak box camera.

My father and I were up early the next morning. The weather was sunny but cool, and I was trembling from the cold and from

excitement. The dual exhausts rumbled as the little red roadster drove through the neighborhood to 82nd, then south to Oregon City. We were on Highway 99, the main road in the state: It was a narrow, bumpy two-lane road! I remember how good it felt driving along with my father; the car ran swell, the top kept off the sun and wind, and we were going to the races.

Only two things marred the

trip. One, we were stopped twice in Salem by the State Police so they could check the roadster over. The second time, the cop repeatedly asked me to move my foot from the gas to the brake, to see if I could do it quickly. This was a stock height Model A! We didn't get a ticket, but I'm sure I would have if my father hadn't been along. The second misfortune to befall us was the white patch that grew in the left front

Engine in Austin's T coupe was 1937 Ford 21 stud V-8 with 1936 heads. Austin cast his own four-carb manifold, with pairs of carbs placed back to back. Guy at right is Paul Downing; he was going to ride down with me, but got there somehow.

tire; the cord began to show, and it grew larger as we returned home, but the tire held.

When we did get to the Eugene strip, there were perhaps 20 cars competing, and perhaps twice that many spectators. But there was enough activity to get my glands stirred, and I was knocked out by some of the cars. There was Al Rogers' neat '28 A-V8 roadster (#615B), a car I'd get to ride in later in the summer, after I'd joined his club, the Road Angels. His rod had been built by Jerry Martindale, with bodywork by Tom Story. It had been ma-

roon, but primer was popular and Al had the glossy paint covered with gray primer. It had a full-race flathead, highly chromed, with a pair of neat air cleaners unlike any I've seen since. It also had a chromed rear end, and people were practically begging to crawl under to polish it! The frame was stepped in back, had a dropped axle and was as low as you could get and still run fenders.

Primered '40 Ford Coupe

In the second photo, there is a primered '40 Ford coupe that

could have belonged to either Ralph Johnson, who appears to be driving, or Jim Beauvais, who is standing beside the car. Both owned '40 coupes typical of that period: blacked-out, skirts, whitewalls, pipes. Jim had a full-race flathead built during the next winter and drag raced it through the 1952 season. I don't know what happened, but a year or two later I saw the coupe's body and frame, less front end, loaded on a flatbed truck with other scrap metal headed for Schnitzer and Wolfe. Jim's was always in primer, but I seem to recall that Ralph's '40 coupe was painted gold later on. Ralph was a student at Portland State, but he found time to have a really hot 296-CID flathead built; it was the first in our area to run a Potvin Eliminator cam. The coupe really cooked with that engine, and in the summer of 1952, Ralph put it into a channeled, fenderless 1930 Model A roadster; by 1953, he was running it in a '27 T-bucket that was almost a rail job, and it was a contender.

Waist-high '27 Ford

There are two shots of a nutty hammered '27 T coupe. Built by Kenny Austin, this coupe was chopped and channeled until it was slightly over waist-high. It was fast and trick. For example, it used a 1937 Ford 21-stud engine with 1936 heads; this allowed the radiator hoses to run straight to the radiator. It also had a four-carb intake manifold designed and cast by Austin, who was an engineering student at Oregon State College. For the Expo show in February, 1952 he painted it green. The following summer it had a brand-new Ford OHV six, with a fuel-injection setup built by

Clarence Everett's two draggin' wagons: '27 T-V8 pickup in background; '33 Plymouth chassis with '34 Chrysler Airflow straight-eight engine and overdrive transmission in foreground.

Austin. He later sold the coupe to Gordon Sully of Portland, who raced and exhibited the car for years. I heard that it went to Alaska in the 'Seventies, then to California.

There's a poor photo of two cars parked together. I can easily recognize Clarence Everett's funny car—funny because it was so high and heavy. It was a '27 T body with a '37 Ford pickup box, mounted on a mid-'30s Ford chassis. It had a '37 Ford truck grille, '34 Pontiac eight side panels and a piece of railroad track as a rear bumper. But it was a draggin' wagon, with a hot flathead V-8, and Clarence drove it across the country one summer. Beside it is a car I do not remember, but it's probably one Clarence told me about years later. He ran a bare '33 Plymouth chassis, stripped except for a bucket seat. He used a stock 323-CID Chrysler straight-eight engine, transmission and overdrive unit from a 1934 Chrysler Airflow. He accelerated through

Looks like really neat '29 roadster, with '32 grille, Kelsey wires, all road equipment. Last halfway decent photo on the roll. I'd love to know what else I took photos of!

second and high gears—"in low gear it'd smoke the tires off." The fastest drag car was a gutted 1934 Ford coupe, and Clarence said that from a rolling start he beat the coupe by ten car-lengths!

This was a super day in my book, and when the guy on the PA system said, "What about running the red roadster?" I was ready. But my father said no, and as I looked at the white cord showing through on the left front tire I had to agree. So I grabbed the camera, wandered the pits and snapped some photos—the start of something I'm still doing 45 years later.

Clubs

I'm reminded that the only thing I've ever joined in my whole life was a hot rod club, the Road Angels.

During the 'Fifties, if you were even a casual hot rodder you probably belonged to a car club. Put duals and skirts on your '36 Ford sedan and you qualified for membership in the Road Knights, Gear Grinders, Hi-Revvers, or whatever your club was called. You got a nifty cast-aluminum plaque with a club name to mount on the rear bumper, and the right to stand in the parking lot after a club meeting, kicking tires, listening to lies and telling a few yourself. It was great fun, and I'm reminded that the only thing I've ever joined in my whole life was a hot rod club, the Road Angels.

That clubs existed is a paradox, because hot rodders by definition are individuals, loners, mavericks, outlaws; they would seem the least likely people to want to meld into an organized group. But it happened almost from the start with the Outriders, a So-Cal club formed in 1932, and by 1939 there were dozens of clubs in the So-Cal area. By 1950 hot rodding had spread across the country and there

Members of Dukes club line up to drive to garage for safety inspection performed by club members. Photo taken in 1955 shows trend toward newer cars.

A pair of plaques from old California clubs. The Throttlers club was largely responsible for formation of Southern California Timing Association (SCTA) in 1938, so the club's early plaque lacks SCTA designation; slightly later Sidewinders plaque includes it.

were clubs in towns with only two or three rodders.

Clubs were important for several reasons. A club allowed people with similar interests to get together to discuss building problems and to view each other's machinery. There were no swap meets during the 'Fifties, but at a club meeting you might locate that hard-to-find part for your rod. Clubs also allowed members to socialize. Most rodders were single, in their teens or very early twenties, bereft of the high school social scene and too young to go to bars; a club that had dances and picnics offered a possible social structure.

From the beginning, car clubs were made up of people from a limited area of the city, so you might know members from high school or from the local garage.

Car clubs were masculine by nature (I knew of only one woman who belonged to a car club), and they created an opportunity for men to get together, talk, bench race, give

encouragement and to help one another, which—at the risk of being called *sexist*—is something I think men need.

I have another theory for the popularity of car clubs, and it has to do with the lack of other activities in those days. Leisure time was spent at a movie, in a tavern, perhaps playing sandlot baseball or doing some fishing. Today there are so many more options—young people have rock bands, make videos, films, tapes, build computers, watch 32 hours of TV a week, and jet off to Europe for brief spells. In the early 'Fifties I didn't know anyone who had been to Europe, except vets who had gone via LSTs.

A sense of belonging

A car club gave one a sense of belonging and a sense of identity. The car club I joined, the Road Angels of Portland, might have been typical. Formed in 1950 by several guys who had gone to high school together, it disbanded in December of that year when 17 of its 25 members

were drafted in one week and sent to Korea. It was reorganized in June 1951, and when I joined in August it again had about 25 members. They ranged in age from 16 (me) to perhaps 24. Several were married, one (me) was in high school, a couple were in college, but most were working at blue-collar jobs.

Most members lived in the southeast part of the city and had gone to the same high school, so the car club was in a way an extension of their high-school social club. We met weekly in the banquet room of an Italian restaurant, conducted business, and then cruised to Bart's Drive-in (later The Speck) two blocks away, where we checked over each other's cars.

From the beginning, car clubs were made up of people from a limited area of the city, so you might know members from high school or from the local garage.

A club jacket and two T-shirts from the 'Fifties. Road Angels of Portland, Oregon helped form early Columbia Timing Association (CTA) in 1951. T-shirt on right was earlier than one on left.

The Road Angels on a beach trip in 1951. Norm Cahill, club president, sits on fender of '40 Ford coupe owned by Jim Beauvais, rather than fender of his own '40 Merc convertible.

The members over 21 or who had passable fake ID, walked across the street to the Creston Tavern where they "consumed some suds."

Those were exciting times. Hot rodding was new, and things kept changing. The Road Angels were instrumental in forming a new timing association, and in securing an airport for a drag strip. It also got the use of a long airstrip in a remote part of the state where one-mile timed runs were held. The club, alone or in conjunction with another club, held reliability runs, a beach trip, a picnic, a couple of dances, and a wild stag party with kegs and risqué films!

Public image important

Hot rodders were very conscious of their public image.

The popular press had branded them *outlaws*; and while a few celebrated that image, most tried to change it. The club plaque on your car gave you an identity; it said, "Here is who I am." And you didn't want your driving habits to reflect badly on the club, so you refrained from peeling rubber or rapping your pipes.

But the social concerns of most clubs went beyond a safe-driving program, extending to public relations. Most clubs had a policy of asking members to help motorists in distress. If you saw someone with a flat tire, you helped the person. And, before leaving, to make it clear that you were not acting as an individual but as part of a movement, you gave the stranded motorist a card that read: "You have been

Dukes club had plaque resembling finned high-compression head.

Leadfoots (leadfeet?) was early club from Oregon City.

Two Portland club plaques from the 'Fifties. Road Knights, formed in 1952, still exists.

assisted by a member of (name of club), a hot rod club dedicated to safety."

When the NHRA was started, it used that last phrase as its motto. Numerous campaigns were organized to create better public relations. For example, members of my club gave blood to the blood bank and, by offering rides in real hot rods, got others to give blood. For this program, the Road Angels won *Hot Rod Magazine*'s public service award in 1952, presented by the governor of Oregon.

During the 'Fifties clubs thrived. An interesting trivia question would be to ask how many clubs there were in the U.S. during that decade. But of course there is no answer—no one knows. Three or four guys out in the sticks could, over a few beers, decide to become a club; they could call themselves the *Untouchables* or the *Gear Heads* or whatever, make a rough drawing of a plaque and have it cast up and on their cars in a week or so. Any large city had at least one foundry that would make a pattern and cast plaques, providing you ordered at least ten of them. Stylized Emblem of Los Angeles provided that service through the mail. A foundry in Chicago that specialized in club plaques had, until recently, the patterns for over 5,000 plaques. If you were a hot rodder, you had to have a plaque mounted on the bumper or hanging under it.

Big in the 'Fifties

Clubs were big in the 'Fifties, but most disappeared during the 'Sixties. During that decade rodders turned to sports cars and muscle cars, but it's not clear to me why they didn't continue to develop clubs built around their new interest. Perhaps clubs are more closely associated with rodding, because with the marked increase in the numbers involved in street rodding during the 'Seventies and 'Eighties, clubs have returned in droves— and probably for the same reasons that clubs were popular during the 'Fifties.

From Hot Rod Magazine, *March 1955.*

Street Was Fun in '51

Looking back, I realize that this might well have been the first reliability run held in the area.

In November 1951 I participated in my first organized hot rod street event. In August I'd joined the Road Angels, a hot rod club. The Road Angels and several other clubs belonged to the governing body, the Northwest Timing Association. The NWTA ran drag races in Eugene, Oregon, about 120 miles south of Portland. Some of the leaders of two Portland clubs felt a need to promote activities in the Portland area, where, after all, most of the people lived. The two clubs, the Road Angels and the Ramblers, broke away from NWTA and formed a new timing group, the Columbia Timing Association (CTA).

They needed an event to promote the CTA and to bond members of the two clubs, so the presidents decided to hold a reliability run open only to members of both groups. Looking back, I realize that this was

Rodders gather before the run: at left, Al Drake, in baggy tweed pants and letterman's jacket, looking amazed and 16. Others are (left to right) Rich Redmond, Chuck Blanchard, Norm Cahill, Hugh Minsker, Red Blivens and Al Rogers. Guy at right might be Don Selden.

Bud Parham's '23 T-V8 on its first outing (lacks headlights, wipers, etc.).
Parham (middle) was dressed for nippy November weather.

probably the first reliability run held in the area. I know that about the same time, and perhaps a little earlier, members of another club, the Mobileers, had cruised to Mt. Hood and Long Beach, Washington in a caravan, but that was different. A reliability run required that the driver and co-pilot guide the car over a measured route of several miles and arrive back at the starting point within a certain time limit. The run promoted togetherness and also safe driving.

Juices flowing

I was excited about participating in the run. I'd driven my roadster to Eugene a couple of times to Madras for one mile runs to spectate at the drag races, hit the local drive-in restaurants, and done some street racing, of course. But this would be the first legitimate street-rodding activity where I would play an active part. Unfortunately, I wouldn't be quite as active as I would have liked. The month before I'd wrecked my roadster when I turned left in front of a '39 Chev which I still maintain did not have its lights on. (OK, I'd only been driving for about four months, and I probably wasn't looking where I was going!) The Chev hit the right front tire squarely, wrecking the axle, one

wishbone and the right side exhaust pipe. I could've had it on the road fairly quickly, but of course I completely disassembled the car and it didn't see pavement again for the better part of a year.

Cruising the back roads

But my spirits were only slightly diminished. The notion of such a run got my juices flowing. The Saturday night prior to the run I was flopped on the living room floor reading a year-old copy of *Hot Rod Magazine* with extensive coverage of the Pasadena Roadster Club Reliability Run. The photos showed roadsters of all types gathered in the Bowl, lining up for the start and cruising the back roads.

This run was somewhat different, in that only a few rods and customs showed up; most members came in "chair cars." I think I came by city bus, or perhaps my father loaned me his 1942 Lincoln Zephyr, I can't recall. But I do remember being a little disappointed by the lack of roadsters and coupes as I arrived at the run. We met in the parking lot of the Il Travatore restaurant at 52nd and Foster, where the Road Angels held meetings. On the lot were Rich Redmond's '39 Merc tudor, stock except for dual pipes; Don Selden's '50 Ford with a little body work and a straight bar grille; Chuck Blanchard's '49

Chev convertible, cream with red primer spots indicating he was working on it; and others of that type. Norm Cahill drove his '40 Merc convert, a nice semi-custom, still in primer; his brother, Bill, drove his '41 Chev coupe, which had been "in-progress" for several years but which eventually would become a sharp custom. Al Rogers had recently sold his neat '28 A-V8 roadster and had bought a '49 Ford coupe.

Handled like a dream

I can't recall the other cars in attendance, but I do remember when Ramblers President Bud Parham drove up in his '23 T-V8 roadster pickup. This was the

car's first outing; it was still in primer but it looked so neat. The proportions were just right and Bud, a machinist, had built it right. I was told that it handled like a dream, and the way Bud maneuvered it in traffic made me a believer. It had a stock flathead V-8, but that engine provided plenty of beans for the light rig. As I recall, Bud broke all records in covering the course, but he had fun. Two months later, with chartreuse-yellow paint and a little chrome, it was shown in the city's second hot rod show. In

We must have been doing something right because we won.

Al Rogers had sold his '28 A-V8 roadster, and had just bought this '49 Ford coupe. He later drove it to San Diego, where it was stolen and found stripped in Mexico. He used insurance money to buy super-neat '29 roadster on '32 rails.

STREET WAS FUN IN '51

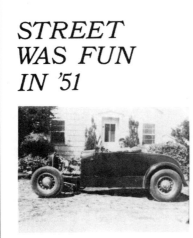

Albert Drake

Al Drake's book, Street Was Fun in '51.

that form it appeared in *Hot Rod* (May 1952) and later, painted blue, with red-and-white flames, it was on the cover of *Rod & Custom* (May 1956). Then, like so many other neat rods, it disappeared.

We lined up for the start, and I was co-pilot for Jim Bartlett. I think the car was a 1942 Chevrolet, something uninteresting. But we must have been doing something right because we won—he got the trophy but now, 46 years later, I want half the credit! The trophy was presented in the banquet room, and then we all enjoyed a big spaghetti dinner, plus a lot of bench racing. Hot rodding was a new activity, and I remember thinking: I hope it lasts a while! This was fun!

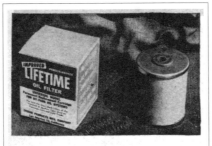

CUT DAILY DRIVING COSTS! Improved Lifetime oil filter lets you drive 10,000 miles without changing oil. And amazing "Perma-Bronze" cylindrical element lasts *forever*— no more buying new filter packs. Stronger, more efficient, greater filtering area. *Removes* all harmful particles, yet retains expensive additives. 10-year guarantee! Universal conversion element for most cars, $6.95. Full-flow type, $11.95. Complete unit with housing, $12.95. Shipped postpaid. Item #1.

A SMART CUSTOM TOUCH without costly body work! Handsomely designed "Smoothee-Lites" lengthen and beautify the lines of your 1952-54 Ford. Simple installation. No body alterations. No wires or lights to change. Easily adapted to many other cars. Either prime-coated for "frenching" or paint matching, or triple chrome plated for immediate use. Primed, $8.95. Chromed, $9.95. Item #6.

HAS YOUR CAR LOST ITS ZIP? Does it burn oil? Sound like a "klunker"? Don't run it off a cliff or spend big money on an overhaul. Just remove spark plugs and squeeze Holt's Piston Seal into holes. Holt's forms self-expanding seal, stops oil burning and piston slap. Restores compression and power. Treatment lasts 10,000 miles. Lloyds of London insures Holt's against harm to even finest engines. Full treatment $4.95, ppd. Item #7.

TIRED OF SPARK PLUGS THAT SKIP AND MISS after first few weeks? Triple Fire Airplane-Type plugs are guaranteed 20,000 miles on mileage basis! Design features three heat-resistant nickel alloy electrodes instead of usual single steel point. Heat varies resistance, causing points to fire in rotation; *triples* performance, reliability and plug life. Lifetime "Cardo" insulators give wide heat range. Terrific value! Only 89c per plug ppd. Item #2.

USERS REPORT INCREASED GAS MILEAGE with the precision-built Gane-Master Fuel Pressure Regulator. Large, sensitive diaphragm smooths out fuel pump pulsations —permits ideal fuel-air mixture. Gane-Master prevents vapor lock; eliminates gas waste, stalling, flooding, and frequent carburetor adjustment due to excessive pressure. Will quickly pay for itself on any car or truck. Only $7.95, postpaid. Item #3.

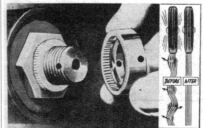

GET 5,000 EXTRA MILES PER TIRE . . . safer, more accurate steering, with a pair of "Educated Nuts." Sensational engineering development makes front wheel bearing adjustment 10 times more accurate! 60-point micrometric head locks bearings in *exact* precision adjustment—saves tires, bearings, brakes, steering—even eliminates most brake squeaks! Actually *easier* to install than conventional nut! New low price, complete for any passenger car (specify), only $2.98 per pair ppd. Item #4.

Newhouse Automotive Industries ads from December 1954 issue of Hot Rod *Magazine.*

The National Hot Rod Association

To bring together a bunch of hot rodders into a national organization was pretty remarkable.

At mid-century hot rodding was booming in California, and slowly spreading to far-flung cities and towns across the nation. In March 1950, Wally Parks, the editor of *Hot Rod Magazine*, used his column to announce the groundwork for an association that would bring several timing associations, from So-Cal to Denver, into a blanket governing organization. Parks also noted ". . . it was brought home to us that this sport has definitely reached a nation-wide status."

A year later, in the March 1951 issue of *Hot Rod*, there was a full page "letter," ostensibly written by Bob Cameron from Chicago, that asked the question: "Why *Not* a National Hot Rod Association?" It outlined in detail the need for such an organization and how it should function. By the May, 1951 issue the magazine announced that the National Hot Rod Association (NHRA)

Original NHRA charter member decal for a rod's windshield.

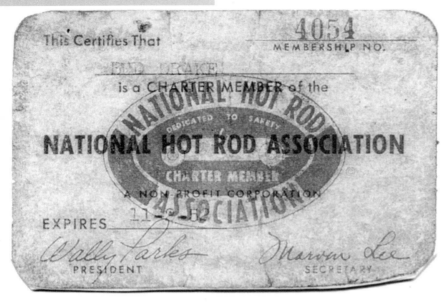

Author's original NHRA membership card.

was a reality, starting with $1,500 borrowed from the magazine. The organization's stated purpose was: "To promote safety, sportsmanship and fellowship among hot rod enthusiasts through the organization of clubs and associations, encourage a mutual exchange of beneficial views and sponsor educational and safety programs to the end that the hot rod sport will be better regulated and conducted on higher standards, resulting in its more favorable acceptance by the press and public and greater benefits to its active participants."

The first president was Wally Parks, the vice president and treasurer was Ak Miller and the secretary was Marvin Lee, hot rodders all. The first field director was G. H. "Tiny" Snell, from Reno, Nevada. Membership dues were $2 a year (up from the $1 that Cameron had suggested), and of course I sent in my money pronto and became charter member number 4054.

To bring together a bunch of hot rodders into a national organization was pretty remark-

able. Among the many good things that the NHRA did to promote hot rodding in those early days was to publish a newsletter, *Drag Link*, starting in January 1955 (later called *Tie Rod*), that linked together rodders who often had no contact with other rodders. From the beginning it distributed the kind of literature rodders needed, such as information on how to form a club or a timing association. Because of the NHRA booklets, clubs proliferated like crazy. In Portland, Oregon there were two clubs in 1948, and no more than four clubs in 1951, all formed before the NHRA was established. By 1954 there were 44 Portland-area hot rod clubs! That's the kind of influence the NHRA had in those early years.

Today the NHRA still flourishes, and Wally Parks still serves as its president.

From November 1956 issue of Motor Trend Magazine.

Not-So-Hot Rods

The majority of hod rods in the '50s were certainly not show quality.

When we think of a 'Fifties rod or custom we usually think of a sleek machine with perfect paint, chrome and upholstery. But in fact such machines were rare. There were many, many hot rods and customs on the streets back then, and the majority were, if not rough, certainly not show quality. These cars were being driven every day, were usually unfinished, and were old cars to start with.

Plenty of unsafe cars were on the road with worn-out front ends, burned-out lights, thin tires. Most 'Thirties cars had mechanical brakes with worn clevises and pins. Even worse were the "cabledraulic" brakes on the 1937-38 Fords, with rusty or stretched cables.

Of course, we didn't want cars with mechanical defects or shoddy workmanship. The cars we had seen in magazines, and a few we had seen on the streets of Portland, had shown us the ideal:

1932 Ford 5-window coupe might be typical 'Fifties rod: it has mechanical brakes, stock '32 V-8 engine, etc. Channeled until fenders rub on rear tires. Radiator in stock position is several inches higher than the cowl.

Even Californians can build imperfect cars. This appears to be a '27 T coupe with top cut off. Not perfect, but cute!

sleek, flawless metal, all chassis parts cleaned and painted or chrome-plated, a spotless interior. That was the ideal we all, consciously or unconsciously, pursued. But the result generally fell far short of the mark. It's hard to be perfect. A car without fenders will throw mud and water across the side of the body. Oil and gas will leak over an engine and on the firewall. Muddy feet will soon track up the carpet.

But the flaws were inherent in the building process. Few cars in those days were disassembled and rebuilt; most were built piecemeal, over a period of months, and many were never finished. Most hot rods had unpainted chassis, or had paint only on the parts that showed. I remember sitting in the driveway

on a warm, sunny day painting the front suspension on my A-V8 roadster; I was painting it with aluminum paint so it would appear to be chrome-plated. The problem was that I didn't disassemble the suspension, and I didn't clean the parts thoroughly. Within a week or two even I realized it looked cheap, so I painted it black—with a brush, without disassembling the parts and without further cleaning! There were rough edges, places where parts from two different cars would refuse to merge. Holes in the firewall, oodles of old wires hanging from the dash; rough welds, lousy workmanship, bad ideas, botched hopes and aborted plans. We desired perfection but had to settle for the humanly imperfect.

Some cars were clearly

illegal: they lacked fenders, horn, windshield wiper or other essential road equipment.

Some cars were clearly dangerous: they were worn-out or badly built. The mechanical defects were compounded when an owner dumped in a hot engine or made shoddy modifications. Mechanical brakes got out of adjustment. Rough welds had so much slag they looked like a lava flow.

Some weird engine swaps clearly taxed the builder's ingenuity. I recall an A-V8 conversion where the builder used pieces of a wooden two-by-four for motor mounts. I recall another flathead V-8 in a Model A coupe where the builder split the wishbone and *wired* the ends to the frame. Whoever put the V-8 in my roadster installed an Oldsmobile steering column and box; the box located so low it hit every bump and curb, in addition to placing the drag link at a severe angle. There were always little things one never got around to doing; for months I drove the roadster without a headlight switch, turning on the lights by crawling under the car and twisting two wires together.

Even simple things like proper headlight brackets seemed insurmountable. You could always identify a fenderless car coming at you at night because the headlights shook so badly. My roadster's headlights were mounted on the frame horns, and cars were constantly backing into them, knocking them out of adjustment. And there were bald tires, leaky gas tanks, rusty water flying back from a bum radiator—all this as opposed to the "typical" beautiful street rod of today.

But it's important to realize that those cars were used for daily transportation. No one I knew kept a car in the garage to be taken out only for car shows or an occasional drive. They were driven everywhere, in all kinds of weather; parked in places where they were subjected to rain, bad drivers and possible vandalism. One had to accept the imperfections of chipped paint, small dents and worn upholstery.

Everyday drivers

As Dee Wescott told me recently, confirming my estimate:

"A lot of stuff in those years was never finished. Now you go to shows and look at these cars that are supposedly 'Fifties cars, everything underneath them is chrome-plated and prettied—it wasn't that way. People in the 'Fifties *drove* their cars. The outsides were nice. A lot of beautiful, beautiful cars, and then you look inside and there's a blanket thrown over the front seat because there wasn't any money for upholstery."

These cars were driven every day and sometimes during the

One had to accept the imperfections of chipped paint, small dents and worn upholstery.

This appears to be a '27 Ford Model T coupe body, less roof, mounted on a stock Model A chassis with '29 A fenders. Unusual treatment is seen with dipped doors, one-piece windshield from mid 'Thirties car. Car sat at station on S.E. Foster and 53rd; car was wrecked a couple weeks after I took this photo in 1952.

time the drivers were making major alterations. I remember seeing a guy with a '34 Ford 5-window in the area where I lived; he was young, married and already a father. The coupe was apparently his only transportation, and each week you'd see it in a different stage of completion. Then he decided to hammer the lid and one day he drove past with the entire roof cut off. A few days later he came by with the chopped top tack-welded in place. He didn't have the glass cut yet, not even the windshield; it was raining, and he had his family with him. It took him a month to get the job done, and he drove it all the time.

I drove my roadster every day—when it wasn't disassembled—for over three years, and for most of that time it was my only transportation to school and work. I drove it through a lot of rain, the front tires throwing water at the place where the side curtains should have been, and sometimes I had to work the windshield wiper by hand.

There were about 50 extra holes in my car's firewall. It had a '39 Ford dash when I bought it, with lots of wires leading to nothing; I put in a '40 Ford dash, complete with all the extra wires. My father leaded in the '32 shell but failed to cut out the crown around the radiator cap so it had an awkward peak. I took off the outside door handles, but rather than lead them in I screwed pieces of metal over the openings. I never did lead in the holes in the cowl that had held the spare-tire support rod. Safety glass in the windshield was crazed, yellow and full of bubbles. The top got shabby, so we gave it a coat of top dressing that gave the material a cheap shine. The front tires were smooth as a baby's behind.

Driven in primer

Many, perhaps most, rods were never given a color coat but were driven in primer. My father and I painted mine—right in the driveway, where we picked up some dust and bugs. We painted right over a couple minor dents; it was an imperfect job, but the car was red! Then we noticed all this stuff hanging underneath the car—wires and exhaust pipes and mufflers—and my father got the idea of putting a 10-inch piece of sheet metal below the body, from the rear fenders forward to the cowl; held on with screws, it concealed all that messy junk, but the piece itself didn't look too great.

I got rid of these pieces of sheet metal the next fall when I channeled the car; I also got rid of the entire floor pan. Dropping the body left a space between the body and the frame that was obvious when the door was open. Channeling also burned the paint off the lower cowl on both sides, and on the rear fenders when I bobbed them with a torch. I began to scrape all that thick red paint off the body, then quit, and the bare metal got rusty. I finally gave the car a coat of primer, without much preparation, and it was again all one color.

I kept driving it, rain or shine. But I don't want to make that sound like a punishment—it was fun, most of the time. With the side panels and hood on the engine heat came through the numerous holes in the firewall and back into the cockpit, where it was nice and warm.

From March 1955 issue of Hot Rod Magazine.

Top Rods

Those builders were artists, real craftsmen, impatient with shoddy workmanship.

There were plenty of hot rods in the early 'Fifties in Portland, Oregon, but only a few were exceptional.

It didn't take a whole lot of money or brains to build a rod in those days. Find an early 'Thirties Ford, remove the front fenders and running boards, put a chrome air cleaner on the carburetor and you were in business. There were degrees of sophistication, but many cars never got beyond that stage. Moreover, a lot of the workmanship was pretty awful: rough welds, crummy paint, botched bodywork. We yearned for perfection, but most builders were nowhere near that state of grace.

A few, however, were, and they showed us the examples of construction that we should strive for. Those builders were artists, real craftsmen, impatient with shoddy workmanship—the

Bud Parham's '23 T-V8 pickup had perfect proportions. Bed was shortened, rear fenders were '29 A, had '32 grill and chrome outside headers.

Tom Story's ex-track roadster converted to street use. It had '28 A rear section and doors, '30 A cowl, Dodge windshield and hand-made race car nose.

Larry Eave's 1932 Ford roadster was cut three ways: sectioned, narrowed and shortened. It was also chopped and channeled, which put the tops of the doors at belt height. I took the photo in 1952 before the car was wrecked at Bonneville. It's the only photo showing this car with hood side panels.

cars that they built emphasized the distinction between show quality and the vast legion of average hot rods.

For example, there was a remarkable '36 3-window coupe that I saw only once, and I'd love to have a photo of the car. I saw it on the first spring day of 1951—I mean the first *real* day of spring, after weeks of rain and gray skies. The sun was out, life was beautiful, and the only cloud on the horizon was the fact that my own roadster wasn't finished. On this particular day the streets were suddenly filled with convertibles with the tops down. And I was riding the bus!

When it stopped at 52nd and Foster I saw in the Dairy Queen

parking lot a radical coupe; I jumped off the bus and crossed the street, knowing that I would have to walk the rest of the way to the Oregon Theater because I had only enough money for the bus ride home. But the look was worth the walk: the car was a 1936 Ford 3-window coupe that had been channeled, with the running boards removed, the rear fenders raised and leaded to the body, and '39 Ford front fenders and deluxe grille installed. Although unchopped, the car was extremely low with just a tad of the wide white sidewall showing beneath the skirted rear fenders. Even in gray primer the car was a winner! It lacked a hood—given the combination of '36 cowl and '39 fenders, I assume that the driver didn't intend to put on a hood—and the exotic engine was clearly evident. The driver told me it was a '50 Merc block, brand-new, just out of the crate, with Edelbrock

Glenn Koko's '28 A-V8 had filled '32 shell; leading edge of front fenders were also filled. This roadster was Koko's daily transportation. Taken at 1952 "Speed-O-Rama" show. Roy Burke's TQ midget, built by Orville Withey.

heads and lots of chrome. But what made it especially interesting was the carburetion—the manifold, probably an Edmunds, used two '49-50 Mercury "side-draft" Holley carbs, a novel set-up. That car represented big bucks, and I've often wondered who owned it and what happened to it.

The possibility of seeing cars

like that, even once, supplied a kind of adrenaline to my life. The obsession of finding such cars made even casual side trips around Portland pretty interesting, and I believed that I knew of

The possibility of seeing cars like that supplied a kind of adrenaline to my life.

Bill Peterson in his neat red '32 Ford roadster, built 1955-56. Car had mild Merc flathead, all-white Naugahyde interior, flipper hub caps, and was featured twice in Hot Rod Magazine. *Car now has Chevrolet V-8, is otherwise unchanged.*

Wes Strohecker's '27 T roadster was mounted on '32 frame; painted black with eggshell-white rolled-and-pleated interior. During the 'Fifties this was the only car I saw on the street with a Halibrand quick change; I recently learned it came from Del McClure's big car, which was wrecked in a race.

Story could have simply mounted one on a set of rails—what he did do shows the kind of imagination and ability he had. He combined a '28 Model A roadster rear section and doors with a '30 roadster cowl; the windshield was chopped from a Dodge roadster; the rear fenders were bobbed '28 Ford, mounted higher on the channeled body, and the front fenders were cycle type. Story was a first-class metal man: an Indianapolis race car type nose was pounded from 20-gauge sheet stock, and the three-piece solid hood had a large bubble for the generator. Although channeled, the car sat comfortably high, because of a stock frame and a stock-height front axle. Large chrome headers carried out the race car theme, and as they tapered back alongside the body they concealed the underside of the car and made it appear lower. It had big and little tires, with wide white sidewalls, a 1941 Ford instrument panel (the only thing about the car that I disliked because it detracted from the race car theme) in a padded dash, a chrome front end,

the existence of most hot rods in town. Of course, once I got my own roadster running the search got easier and more extensive. My only regret today is that I didn't have a better camera and more money for film; I'd love to see some of those rods again, if only on paper.

$1,800 roadster

Another exceptional car was an old track roadster that had been converted to street use. I'd seen a photo that Dick Martin had sent to *Hot Rod* in 1949 when it was owned by Jim Hill; in 1951 I saw the car at Glenn Volz's Salem Speed Shop. Later that year it appeared in my neighborhood, owned by Jack Johnson, who traded a brand new Olds 88, worth about $1,800, for the roadster—that was a helluva lot of money in those days. The car had been built by Portlander Tom Story in 1946-47 as a competition machine. There were plenty of solid roadster bodies around then and

Tom Story also built this sports car in 1950. It combined a Willys frame, Ford V8-60 engine, new Chevrolet and Pontiac fenders; the rest of the body Story pounded from aluminum, and it was flawless. Paint was dark-green. In 1951 the car was sold and it disappeared.

Bo Knab built this '32 Ford 3-window coupe in 1949-50. It was chopped, channeled, had fully chromed front end and full race Merc engine. Paint was very purple. Taken at Scappoose drags.

column shift, a neat padded top, and the car was painted metallic-bronze.

The '48 Merc engine, built by Blackie Blackburn, ran a Shanafelt manifold, Edelbrock heads, big intake valves, a full race cam and a stroked crank that was the first statically and dynamically balanced unit in the Northwest. The car was very fast on the circle track; it reportedly turned 108 mph in the quarter and 134 mph top end. It was a beautiful, well-made, well-designed machine, and would drive people nuts if it were to show up at a rod run today! Peter Sukalac did a feature on the car in 1955 for *Rod & Custom*, when the car was owned by Ed Brooke;

Roger Simonatti built this cute pickup in 1953 using '32 Ford cab, front fenders and grille, Model A bed and rear fenders. Big Merc engine, dual chrome stacks beside cab. Cab was channeled but not chopped, and truck had more of a rake than is apparent here. Paint was light yellow. Truck is still a street rod 40-some years later.

the article was entitled "Old Roadsters Never Die" and ended with this line: "This rod doesn't have a chance to deteriorate—like fine wine it ripens with age." About that time I saw the car at Keith Randol's garage; the grille and nose had been pushed in, as had the panel below the decklid, and it was generally beat up. I never saw the car again, although I find it hard to believe that something so beautiful could disappear.

A real grade-B production

One night Jimmy Strand and I rode the bus, then hitchhiked, and finally walked up 82nd to the Granada Theater to see a film called *Hot Rod*. It was a Monogram release, a real grade-B production starring Myron Healy, Art Baker and Jimmy Lyndon. The plot was worse than the acting, but what I enjoyed were the cars—real California hot rods!—and the sense of community that the rodders shared. To be part of a group, working together to build rods, shooting the breeze late at night in a cozy garage, that was what I desired. A few months later I learned that the Montavilla area around the Granada Theater was a hot bed of car building activities—more real and much more interesting than the version shown in the film *Hot Rod*.

At the Montavilla Garage a young mechanic named Don Krueger owned *four* rods—a gray-primered '36 3-window coupe, a '36 Ford tudor, a fenderless '25 T bucket with a Riley two-port, and a white full-fendered '28 Ford roadster with a hot four-cylinder flathead. Down the street Willy Wagner was building a super-low '29 A-V8, and farther yet Jerry Taylor was installing a new Chrysler V-8 in a full-fendered '32 3-window—the first such installation done anywhere.

Top-buck production

Across the street from Montavilla Garage was the Chevron station owned by Bob Newcombe where Larry Eave was building his radical roadster. It was a '32 Ford roadster body that had been cut three ways: sectioned 4 inches, narrowed 5-1/2 inches, and shortened 9 inches by Inky Sterling. The frame was stepped 9 inches in the front and in the rear (the first time I'd seen a frame with a double step), and the body was channeled 5 inches. The car was very low; the top of the door came to my waist, and the molded rear fenders were almost flush with the top of the rear deck. This was a top-buck production, an exceptional car; it looked like a rolling advertisement for the So-Cal Speed Shop. The body was painted white enamel and the running gear was black; it had Kinmont disc brakes, a Norden race car center steering assembly, a full Stewart-Warner dash, a rolled-and-pleated red-and-white Naugahyde interior, and a DuBrille top. It had a trick engine too: small bore and short stroke, with a Norden 180-degree crank and cam, a Harman and Collins

Carl Jensen built "Tinker Toy" in 1958. '29 A roadster pickup was bright-red, with fully chromed 303 Oldsmobile running three carbs. Car now has late Ford V-8 and minor changes, is still on the street.

Bob Knowles and his 1932 Ford highboy roadster in 1957. Car was state-of-the-art with dropped axle, chrome front and rear end, metallic-blue lacquer paint. blue-and-white rolled-and-pleated Naugahyde interior, white sidewall tires—it even had a top and side curtains!

This was a beautiful roadster, but I suspect that Eave was less interested in beauty than in speed.

magneto, Edelbrock heads, and numerous intake manifolds—a two carb, a three carb, and a four carb, and a dual manifold that mounted two of the '49-'50 Mercury Holley four-bolt carbs.

This was a beautiful roadster, but I suspect that Eave was less interested in beauty than in speed. Upholstery kept things sanitary, but it didn't make the car go faster. And Eave was a racer! You sensed that by the lack of chrome on the engine. A street racer would run chrome acorn nuts on his engine, but a real racer would run hardened-steel head nuts and washers so he could get a true torque reading. The editors of *Speed Age*, a racing magazine with a distinct anti-hot rod bias, knew that

Eave was a racer and so they featured his car on the cover. He raced in local legal drags, and at Bonneville in 1952, where, on a return run, the car was struck by a spectator's car and badly damaged.

Perfect proportions

Bud Parham's '23 T-V8 pickup not only looked good and

handled well, it was a low-bucks project. Parham, a machinist who later ran a speed shop, did all the work himself, and he did it right. The frame was Model A, as were the rear fenders and box; the body was a '23 T, the grille was a chopped and filled '32. Parham assembled these components in such a way that the result was a perfectly proportioned machine—it looked exactly right from any angle. Although it had a nearly-stock '48 Mercury engine, the little truck was fast and it handled beautifully. The paint was yellow; the interior was done in flat Naugahyde in gray and orange—not expensive, but very neat!

Daily driver

A good example of a beautiful rod that was used as a daily driver was Glenn Koko's '28 A-V8 roadster, originally built by Al Davis. Full-fendered with a dropped axle, it had an adjustable rear crossmember so its height could be changed. Much of the car's metalwork, including filling in the front fender outline, building the panel between the frame horns, and fitting the '32 grille shell had been done by Tom Story. These minor changes gave the car a distinctive appearance. Painted bronze-gold, it had new white sidewalls, and a new louvered three-piece hood. The upholstery was maroon and tan, and the white top had a headliner of tan vinyl. A feature of the car was its finned-aluminum six-gauge panel; five of these were cast by pattern maker Al Davis, and they're beautiful and rare. Of the five, two can still be accounted for—and I have one of them!

I can recall only three hot rods that had race car noses, and Wes Strohecker's roadster was

one of them. A black '27 T body on a '32 frame, it had a chrome-plated front and rear end; the interior was done in bone-white rolled-and-pleated Naugahyde. Because it had a race car nose and was fenderless—even when driven on the street—it looked to me like a true California hot rod. It also had exotic things like a Halibrand quick-change rear end, sprint car steering wheel, and race car type chrome tubing radius rods—features almost never seen on hot rods of 45 years ago. I learned recently that many of these parts came from Del McClure's sprint car, which had been wrecked. It was high bucks, and one of the finest street rods around. It went too—the '48 Merc engine was bored 3-5/16 inches, with stock 3-3/4-inch stroke; it had Evans heads and triple manifold, special ignition, and all the goodies. In

1952 Wes drove the car from Portland to Bonneville, put tall tires on the rear and, without even changing the spark plugs, drove it through the traps at 128.82!

Sometimes, when I'm pondering, and grow tired of pondering the economy, the global situation, or the location of toxic dump sites, I ponder what it would be like to drive one of the above-mentioned hot rods to a national meet—say, Merced or Lodi or Columbus—and if I ponder real hard I can imagine the look on faces when they see the car. I know most people would have to admit that now, as then, these are indeed Top Rods.

"This exceptionally beautiful roadster with a Cadillac engine was displayed at the 1955 Ford show held in Dearborn"—from Best Hot Rods *Number 2, 1955.*

Hot Rod Mart

I loved to read about the parts, just to know they existed.

It was not easy to find used speed equipment in my area of the country in the early 'Fifties. You had to either search constantly or be pretty lucky to find a used dual manifold for a flathead Ford V-8, and heads were non-existent. Production of Ford and Mercury 24-stud finned-aluminum heads did not get going until around 1948, apparently in the early 'Fifties the demand still exceeded the supply. They were seen on engines at circle tracks and drag strips, creating the illusion that they were readily available. Darn few were seen on street machines. You could buy new finned aluminum cylinder heads—but they cost $75—more than most guys had in their entire cars!

I must have had trouble finding a dual intake manifold also. Why else would I have had my father drive me to Coast Auto Supply where I got a brand-new Edmunds dual intake manifold with linkage and gas lines for $37.50—or half of what I had paid for a complete, running 1929 A-V8 roadster! I remember seeing one used dual manifold—a Thickstun, I believe, in the "Thrifties" section of our newspaper for $12, but I didn't call. The fact that I remember that ad so vividly is proof to me at least that that was a singular example of speed equipment in the newspaper.

Nash "twin-8" ignition

Somehow my father learned of a special ignition for the flathead Ford V-8 engine in my roadster and we drove to a guy's house across the river in Vancouver and bought it. It was built locally by Blackie Blackburn and machined by Bud England. It combined a 1934 Nash "twin-8" distributor and a 1949-53 Ford shaft. That huge distributor head contained dual points and condensers, and operated with a pair of 6-volt coils. One of the dumbest things I've ever done was to let that distributor go when I sold the engine to a guy in Longview, Washington.

In the fall of 1951 my father and I removed the hydraulic brakes from a wrecked 1942 Mercury, and I noticed a dual manifold on the basement wall. It was a Lance, a manifold cast in Portland; it was for sale, probably for very little, but we didn't buy it. My father did buy a pair of 1937 DeSoto bumpers because we knew they were always hard to find.

In early 1952 someone connected with the Road Angels had a 1935 Ford coupe for sale with a hot (probably worn-out) 1935 engine topped with Eddie Meyer 21-stud finned aluminum heads and dual manifold. I was tempted, but as usual, I had no money and I don't know where the engine and the car went.

HOT ROD MART

Requirements of "Hot Rod Mart" are: limit of 25 words per ad, not including name and address. Ads will be placed in this column on a first come, first served basis. We reserve the right to edit ads when necessary. We are not responsible for the accuracy of description, but we will reject any obviously misleading statements. No ads will be knowingly accepted from commercial firms. A charge of $2.00 per ad will be made and must accompany each ad. Only one car may be listed in any one ad. This limitation will not apply to parts or equipment, however. Send to Hot Rod Mart, 5959 Hollywood Blvd., Los Angeles 28, Calif.

Due to the normal delay in publication, allow at least two months from the time your ad is received until the time it is published.

SELL—'48 Lincoln continental hardtop, Chrysler V8 engine, radio, heater, overdrive, good condition. Best offer or will trade for ?. William Stocker, 417½ Clay St., Fillmore, Cal.

SELL—'32 B roadster, 36,000 miles, always garaged, strictly original and complete, absolutely no rust. Easily sold in U.S. Used 3 months a year. Photos on request. D. J. Asher, Box 233, Dunnville, Ontario, Canada.

SELL—'32 Ford model B, excellent A1 condition, inside and out, bumper to bumper, 45,000 miles, Worth $400, must sacrifice to best offer. Raymond Kirpes, 593 Hill St., Dubuque, Iowa.

SELL—'32 Ford roadster in perfect original condition, $300. John Yannone, 2 Bridge St., Newburgh, N.Y. Phone 7378.

SELL—8 new JE pistons, 3 5/16 x 4 with Grant rings, $40. 8 new Vanisel pistons, 3 5/16 x 4 with Grant rings, $45. Ralph Piersall, Richmondville, N.Y.

SELL—H & C full cam, $20 Stewart-Warner tach, $15. Almquist dual intake, $20. Mallory coil, condenser and points '49-'53 Ford, $15. Ralph Piersall, Richmondville, N.Y.

SELL—'54 Ford business coupe, stick shift, 3.90's, power brakes, R&H. Bored and stroked 296 cu. in. OHV Merc, dual Stromberg 4-throats, Edelbrock manifold & pistons, Lincoln valves & springs, headers, "Magspark," good cam, balanced, Silver "E" shocks, road race tires, etc. A few spares. See July, Sept. '54 & Jan. '55 HRM. Best cash offer around $2250 for this exceptional performing street machine. Will deliver within 500 miles after sale. Racer Brown, 5959 Hollywood Blvd., Los Angeles 28, Cal. HOllywood 2-3261.

SELL—'40 Buick 4 door convertible, black torpedo body sound with clean white top. Recently rebuilt engine fully loaded except for cam. Best offer over $300. Jack Barense, 3060 Washtenaw Rd., Ann Arbor, Mich.

WANTED—A used Micro Midget. Richard Walsh, 6 Third St., Garden City Park, L.I., N.Y. Pioneer 6-4348.

SELL—'34 Ford convert, Olds 88 engine, chopped top. Lincoln transmission, F 100 truck clutch, column shift, leather interior, SW dash, new paint, body restored. Won trophy for best in its class in Huntington Motorama. $695. J. Peter Mahaffy, 138-43 226th St., Laurelton 13, N.Y. Laurelton 5-7473.

SELL—'32 Ford full fendered roadster, hydraulics, pleated leather upholstery, new 3⅜x3⁵⁄₁₆ Merc engine, Lucas ignition, WW's, show perfect. Best offer over $900. John McQueen, 11156 So. Raymond Ave., Los Angeles 44, Cal.

SELL—Buick convert, 1947-56C, H&C ¾ cam, alcohol injection, three carbs, headers, duals, milled head, 7.50x16 rear, 6.50x16 front new WW's, air lifts, new upholstery, new two-tone paint, customized, safety belts, R&H, low mileage, perfect, $450. Jordan King, 7 Collegeview Ave., Poughkeepsie, N.Y.

SELL—Nearly new 7500 rpm Sun tach, $20. Perfometer, $15. SW fuel pressure gauge, $5. Jordan King, 7 Collegeview Ave., Poughkeepsie, N.Y.

SELL OR TRADE—'41 Lincoln convert '50 Merc engine, new clutch, brakes, carb, fuel pump, good tires $85. Or trade for Chevy speed equipment. Joe Fogel, 28-02 141 St., Flushing 54, N.Y. IN 1-4593.

SELL—'42 Lincoln continental hardtop, excellent condition, '53 Lincoln engine, solid tappets, dual carbs, overdrive, heater, radio, backup lights, WW's. Will deliver anywhere. $2200. Clarence Everett, 3425 Dallas Rd., Salem, Ore.

SELL—Set of 4 hot rod fenders, $12. Four Calnevar wire wheels, $20. Three Buick two-barrel carbs, $7 each. Zebra covered bucket seat, $7, other miscellaneous parts cheap. Robert Tews, Wartburg College, Waverly, Ia.

SELL OR TRADE—Have two Smith "Jiggler" heads in good condition, would like to swap for 2 Ardun heads in good condition. Will pay cash difference; to fit Ford 60. W. Frank Sharp, Jacksboro, Tenn.

SELL—Cord ambulance 1937-810 series 7 passenger limousine, new engine, tires, good body. $550. Joe Jageers, Funeral Home, Athens, O. Phone 31567.

SELL—Dismantled '54 Morgan + 4, and '53 Singer 1500, '52 Volkswagen, 4 Fiat 500's, will sell whole or parts. Fiberglass, blower, seats, instruments, collection of items, all excellent. John Naylor, Jr., 105 North Line Dr., New Orleans 20, La.

SELL—Sprint car, body, frame, running gear, less engine. Short wheelbase and light weight make it an ideal dragster. Asking $50. Sparkers Hot Rod Club, Box 289, New Providence, N.J.

SELL—248 GMC complete, less head, balanced, .100 over, Jahns pistons, rings, grooved crank, ¾ HC cam, new rod-main bearings, light pushrods, never run. $150. Allen Bridle, 3130 W. 46th St., Cleveland 2, Ohio.

WANTED—Shop manual for 1932 Ford V8. Also book entitled "Ford Models A, B & V8 Cars" by Victor Page (1934). Karol Wilkosz, 1547 N. Talman Ave., Chicago 2, Ill.

WANTED—For '32 Chevy coupe, radiator, radiator grille and chrome shell. New or used, must be in good condition. Raymond Griffin, P.O. Box 1773, Montgomery 2, Ill.

SELL—205 issues of automotive, engine maintenance and hot rod books and magazines in good condition. Valued over $60, sell for $35 cash or best offer. John Mason, 279 Liberty St., San Francisco 14, Cal. HI 8-2378.

SELL—1952 K-2 Chrysler-Allard, excellent condition, low mileage, unusual extras, write for details. $2250. Dick Colgan, Church IV, Room 22, Troy, N.Y.

SELL—Judson supercharger for flathead Ford, Merc, adaptor for Nash Rambler, used 2 hours, $100. Dick Colgan, Church IV, Room 22, Troy, N.Y.

SELL—Olds dual quad manifold complete with Carter 4 barrel carburetors and Hellings air cleaners. Complete Mallory Magspark distributor. Will fit '49 to '54 Olds, $150. William Hermes, 90-16 171 St., Jamaica 32, L.I., N.Y. OLympia 8-6554.

SELL—'35 Chevy coupe, dual manifold, cams—Howard SU9, ¾, aluminum flywheel, 216 or 248 cu. in. blocks with full oil pressure system. Sell parts single or assembled, any combination. Joe Bosworth, 931 Sixth, West Lafayette, Ind.

SELL—Two Merc 4 in. shafts, $30 each. 8 pistons, new, 3⁵⁄₁₆ Semi 4 in. stroke 4 ring, $18. Vertex mag '49 through '53 Ford, $65. Tach complete, $20. A. R. Liebeler, 210 13 St. No., Columbus, Miss.

SELL—'50 Olds V8 engine complete, heads milled .080, Herbert 285° roller cam, flywheel, clutch, pressure plate, McBar adaptor for 49-51 Ford, Merc, $400. Addison Roberts, 707 W. Blvd. St., Marion, Ill.

SELL—Chrys. V8 roller cam 270 Herbert, exc condition, $70. New Chrysler V8 Edmunds dual intake manifold, $40. New Olds Rocket dual manifold, Edmunds, $40. G. S. Potter, 327 West 117 St., Hawthorne, Cal.

SELL—Cadillac dual quad intake manifold, Nicson, used 100 miles, like new, $40. '40 Ford complete front and rear end, hydraulics, hubs, $10. G. S. Potter, 327 W. 117 St., Hawthorne, Cal.

SELL—Ford stock transmission, late gears, $15. 59A crank slightly used, $10. 10 in. Auburn clutch and disc, heavy springs, new, $12. Cad trans., excell., $15. G. S. Potter, 327 W. 117 St., Hawthorne, Cal.

SELL—Chevy parts all brand new. 3.55-3.70-4.11 gears, $12. '49-53 radiator, $25. Voltage reg., $5.50. Many chrome accessories, spot lights, mirrors, air filters. G. S. Potter, 327 W. 117 St., Hawthorne, Cal.

SELL—Chrysler V8 to Chev transmission adaptor, complete with accessories, $35. Chrys. V8 Cunningham type 4 carb log manifold with carbs, air filters, linkage, $100. G. S Potter, 327 W. 117 St., Hawthorne, Cal.

SELL—Chrysler V8 torque converter new, excellent for street roadster, $50. 2 SW gas heaters practically new with attachments for any car, $15 each. G. S. Potter, 327 W. 117 St., Hawthorne, Cal.

SELL—'34 Ford convert, clean body, solid late engine. Would make good show car. $285. Bob Burgess, 128 E. Clay St., Stockton, Cal.

SELL—Used Wayne head assembly, perfect condition. Fits '37-51 Chevy Hi-torque except Powerglide. 8.5 to 1 compression ratio, dual intake, exhaust, BXOV-2 carbs, linkage, Mallory dist and coil, $250. Charles Kehm, Jr., Rt. #1, Box 186K, DesPlaines, Ill.

WANTED—Desperately need ring and pinion set 4.11 ratio from '42-47 Ford ½-ton pickup, open drive shaft type. All inquiries answered. Al Faurot, Pinos Altos, New Mex.

SELL—6 cyl Plymouth-Dodge new Edmunds head, dual intake manifold, linkage, two 97's. $45 or best offer separately or trade for 3.54 gears for '53 Ford. Ed. White, Rt. #2, Box 109, Covington, Va.

SELL—'50 Ford convert, radio, heater, overdrive, ¾ race Offenhauser engine. New top, brakes and Premium WW's. Illness forces sale of this clean, original car, $900. James Grushon, 3469 McLaughlin Ave., Los Angeles 66, Cal.

SELL—'33 Plymouth coupe, channeled, hot '50 Dodge engine, hydraulics, used less than 3000 miles. Must sacrifice. $600 or best offer. Write for details. Mike Giles, 408 No. Court St., Steubenville, O.

SELL OR TRADE—'48 Merc custom chopped, Carson top, dechromed, electric doors, pleated & rolled leatherette interior, maroon lacquer paint. $800 or trade for '52 Ford convert, std. trans. Fred Sowa, 230 So. 10 St., Reading, Pa.

(Continued on next page)

HOT ROD MART

(Continued from preceding page)

SELL—'40 Ford, black, Deluxe coupe, Olds V8 engine, rolled & pleated upholstery, US Royal WW's, 15 in. wheels, radio, chrome grille & window frames, undersealed, $850. Roger Lind, 240 Burlingame Ave., Los Angeles 49, Cal. EXbrook 5-1428.

SELL—Adaptor, brand new for Olds or Cad V8 engine to '32-48 Ford trans., $28 postpaid. J. Cristenson, 3223 N Adams Rd., Birmingham, Mich. MI. 4-9190.

WANTED—Late model Chrysler engine, '52-54. Please state price and condition. John Scherer, 665 Lakeshore Dr., Grosse Pointe Shores, Mich.

SELL—Clean full-fendered '29 Ford roadster ready for V8 and hydraulics. New differential, white top, '32 shell and trans, '49 steering wheel, '39 taillights, $80. Bill Chisholm, 60 Oakwood Crescent, Oakville, Ontario, Canada. Victor 5-1744 evenings.

SELL—Classic Packard '36 convert 4 door sedan, new tires, original and unrestored good condition throughout. Needs no major work. A black beauty. $475 or best offer Peter Sullivan, 111 Beacon St., Greenfield, Mass.

SELL—Classic Chevy '33 roadster, new tan top, new jet black paint, good tires, good running shape. Stylish little car for $350 or best offer. Peter Sullivan, 111 Beacon St., Greenfield, Mass.

WANTED—Overhead valve setup for Ford B, must be complete or repairable and cheap. Also need '40 rear brake drums, rear Model A fenders. R. C. Spurgeon, 325 Milford St., Glendale 3, Cal.

SELL—'32 Ford sedan, partly modified body, stock '36 engine, mechanical brakes. Body, upholstery very good. Write for pictures, details. Larry Rix, P.O. Box 197, Garwin, Ia.

WANTED—New body panel that fits below the deck lid of a '40 Ford coupe, also called tail pan, will pay charges. Richard Louis, R.F.D. #2, Willoughby, Ohio.

SELL—'50 Singer roadster, dismantled. Started to rebuild and refinish but ran out of time. $225. Richard E. Williams, P.O. Box 746, New Britain, Conn.

SELL—New Stromberg 4-throat carb, $35; pair Weiand 8.25 to 1 heads for '39-49 Ford, Merc, like new condition, $30. Raymond Schlachter, P.O. Box 187, Mount Pulaski, Ill.

SELL—Set new Sterling pistons complete with Grant rings, 3⅜ in. bore,, 4⅛ in. stroke, $30. Modified Frenzel supercharger with 2 Zenith 8810 side draft carbs, best offer. Raymond Schlachter, P.O. Box 187, Mount Pulaski, Ill.

SELL—Complete 85 hp Ford engine, milled aluminum heads, magnafluxed crank, adjustable tappets, perfect condition, no cracks, $50 FOB. Raymond Schlachter, P.O. Box 187, Mount Pulaski, Ill.

SELL—Channeled '40 Ford coupe with new wine paint and 15 in. tires. Has chromed hot '48 Ford engine. Would trade for hot roadster. Don Wallace, Rt. #1, Walnut Ridge, Ark.

SELL—'39 Ford 4 door convert, 59AB block, 3.54's, duals, $200 in custom upholstery, top new spring '54. Needs rear fender, paint, otherwise little body work. $175 or best offer. Arthur Broadbooks, Jr., Todd Union, University of Rochester, Rochester 3, N.Y.

SELL OR TRADE—'47 Chevy Spt. cpe., 296 in. GMC engine, overhauled, McGurk manifold & ¾ cam, SpeedOMotive pistons, Grants, Mallory, tach, new tires, heavy front springs, direct shocks, 3.73 gears, short-wave radio, clean, $800. Or swap for late Ford or Chevy. Tony Clark, Box 536, Tarleton Station, Tex.

SELL—McCulloch supercharger for '49-53 Ford or Merc, used four months, $195. T. V. Lewis, 17148 Lorne St., Van Nuys, Cal.

SELL—Mallory Magspark and Mallory dual point distributor as a unit. Complete with car and wiring for '40 and possibly later year Packard 160. $30. E. R. Dickens, 3944 E. 42 St., Cleveland 5, O.

SELL—Hal D.O. on B block also Hal D.O. with 5 main parts; Cragar D.O. Speedway front end chromed. Dick Sawin, 594 Farmington Ave., Hartford, Conn.

SELL—Stromberg 4-throat carb, Weiand manifold, Hellings air cleaner, Mallory distributor, Magspark, throttle kit for '49-53 Ford-Merc. All $90. T. Trudeau, Central School, Edwards, N.Y.

SELL—'31 A-V8 street roadster, stepped frame, channeled, '40 hydraulics, '40 dash, column shift, 59A engine, duals, needs some body work, upholstery. Best offer around $250. T. Trudeau, Central School, Edwards, N.Y.

SELL—'49 Fordillac 5-passenger coupe, '52 Cad engine, dual Cad carbs, Spalding ignition, Herbert 270 cam, stock bore and stroke. Best offer over $1200. Earl Engle, 8150 Womall Rd., Kansas City, Mo.

SELL—Roadster, 30 model A V8 '39 Ford hydraulics, steering and front end. Red quilted upholstery just finished. Body channeled 6 in. A-1 shape, $300. A. M. Anderson, Jr., 20 So. Beech Ave., Highland Springs, Va.

WANTED—Name and address of owner who raced '32 Ford coupe, chopped, channeled, full fendered with flame paint job, on July 4 at Shelton, Wash. Merryl Johnson, 1304 Aberdeen Ave., Aberdeen, Wash.

WANTED—Name and address of owner who raced '34 Ford 3 window coupe, red paint job July 4 at Shelton, Wash. Want Howard M-5 cam for '50 Olds. Merryl Johnson, 1304 Aberdeen Ave., Aberdeen, Wash.

WANTED—Well built stock car trailer, tandem axles with electric brakes, state price and condition first

Hot Rod Mart from March 1955 issue of Hot Rod Magazine.

letter. Will answer. Eastern area preferred. M. W. Suraske, 631 Hewey St., Utica, N.Y.
SELL—'32 Roadster, excellent condition, chopped top, Z'd frame, dropped axle, louvered hood and belly pan, pleated upholstery, Cord dash, full race 59AB, $800. Ronald Donati, 1710-N., Galveston, Tex.
WANTED—'32-37 Cad V16 engine and transmission, must be complete and in running condition. Also owners manual for above. State price and condition. Lloyd Franklin, 110 N. 2nd, Enid, Okla.
SELL—'37 Cord Beverly sedan. Stock throughout. $1000 cash. No trades. Rebuilt engine, new U-joints, good body and interior, new paint, good tires and chrome. Dr. Robert Barnard, Lt., MC U.S.N.R., US Naval Hospital, San Diego, Cal.
SELL—'36 5 window coupe, stock, cycle front fenders, SW instruments, full house Merc, Zephyr gears, ¾ finished. Must sell. Write for details. John Pedler, 1201 Magnolia Ave., Elkhart, Ind.
SELL OR TRADE—'36 Ford roadster, hydraulics, column shift, engine in mechanically good condition, body also. Reasonable offer accepted. Ken Brocker, 2136 Auburn Ave., Cincinnati 19, Ohio. WO 2758.
SELL—Nash '52 Statesman speed equipment, Edmunds head, 2 Carter WA-1 carbs, complete with linkage, used about 1000 miles. $60. Bill Huber, Box 124, Calpella, Cal.
SELL—Complete '49 Merc stock engine with 4 in. stroke and all accessories. Running condition, $100. Five 15 in. wheels fit up to '48 Ford, $4.00 each. Ken Struman, 1519 Ellsmere Ave., Los Angeles 19, Cal. WH 5406.
SELL—'32 Ford V8 sedan, 16 in. spoke wheels, good engine and upholstery. Make offer. Alfonso Gomez, 2112½ Ellendale Pl., Los Angeles 7, Cal. RI 6815.
SELL—Judson supercharger, Buick four barrel carb attached, new in November '54. Complete kit to install in 1950 Ford, including carb linkage and top cylinder oiler, $170. George Carmer, 7929 Thouron Ave., Philadelphia 19, Pa.
SELL—Clayton dynamometer drive-in type, Model 41. Used very little, will pay shipping cost. Carl Badami, 711 Wabash, Kansas City, Mo.
SELL OR TRADE—'39 Ford tudor with ¾ race 59L engine, 4-speed transmission, engine built up May '54, never raced. Excellent body, near new WW's. R. F. Weber, P.O. Box 302, Shaw AFB, So. Caro.
WANTED—Urgently needed new or used full flare fender skirts for '54 Ford F-100 pickup truck. Send description and price. Joe Germuga, 235 Klink Rd., Rochester 10, N.Y.
WANTED—'40 or '34 Ford coupe without engine, chopped or stock, reasonable, good condition. Pay cash, pickup within 150 miles. Send complete description. Richard Allinger, 2577 Manchester Rd., Akron 19, O.
SELL OR TRADE—'32 channeled Ford coupe, full race $3\frac{5}{16}$ x 4, 275 cu. in. Merc engine, hydraulics, fenders, $500. Or trade for MG or pickup truck. Empson Peters, Vallonia, Ind. Phone 3529.
SELL—'51 Humber Super Snipe Mark III, needs differential work but otherwise in very good condition. $550. Will send photograph if interested. Stephen Cheselka, 58-28 83rd Pl., Elmhurst 73, Long Island, N.Y.
SELL OR TRADE—1932 Ford roadster, '54 Cad engine, chopped, channeled, chromed, pleated & piped leather. Most parts new. Plenty fast, immaculate. $1500. Fred Moeller, 364 Ave Rd., Muskegon, Mich.
SELL—Breaking Cadillac sixteen chassis less engine, sell wheels, steering gear, transmission, other chassis and body parts. Write for list. H. A. Summers, Box 7013, Norfolk 9, Va.
SELL—292 GMC, $3\frac{15}{16}$ x 4, 1950 big port head, new valves, line bored mains, Lischien Drag cam, Venoila 8½ pistons, complete rebuilt, never run. First $250. Gerald Gill, Jr., 1822 Kalamazoo Ave. S.E., Grand Rapids, Mich.
SELL OR TRADE—Olds engine, .090 milled and ported, '52 heads, .400 lift cam. Caddy synchromesh transmission, new heavy duty clutch, low mileage. Special starter, intake manifold, extras. Gerald Gill, Jr., 1822 Kalamazoo Ave. S.E., Grand Rapids, Mich.

• MOTOR SERVICE •

SELL—$200 Grand Prix Ford-Mercury V8 magneto used 10 hours, for $100 cash. Set matched, magnafluxed, precision balanced 29A rods $20 cash. R. Schlachter, P.O. Box 547, Lexington, Ky.
SELL—Ford Edelbrock dual manifold $19.50; Chrysler 6 cam, full race, $15; Chevrolet ¾ cam $19.95; Chevrolet shop-made dual intake and split exhaust manifold $19.50. G. Miller, P.O. Box 1417, Vallejo, Calif.
WANTED—Used speed equipment for Ford, Chevrolet, or Plymouth. Will pay cash or trade. Let me know what you have. J. Miller, 170 Woodrow Ave., Vallejo, Calif.
SELL OR TRADE—'51 Mercury convertible, Continental trunk, custom grille, loaded with all extras, new tires and '53 engine just installed. Yellow with black top and skirts. B. Brody, Forest Hills, Knoxville, Tenn.
SELL—Two 59-A blocks, ported, relieved, polished, bored to $3\frac{3}{16}$, tested for cracks, perfect shape, new cam bearings, valve seats, $115 each. B. Groner, Super Highway & Highland Ave., Langhorne, Penna.
SELL—'32 Ford roadster, coral flame red, black frame, 3.27 rear end, dechromed, dropped, everything new. Less engine. Best offer. May be seen at Langhorne Speed Shop. B. Groner, Super Highway & Highland Ave., Langhorne, Penna.
WANTED—V8 DeSoto engine complete. State price and condition. Also cam and solid lifter for same. D. June, Theresa, N. Y.
SELL—Edelbrock tall manifold $20; ¾ Iskenderian cam with gear $20; Federal Mogul 21 stud heads, fit '32 to '38 Fords $30. L. Matustik, 3924 Council Grove, St. Louis 20, Mo.
SELL OR TRADE—Cheap. Freiman universal type dual manifold, 2 Chandler-Groves 94 carbs. Interested in headers and pipes for '41 Ford. J. Stoll, Box 163, Superior, Ariz.
SELL—Stutz eight transmission, complete, '32, $70. Flywheel and clutch assembly available. J. Harvey, 8102 Imperial Ave., Lemon Grove, Calif.
SELL—Mercury engine, full-race, stroked, never run. Owner shipped overseas. $475. Mrs. B. Allen, 548 N. Valencia, Covina, Calif.
WANTED—'37 Ford pickup; body, box, fenders, hood, and running boards must be perfect. Send description, price, and photo. Would prefer car located within 500 miles. B. Neumeister, 1015 Highland Ave., Pueblo, Colo.
SELL OR TRADE—'36 Cord sedan in running condition, $475 cash or swap for rod or roadster or what have you. J. Xifos, 40 W. 93rd St., New York, N. Y.
SELL—Customized sports car built on '32 Stutz frame; 3 fins in rear like Le Sabre; Studebaker grille, chromed Stutz engine available; write for photo and info. L. Needy, 9000 Pollardy Lane, St. Louis County 21, Mo.
WANTED—For Model T Ford—D. O. Miller head and transmission, D. O. Fronty parts, tubular rods, starbeam rods, special rear end gears, Hartford or Hassler shocks, etc. F. Rand, 395 Freeway & Washington, Escondido, Calif.
WANTED—For 'A,' 'B' Fords—Pop Evans head, magneto drive, Hartford shocks, aluminum water pump, tubular rods, starbeam rods, any aluminum head, Franklin steering, etc. F. Rand, 395 Freeway & Washington, Escondido, Calif.
SELL—Uncompleted Ford roadster, '32 chassis, hydraulic brakes, dropped front axle, '42 mill, headers, Evans manifold, chopped flywheel, 'A' body; needs only finishing touches. $200. M. Moffit, R.R. No. 1. Mechanicsville. Ia.

SELL OR TRADE—Customized '50 Ford club coupe with souped '50 Mercury engine, extra instruments and equipment. Also slightly damaged '52 Nash grille and miscellaneous items. Lt. R. W. Althoff Hq. Sq. ATLD-MATS, Westover AF Base, Mass.
SELL—Dago axle $12, two dual Weiand manifolds $15 apiece, rear '40 hydraulics $10, 59A block $30 '34 transmission $10, two B grilles $8 apiece. Tom (Stroker McGurk) Medley, Hot Rod Magazine, 5959 Hollywood Blvd., Hollywood, Calif.
WANTED—'29 A open pickup body, or a real "Uncle Daniel" '29 A Tudor, tachometer and drive. Tom (Stroker McGurk) Medley, Hot Rod Magazine, 5959 Hollywood Blvd., Hollywood, Calif.
SELL—Ford, '32 3-window, perfect, 67,000 miles, stock body, stock '52 Mercury engine, hydraulics, sealed beams, 8.20x16 rubber. Photos on request. $750. S. J. Wheelock, 6557 Lemarand Ave., San Diego 5, Calif.
WANTED—Used V8 60 speed equipment, KK midget body, frame, and midget parts, wheels, tires, front and rear ends, headers, pipes, etc. P. L. Kellar, 2514 Midland Ave., Syracuse 5, N.Y.
SELL—New 24 stud V8 aluminum heads, not finned, stock compression (can be raised) $35; '48 Columbia overdrive $75. Want '49 Mercury carburetor and intake manifold. D. Haack, Lindsay, Okla.
SELL—Three '35 Ford 16" spoke wheels, $2 each; '32 Ford radiator and grille $10; Winfield model S $1\frac{5}{16}$" carburetor $3. Will ship. M. Wright, 100 McLarea St., Red Bank, N.J.
TRADE—Excellent '32' full-fendered Ford roadster, late chassis equipment, ¾ engine, new top, upholstery, rechromed full windshield, windwings, stock appearance, for Ardun equipped Ford. O. L. Vosburgh, 16248 Sherman Way, Van Nuys, Calif. ST 0-6634.
WANTED—Left front door for '28 or '29 model A touring car. Roadster or open type pickup door will also fit. Will pay freight. R. Vanatta, 328 S. Grener Road, Columbus, Ohio.

...

SELL—Roadster pickup '28 Chevrolet, new mill, three-port Olds head, header, 1⅞" valves, Johns pistons, 4" Dago axle, new upholstery, battery, tires, etc. $135 or ? K. D. Reynolds, 3957 Huron Ave., Culver City, Calif.
SELL—New '52 Cadillac four barrel Rochester carburetor and intake manifold, $50 for both. New Spalding dual coil ignition, '49-'51 Ford and Mercury, $40. B. Forney, 135½ S. Hazelwood, Youngstown, Ohio.
SELL—$100, Ford '51 transmission—clutch, bell housing, overdrive, steering gear, all controls, or trade for spool rear end or quick change rear for Ford. Want magneto for Ford six. B. Morse, 18 Myrtle Ave., Frankfort, Ky.
WANTED—1932 Ford hydraulic brakes, column shift, one half or three quarters Mercury engine—sedan or coupe. D. Grossman, 10128 Colwell Dr., Sun Valley, Calif.
SELL—'32 Ford coupe, whitewalls, hot Mercury engine, hydraulics, column shift, maroon lacquer, all chrome front end. See to appreciate. K. Lawrence, Rt. 2, Box 56, Fillmore, Calif. Phone 529-R.
SELL OR TRADE—'32 Ford roadster, featured March '52 Hot Rod Magazine, pages 18-19, "Washington Show Winner," full mill, channeled, excellent condition. Best offer, cash or trade. C. L. Crowther, 4311 Rokeby Road, Baltimore 29, Maryland.
SELL—Winfield R-1 cam, run just 1,000 miles. $25 cash. E. Israelson, 128 So. Reno St., Los Angeles 4, Calif.
SELL—'50 Ford convertible, $4\frac{1}{8}$x$3\frac{5}{16}$, Edelbrock heads, Edelbrock 3 carb manifold, complete Mallory ignition, full-race cam, ported and relieved. Chrome accessories, whitewall tires. Must sell. A-1 shape. 5000 miles. F. Carfagno, 313 East Penn St., Norristown, Penna. Phone NO 5-7398.

WANTED—New front fenders, chrome grille, hub caps, new or used windshield frame for '36 Ford Phaeton. J. L. Rhinehart, 829 Ontario St., Harve de Grace, Md.
SELL—Mercury engines, 1 full-race '48 and 1 road engine '50. Both fully equipped, like new and ready to go! Sacrifice at $450 and $250. C. Cagle, 15951 E. San Jose St., Puente, Calif.
SELL—Four barrel Ford engine formerly in sprint car with McDowell OHV, track cam, 4 inch exhaust header, etc. Rebored, rebuilt with J.E. pistons, $250. T. R. Smith, 3103 Woodland Ave., Louisville, Ky.
WANTED—Lincoln Continental rear body sections, or complete hardtop body, '48 preferred. Will consider car or body in any condition. Price, description, location. R. F. Glah, Sr., 113 Ridgefield Rd., Newton Sq., Penna.
WANTED—Edelbrock Super dual manifold and Edelbrock 8 to 1 heads for '49 Ford. Also Belond dual system for same car. Will consider other makes. D. Bottelli, 168 Oakland Rd., Maplewood, N.J.
SELL—'40 Ford V8 engine, 85 hp, complete with all accessories incl. new clutch, pressure plate. Good condition. $75 cash. Consider trade for '50 engine. J. Kane, 3538 Kelton Ave., Los Angeles 34, Calif.
SELL OR TRADE—Two WA-1 Carter carburetors, fit most single throat two-bolt manifolds, off '52 Hudson Hornet, never used. Want Olds or Ford equipment or anything. G. Williams, 303 S. 5th Ave., Pocatello, Ida.
SELL OR TRADE—Edmunds dual manifold, air filters, linkage and Rochester carburetor, for V8 Olds, 1949 and later. $50 or trade for gun by Colt, S&W or ? M. Bernardy, 344A Summer St., Somerville 44, Mass.
SELL OR TRADE—Stock '29 A Ford roadster, good shape, new A engine. Sell for best offer or trade for Ford pickup or what have you. G. Beery, 1919 LaSalle St., Racine, Wisc.
SELL—McCullough supercharger. Last model with spare gears and bearings. Also water pumps, sheaves, and idler gear. Less than 500 miles on unit. $110. J. R. Dunbar, 1510 Washington St., Golden, Colo.
WANTED—'31 Model A Ford touring car body, with or without fenders. Will pay reasonable price. Must be in Southern Calif. B. Enigenburg, P.O. Box 608, Fallbrook, Calif.
SELL—'32 Ford convertible. Car is original except for new 16 in. tires and wheels. Phone Wabash 6213 after 5 p.m. B. Robertson, 2859 N. Meridian, Indianapolis, Ind.
WANTED—Columbia rear axle for '32 roadster. J. Gajewski, 752 N. Van Ness Ave., Hollywood, Calif.
SELL—Smithy dual exhaust system for 88 Olds. Used one month, $20. Six new and used Hollywood mufflers $1.50 to $7.50. Three sets lowering blocks '49-'52 Ford, $3.50 set. D. Fern, 205 Washington St., Holly, Mich.
SELL—Four-barrel engine, dual carburetors, race cam, Simmons head, magneto, pressure oil system, 4 in. bore, ported, big valves, A-1. Best offer over $150. W. E. Hay, R.D. No. 1, Dover, Ohio.
WANTED—'42-'48 Lincoln overdrive transmission, '49-'51 Ford V8 Mallory distributor and coil, '49-'51 Ford V8 dual or triple intake manifold. Send information, price. M. Hayes, 460 Page Mill Rd., Palo Alto, Calif.

Hot Rod Mart from March 1955, March 1953, and April 1953 issues of Hot Rod Magazine.

HOT ROD MART

Requirements of "Hot Rod Mart" are: limit of 25 words per ad, not including name and address. Ads will be placed in this column on a first come, first served basis. We reserve the right to edit ads when necessary. We are not responsible for the accuracy of descriptions, but we will reject any obviously misleading statements. No ads will be knowingly accepted from commercial firms. A charge of $2.00 per ad will be made and must accompany each ad. Only one car may be listed in any one ad. This limitation will not apply to parts or equipment, however. Address all ads to Hot Rod Mart, 5959 Hollywood Blvd., Los Angeles 28, Calif.

SELL—Full-race Cragar engine with all accessories including B transmission; 5000 miles since building; construction cost $600; price $450; F. Hehr, 12209 Braddock Dr., Culver City, Calif.

SELL—'36 Ford roadster, has hydraulics, column shift, 15" wheels, Columbia 2 speed rear end, generally solid, no engine. Make offer. A. B. Lyons, Box 101, John Day, Ore.

WANTED—Used speed equipment for '51 Mercury: aluminum heads, Ardun heads, dual manifold, supercharger, semi-cam, adjustable tappets. Give condition and price in first letter. Lt. L. H. Guenther, Hq. 64th Troop Carrier Gr., DAFB, Greenville, S.C.

SELL—'32 Model B Ford 2-door. Never been wrecked; body excellent; engine fair; interior poor; 16" wheels. Photo on request; best offer. H. Cowell, 314 Dubelett, Weatherford, Tex.

SELL—270 GMC engine, 12,000 miles on 1950 head assembly, Stellite valves, full-flow oil filter, three-quarter cam, Rockford truck clutch. $150. E. Patton, 5249 W. Dunbar Road, Monroe, Mich.

SELL—'50 Mercury crankshaft, newly reground, $25; set of 3⅛ pistons, ⅛ low crown. Driven 1200 miles. $10. E. Patton, 5249 W. Dunbar Road, Monroe, Mich.

SELL—'48 Plymouth club coupe, near perfect condition throughout; new paint; whitewalls; radio; heater; other extras; stock engine except for planed head; 53,000 miles; $972. R. Swain, 352 High St., Charlestown, Ind. Phone 252-R.

SELL OR TRADE—Midget race car, both 2 cam engine and flat head; tires, wheels, equipment and trailer. Sell or trade for pickup truck. Saturday and Sunday. L. Harrison, 324 N. Ontario St., Burbank, Calif.

WANTED—GMC 3-71 blower; Stewart-Warner Chevrolet tachometer drive kit with or without tachometer; 1936-38 Cadillac transmission. O. Steinke, 809 Ann Eliza St., Pekin, Illinois.

SELL—Ford & Mercury three-quarter cam $15; dual manifold $16.90; aluminum heads $36; headers $14.70. Never used. For information, G. Miller, P.O. Box 11, Del Paso Hts., Calif.

WANTED—Stutz Bearcat 1914-20 Series E, 4 cylinder restorable, or will accept any other Stutz car if in good condition. Send photo and full details. E. Pfannebecker, Latham, N.Y.

SELL OR TRADE—'32 model PB Plymouth coupe, converted for use of Ford V8 engine. Includes radiator, Lincoln transmission, etc., less engine and driveshaft. $50 or trade for good 59A block. Will deliver within 500 miles for gas expenses. D. Davis, P.O. Box 939, St. Petersburg, Fla.

SELL—New Scintilla magneto for Chevrolet or GMC $100; Iskenderian 1024 mushroom cam and adjustable lifters, used $35; Cook adaptor for Chevrolet or GMC $25. B. McClure, 14917 Septo St., San Fernando, Calif.

SELL—Lincoln V12 engine, 3⅛6 x 3¾, adjustable tappets, special cam, dual manifold, F8 truck flywheel and clutch. Used only 20,000 miles, good shape. S. Woodward, Cedar Beach, Belgium, Wis.

SELL—'50 Mercury block, ported, relieved, perfect, $60; 1007B Iskenderian track cam, $28; '47 8¾ heads, $45; dual manifold $38. T. King, 348 Sterling Rd., Kenilworth, Ill.

WANTED—1930-31 Chevrolet coupe or roadster. Must be in perfect original condition. Preferably in the Tri-State area. Send pictures, details and price. A. Rogers, 613 Washington Ave., Niles, Ohio.

SELL—2 new 4 cylinder Chevrolet engines, full-race, built by Ansen. Olds 3-port heads, magneto. Two place 96" wheelbase chassis. All $225 or trade. H. Brooks, 611 E. Providencia, Burbank, Calif.

SELL OR TRADE—'50 Olds 88 powered '48 Studebaker Commander convertible. Heads polished, milled .100, '51 Hydramatic, what have you? Write for complete information. G. Gill Jr., 1822 Kalamazoo Ave. S.E., Grand Rapids 7, Mich.

(Continued on page 81)

Hot Rod Mart from May 1953 issue of Hot Rod Magazine.

Not much used speed equipment

I mention these specific examples because they seem proof that not much used speed equipment was around. I'm sure there were heads and manifolds that I didn't see, but darn few, I'll bet. Not until around 1954, when supply caught up with the demand and as the new OHV engines were being introduced, did flathead Ford and Mercury speed equipment become abundant.

But before that, probably in early 1952, I wrote a letter to *Hot Rod Magazine*, saying, among other things, "...about having a colummn (sic) for parts wanted & for sale." I assumed that *somewhere* in the country there were piles of used heads and manifolds, dropped axles, 1932 Ford grilles and '39 taillights and a hundred other speed and specialty items that I coveted. Of course, I had no money to buy those things, should they turn up. But then, as now, I loved to read about them, just to know they existed. The idea for such a column was not an original idea because from the start *Motor Trend* had such a column devoted primarily to antique and classic-car afficionados. In fact, at the same time I wrote a letter to the editor of *Motor Trend*; I enclosed a dollar and an ad: "Wanted: 'A' dropped axel (sic), used, tube radius rod's (sic), triple intake manifold for Ford V-8." I also indicated that I wanted to correspond with someone my age in California who was interested in roadsters and the dry lakes.

Easy to sell

Today those letters interest me for the perspective they offer, indicators of what I was thinking during those distant days. They had no effect on policy at *Hot Rod Magazine*, primarily because I never *mailed* that one (that too tells me something about myself back then). In the January 1953 issue of *Hot Rod Magazine*, a used parts column was started with the announcement, "Somebody wants that old Model 'T' Rajo head you thought was obsolete; yes, and that ancient Winfield DD carburetor, too. What's that under the bench—a pair of heads for a Merc? Man, what a fine supply of 'goodies!' All of those things are easy to sell and here's how." There followed directions on how to write an ad and where to send it, along with $2.00.

Federal-Mogul heads $30

In March 1953 the first column appeared and, although brief, I saw all kinds of things I absolutely *needed*! Such as that '32 Ford roadster located in far-off Pennsylvania, or that unfinished roadster in Iowa, a country where I had never been. But the best deal in that month's column were the Federal Mogul heads for the 21-stud Ford V-8 engine, and priced at only $30! If I had bought them, simply put them on my garage wall to look at for 45 years, it would have been a better investment than if I had put the money in stocks. But of course that running '36 Cord sedan for $475 was nothing to sneeze at...

Gettin' Down!

A cool set of wheels was distinguished by its degree of lowness.

In the 'Fifties a cool set of wheels, whether rod or custom, was distinguished by its degree of lowness. The streets were full of tall, stock-height cars and the way to make a machine rakishly different was to lower it.

If it was a custom this meant long shackles, in the case of a Ford. They came in 2, 4 and 6 inch lengths, and sometimes a guy who wanted his car right on the deck would make longer shackles by drilling holes in pieces of flat steel. Lowering blocks were used for Chevrolets and other GM and Chrysler cars.

Shackles or lowering blocks could be installed in the backyard in an afternoon, and they would put a car's rear end close to the ground. The ideal amount of drop would leave just a smidgen of white sidewall showing under the rear fender skirt. That one alteration made a car look neat. And all kinds of cars were lowered! I remember a sharp 1939 Chrysler Royal coupe with a 6-inch drop. I always liked

Bill Wagner's '29 A-V8 roadster at the Eugene drags, 1951. The Model A frame was stepped both front and rear, had suicide front suspension, body channeled. Wagner was tall, and his knees stuck up above the doors—like a Stroker McGurk cartoon! Note height of steering wheel.

Al Roberts spent his military stint in Korea thinking about building "the world's lowest tub". When he was discharged in 1954 he built a super-low chassis, then channeled a '27 T body over it. The car had a narrow bellypan that offered less than 1 inch of ground clearance.

that model, but those bodies were bulky and the drop completely changed the appearance of the car, emphasizing its smooth lines. The owner later added skirts and whitewalls, and he leaded in the hardware on the long deck lid.

It looked great!

But dropping a car to that degree caused problems. With long shackles there was a lot of side sway, even with a sway bar. And when you took a sharp corner the body would rub like crazy on the tires. If you were foolish enough to put shackles on the front as well as the rear you had a car whose handling was as loose as a goose. No street is absolutely smooth, and in a lowered machine, with limited spring travel, you feel every expansion strip. It's worse on a road with bumps, and if you hit a pothole, there's a good chance that the car will "bottom," meaning the inactive spring allows the floor of the car to come in violent contact with the differential. Tailpipe extensions get flattened. Driveways have to

be taken at an extreme angle. In those days many lowered cars were also blacked out—that is, they'd had the chrome removed and the holes filled with lead— and the shock of hitting bumps would often pop the lead from the holes.

Torching Springs

A hot rod like a Model A was harder to lower. The first thing to do, if it hadn't already been done, was to swap the original tall wheels for a set of 16-inch (or a set of scarce 15-inch) wheels; this would bring the car down several inches. A dago axle would drop the front end 2-1/2 inches, but it was somewhat expensive ($25 outright) and the installation was somewhat complicated, especially if you intended to keep the mechanical brakes. You couldn't use long shackles because the spring is directly over the axle, but there are ways of dropping the spring. A favorite method, back in those days when lowness was more important than comfort, was to remove two or three leaves from the spring. I did this on the front

of my Model A; it lowered the car all right—and dropped the crank pulley against the tie rod! If you were willing to wrestle the spring in and out of the car, you could take the main leaf to a spring shop and have the eyes reversed; this would drop the car half an inch without diminishing spring action.

An easier method, one that could be handled by the corner garage, was "torching" the main leaf. Heat was applied until the main leaf was V-shaped near its ends, which put the V very close to the axle.

Step, chop & section

Even if one used all those methods he still had a pretty tall machine. There were several other ways to lower a car, but they involved a fair amount of work. For example, a good way to lower the frame was to "step it;" this involves cutting the rail ahead of the rear crossmember and welding in a vertical section. The car is lowered an amount equal to the new section, but the original spring action is maintained.

A dramatic way to lower a car is to chop the top—that is, remove a section of metal, from 2 to 4 inches, and weld the roof on again. Another dramatic method is to section a car; this means taking a horizontal section of metal from the body and rejoining the two halves. These methods seem much more popular today. In the 'Fifties one occasionally saw a car with the frame stepped, rarely saw a chopped job, and looked in vain for a sectioned car. Open cars were chopped, but to chop the top on a closed car was simply too big a job for most builders. One often hears someone reminiscing about a "chopped-and-channeled" car he saw 'way back when, but usually the speaker is mouthing a catch phrase. Chopping, no; channeling, yes.

Channeling

If it hadn't been for channeling there would have been lots of tall rods. Channeling is a fairly simple method of lowering a car, and it works well on early model machines. To channel a car you simply cut away the floor and body supports, drop the body over the frame, and build new supports. You might channel a car the width of the frame, welding the bottom of the body to the bottom of the frame, or you might drop the body an extreme amount, getting it right on the ground; if you left the frame in a near-stock position and dropped the body a lot you could use the rails as an armrest!

Cutting the supports away and building new supports was deceptively easy; then came the hard work. Channeling made the car lower but changed the relationship of everything: the seats had to be cut down, the steering column cut or dropped, a new floor and firewall built, new throttle linkage made, the radiator cut an amount equal to the channel job or placed ahead of the front cross member and dropped. And if the radiator was moved forward a new hood had to be built.

And, in most cases, when you channeled a car there went the fenders! By law you had to have something over the tires, so the builder would often trim the rear fenders and mount them higher on the body. For the front he'd build a set of cycle fenders.

This was done by cutting a spare-tire cover into two halves, one for each front wheel, and building brackets that attached to the backing plates; the fenders then rode with the wheel independent of the body. But it was hard to build brackets that would stay on the car. Mechanical-brake backing plates are curved inward and lack a flat surface; welded brackets wouldn't last a hundred miles before vibrations broke them. The solution was a sturdy bracket that bolted to the hydraulic-brake backing plate.

Because channeling was so easy it seemed like everything was being channeled. I can recall at least five 1932 Ford coupes owned by friends that were bought in stock, running condition and were channeled almost immediately. A cutting torch took care of the floor and the firewall and some scrap iron was worked into brackets for the body supports. Of course, if you got the body a little crooked the doors wouldn't shut. If they did shut, they'd pop open when the body flexed, which it was doing constantly without a floor pan to keep it rigid. But what excitement we felt as a stocker, after a couple hours under the torch, began to resemble a real California hot rod.

My friend Gary's first '32 coupe was a one-owner 3-window; it had the original green paint, and it was 100% stock (except for a dropped axle). Gary bought it, drove it a few days, then took off the fenders and bumpers. We all thought it looked sharp like that, especially after he'd put dual exhausts on the '32 engine. Then Gary succumbed to the pressure to get it down, make it low! Over a weekend he channeled the body the width of the frame, mounted the grille and radiator ahead of the front crossmember, and built a longer top section on the hood. As that car came past the high school on Monday morning we thought it was the *meanest* looking rig imaginable.

Lower!

He drove it like that for a couple of weeks, and then, dissatisfied, he channeled it again—more! Lower! The body must have been dropped 12 inches, but because the frame

Kenny Austin's '27 T coupe was chopped and channeled—a lot!—and chassis lowered, to put it right on the ground. Although it has headlights, I don't recall the car being driven on the street.

Al is dumping some kind of fuel in tank at Scappoose drag races. Rear tires were "the biggest I could find—they came off an ambulance," Al recalled. He also remembered that there were incredible problems involved in building a car this low. Body had to be narrowed to clear tires. Yes, he drove the car on the street!

was in stock position there was very little room inside the car. You sat on a thin pad and hoped your head wouldn't hit the roof at a sharp bump. One *experienced* the engine: there were no floorboards or firewall so fumes came back where we sat. But there are few thrills in life like the one of climbing into a channeled '32 coupe after a dull day at school, snuggling down among the crossmembers and exhaust pipes, seeing the naked machinery at your feet and the ground a few inches beyond. I can still remember the sound of that flathead. The distinctive grinding of the starter and then the noise of the ragged, choppy V-8; the short shift lever; the sometimes comforting, sometimes claustrophobic feeling of the coupe's tiny cockpit.

A lowered machine looked great, however impractical it might be. It looked like a hot rod—rakishly low. There was intense pressure from one's peers and the general public that caused one to get the car down—low! The first year I drove my A-V8 it was stock height except for

16-inch wheels, reversed eyes in front and a torched main leaf in back. I thought it looked great, but people always asked when I was going to channel it or get a dropped axle, or at least step the frame to get rid of that ugly gap between the back tire and fender. Dozens of people asked why the car wasn't lower (and why it didn't have aluminum heads— something else I couldn't afford). Finally, in the winter of 1952 I bought a dago axle and channeled the body, an act of mayhem I've sometimes regretted.

Another roadster owner who felt this social pressure was my friend, Al Rogers. He had a beautiful '28 A-V8 with a full-race Merc engine and chrome-plated rear end. I mean, it was sharp, with lots of trick details. It was full-fendered, with a dropped axle and stepped frame, and as low as a fendered car could get. But Al took a lot of heat about the car's height and he sold it.

Then he went to San Diego and bought a super '29 A-V8 roadster that had been in *Hot Rod* (April, 1952). It was black, built on a '32 frame, with every-

thing on the engine and under the car chrome-plated. It was the best-handling and best-riding hot rod I've ever driven, with plenty of road clearance, sure steering, thick seats, lots of elbow room and a great ride. These virtues were due primarily to the car's height. It didn't even have a dropped axle!

Al drove the car to Oregon in July, 1952 and almost immediately folks began to ask when he was going to lower it. By the spring of 1953, Al had enough of the kibitzers and he completely dismantled this beautiful roadster, keeping only the '32 rails and the basic '29 body. Everything else he sold or gave away Then he slowly began construction of a new roadster.

He narrowed and stepped the '32 rails, built a suicide front end, and channeled the body over the frame. Called "The Seven Year Itch" when it was on the cover of *Hot Rod,* the car was right on the ground; the whole job took him 13 years, and by then the "resto-rod" look was gaining favor, which meant building them high again!

Around 1950 Cliff Johnson built this radical roadster. The body, supposedly from a Fiat, was channeled over a tube frame; it had suicide suspension in front and flattened crossmember in rear. The car was actually lower than the rear tires! It also had Kinmont disc brakes, tubular radius rods and race car steering.

In the years following World War II there was increased activity in all types of auto racing. This included a fairly new type, the track roadsters, or, as they were often called, *hot rods*.

Track Roadsters

Track roadster racing probably had its origins in the early 'Thirties, when stripped-down stockers competed on a dirt horse race track at a county fair, a promoter's idea to ensure that there would be a crowd. The cars had the fenders, hood and windshield removed to make them resemble streamlined racing machines. They were Model T and A Fords, Studebakers, Hudsons, Whippets and any number of various other makes. In the photos I've seen of early track-roadster-type races there seemed to be as many touring cars as roadsters in the race. Most engines were stone-stock, and if an engine was hopped up, it was done on a tight budget. In general, these open-wheeled machines lacked the sophistication and finish of the race cars

In 1946 "Duck" Collins built a '31 A roadster on '32 rails as a dual-purpose machine; it was great on street, but heavy for the track. In 1947 he built this flathead-powered T-V8 strictly for racing. '27 T, even with pickup bed, weighed only 1,500 pounds. "Kuzie" Kuzmanich was one driver who got the roadster around the track quickly.

they attempted to copy.

Officially, track roadster racing began in 1936 in Southern California with the establishment of rules and scheduled races. A major track was the old Ascot Speedway in Southgate, where as many as 8,000 spectators would gather to see drivers like George and Hal Robson, Don Farmer and Carl Mays compete for prize money. As might be expected, the So-Cal cars revealed a strong race car influence; they were generally showier, with paint and chrome, and faster, with all-out racing engines.

Sense of victory

After World War II track roadster racing boomed in California, spread up the West Coast, and then across the United States. Men who had faced combat and were still looking for action turned to hopped-up cars. Auto racing gave them the intense competition and the heady sense of victory they had experienced overseas; there was joyful celebration and death-defying exhilaration in the exhaust note of a full throttle. If a man wanted to get into auto racing, the port of entry was via track roadsters. It was low in the hierarchy, ranking somewhere above jalopy racing and well below midget auto racing, but it *was* legitimate racing. It was an amateur sport, and was for most people an *affordable* activity.

A builder usually mounted a '23 to '27 Model T body on a Model A frame, hopped up the four-cylinder engine, or replaced it with a flathead V-8, perhaps bolted on a set of juice brakes, and he was ready to go racing. Sometimes he used a Model A roadster as the basis or even a '32, although Deuces were rarely

used because of their excessive weight. Today when we think of a track roadster we think of a T bucket, and most built in the racing heyday used that body. The object was to have a high horsepower-to-weight ratio, which meant building a spindly,

If a man wanted to get into auto racing, the port of entry was via track roadsters.

California roadsters circa 1947: first '29 A has four-barrel engine with Cragar OHV set-up; next '29 and the '34 roadsters have full-dress Mercury flatheads. All three were probably driven on the street.

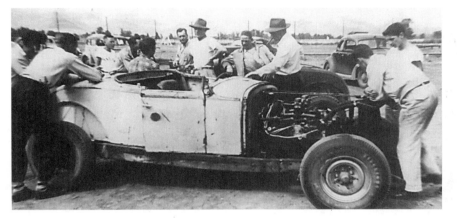

This 1930 Model A roadster body has been mounted on a larger frame, with semi-elliptical springs. It runs some kind of large V-type engine, possibly an Oakland Viking V-8. Car was probably too heavy to be competitive.

gutted, stripped-for-action machine. Often the car was used on the street also—a concept I find quite interesting!

Rolla Vollstedt

Rolla Vollstedt has been a racer for 50 years. He was a hot rodder before WW II, got into track roadsters in mid-1947, graduated to big cars, and has built and owned cars that have run in many Indy 500 races during the past 25 years. He makes a point that there were plenty of hot cars around, lots of youthful energy, and no place where these energies could be unleashed. We're talking about 1945, a full five years before the first official, legal drag strip was established. Rolla told me how track roadster racing originated in Oregon, but the sport followed the same pattern and developed for the same reasons in other places:

"Track roadsters started out with a group of fellows around town (Portland) having Model A roadsters, and most of them had installed Ford flathead V-8 engines. They were hard-pressed for somewhere to run them. They were hopped-up engines, and you wanted to run them some-place, and if you ran them on the streets or highways you got into trouble, so we came up with the idea of racing them on the race track.

"Initially, you would drive your car to the race track, take off the running boards and fenders, tie the car down, and go out and race it…There was lots of competition…"

Len Sutton

Len Sutton drove Rolla Vollstedt's GMC-powered track roadster to many a victory and several championships. He later raced midgets, sprint cars and big cars up and down the West Coast and competed several times in the Indy 500, placing second in 1962. I talked with him recently and he recalled how he got his start:

"In 1946, when I came out of the service, I had been in the Navy, I decided I wanted to continue doing things that were a little exciting. I owned a Model A roadster with a Ford V-8 engine in it and decided after seeing a couple of these (track roadster) races that I could do the same thing. So I put a number on the side of it, joined the association and started racing. That was in August 1946 and I drove two races with that car.

"It was a car that I drove on the street. I think the engine was a '35 or '36 Ford V-8, and the Model A (roadster) was a 1930. There were a lot of them at that time that were put together that way. It had a dual manifold, a Payne, and that's all—other than that it was stock including mechanical brakes. It didn't even have hydraulics. After that initial race I drove it home…It didn't have fenders, they didn't have fenders in those days; it did have a license on it, and it was legal to run on the road."

There's something fascinating about such a dual-purpose machine—a serious race car that is also a grocery-getter. This concept of street and competition car continued for only a year, and by 1947 the cars had been modified so extensively that they could only be used on the track. An example is Rudy Ramos' track roadster which was

Frankie McGowan in George Koch's '27 T roadster pickup, powered by Lincoln V-12, leads Don Moore in Al Reamer's '27 T roadster with Merc Flathead. Taken at Portland Speedway, 1947.

Roadsters dicing it up. Actually, this was a publicity photo for the newspaper. #82 owned and driven by Don Turner. #19 owned by the Clevinger brothers, driven by Don Moore.

designated Hot Rod of the Month in the July 1948 issue of *Hot Rod Magazine.* A '27 T roadster body on a '32 Ford frame, it had a '32 grille and an aluminum hood. The engine, a 1946 Mercury, had been bored 3-5/16 inches and the crank stroked an eighth. It was fully balanced, ported and relieved, ran Sharp heads, a triple-carb manifold, and an unnamed 3/4 cam. The running gear showed a real departure from what had been the norm just the year before. Rather than running a Ford three-speed transmission, the car had a

Stellings in-and-out gear box, which meant that it couldn't be run on the street. It also had neat stuff like a Knudsen full-floating rear end and Franklin center steering.

Safety features

While in the beginning there had been little concern for the driver's safety, by 1948 the rules required certain safety features, such as aircraft bucket seat, a regulation aircraft safety belt and a fuel shut-off valve. Roll bars, however, were not required. In 1948 the Ramos machine won

four out of five trophy dashes. The car also competed at the dry lakes on occasion as a Class C roadster under SCTA rules, where it turned 118 mph.

The development of the track roadster in Southern California did not go unnoticed in other parts of the country. Most So-Cal cars ran with lightweight flywheels, and a few even ran without a flywheel. The 1946 Oregon champion roadster ran a Lincoln V-12 that had its flywheel removed, the only car to do this. By 1947 most of the cars ran without flywheels. They had also been lightened and had faster steering. Midway in the 1947 racing season Manuel Ayulo and Jack McGrath, two of the fastest California drivers, came north to compete. Their cars were faster, handled better, and the two Californians took home the money, leaving the Oregon racers with track records that seemingly would never be broken. But as Dick Martin wrote in *Hot Rod Magazine* a few months later: "Changes were made, and immediately afterwards, Manuel's and McGrath's

In 1948 to run with the big cars, "Duck" Collins borrowed a tail section from Les Anderson's Maserati Indy car and adapted it to his '27 T. Don Moore driving it at the Salem Fairgrounds, a half-mile track.

records, which looked so far away from us, fell along with the big car record at Portland." By the late 'Forties roadster racing was no longer an outlaw activity, although it did not have the prestige or recognition given to seemingly more legitimate forms of racing, such as midgets and big cars.

Roadster racing continued to expand. More racing associations were formed, more tracks were opened to the roadsters, and more races were scheduled. Soon it became possible to race at least once a week, and more often if the owner wanted to haul his car to other tracks. The California Roadster Association (CRA) raced at Carrell Speedway in Gardena, a half-mile dirt track, and at Culver City Speedway, a banked-and-paved quarter-mile track. The California Hot Rods (CHR) raced at the Huntington Beach Speedway, a fifth-mile track, and at Bonelli Stadium in Saugus. American Sports Cars (ASC) held races at Valley Speedway, a five-eighths mile track in Fresno. The North California Roadster Racing Association (NCRRA) raced at Pacheco Stadium and Contra Costa Stadium, both in Pacheco, California. This association, started in 1946. It was so successful that by 1947 it could

Tom Story (standing) built this track roadster shortly after the war. He used the rear doors and section of a '28 Ford roadster body, '30 cowl, hand-formed nose. Car was driven to races, even to some in Washington state. Around 1950 car was retired to the street; it got a neat top, large chrome-plated headers, interior, bobbed rear fenders. Driver is Jim Martin.

To show how sport evolved, in 1948 "Duck" Collins abandoned his old rig, built this '27 T. It had the Merc engine moved back, had reworked Franklin center steering, four-wheel juice brakes, full bellypan and extensively lightened. 1949 photo taken at Hollywood Bowl in Salem shows Gordy Livingston driving, and, from left to right, Merritt Aldridge, Jimmy Francis and "Duck" Collins.

claim that 30,000 fans attended its events.

Those associations served as models for groups in other parts of the country. The Oregon Roadster Racing Association (ORRA) was formed in May 1946; its purpose was to band together people with a common interest, to develop places where roadsters could race, and also as a tool to allow racers and owners to bargain with promoters. In Indiana there was the well-known Mutual Racing Association (MRA)—Dick Frazier, a Mutual racer, was featured on the cover of *Hot Rod Magazine* in 1948, a rare honor because the magazine featured California cars almost exclusively. Another Midwest group was the Ohio

Speedway Association which by 1948 was racing at two Ohio tracks, Berea and Norwalk.

It developed racers who would become famous

Track roadster racing was amateur racing, which explains part of its appeal. There were no legal drag strips where a driver could feel the satisfaction of putting the pedal to the floor. So it was not surprising that it should attract and develop some real hot shoes, some of whom would eventually race in the Indy 500; among them were Manuel Ayulo, Jack McGrath, Troy Ruttman, Dempsey Wilson, Ed Elisian, Bob Vieth, Pat Flaherty, Jim Rathman and Andy Linden.

The evolution of track

Auto racing gave them the intense competition and the heady sense of victory they had experienced overseas.

Roadster racing in Portland got started in 1945, as soon as WW II ended. The early cars were generally also driven on the street (note license plate).

roadsters can be seen in the cars built and raced by Don "Duck" Collins during the years that spanned the sport. Collins, who has wrenched at numerous tracks, including Indianapolis and LeMans, got out of the Navy in 1946 and was anxious to put his street roadster on the race track. His '31 A-V8 had been built before the war, and Collins had rebuilt it in 1944, before he went into the service. A highway accident in early 1946 had put the car on blocks. When he was discharged a few months later, he mounted the '31 body on a '32 Ford chassis, used a hopped-up 1938 Ford V-8 engine that belonged to his partner, "Kuzie" Kuzmanich, and entered the car in the final race of the 1946 season. It ran and handled well, but, as a street rod, it was too heavy to be competitive, as he knew it would be.

For the 1947 season he built a new car, a 1927 Ford Model T pickup, powered by the same '38 V-8 engine. As Collins recalled, "That car weighed only 1,500 pounds, which was pretty light, even though I had a Model T box, not one made out of lighter sheet metal like George Koch had made. My body was probably 150 pounds heavier than his body. The first time out we had fast time, and set a new track record at the Portland Speedway—27.011 seconds."

During the 1947 season McGrath and Ayulo came to Portland, and as a result of their visit Collins decided to build a new and improved car. Collins recalled, "I took my car up into the space I was renting above Blackie Blackburn's garage, above Merchants Delivery. I dismantled it, moved the engine back 12 inches, put in center steering using a Franklin unit,

#57 was built by Al Reamer, Sr. and Westly Wyss in 1947. It was a beautiful car, with '27 T roadster body mounted on 1932 Ford chassis, black paint, red-leather interior and full-race Merc flathead. One-piece nose and hood formed by Art Scovell tilted forward.

Later the car was shortened, lightened (interior gone), with '32 Ford grille replacing the nose. When Don Moore hit the rail hard he broke several ribs, and car was damaged much worse than it appears. Because front and center cross members were replaced and body supports removed, the frame triangulated and pulled body with it; engine fell out of car!

and put on a '27 T roadster body I bought from Norm Snodgrass. We went out to the last race of the '47 season and turned the track faster than McGrath or Ayulo had run earlier in the season—we turned 25.25. Then I built a whole new car for the 1948 season, and I ran that car the rest of the years we were racing."

As track roadsters became

more sophisticated, their speeds approached the times of the big cars, and some big-car owners were defensive, because the hot rods were lower on the hierarchy, they felt. An example was Bob Scovell, who had been racing since the 'Twenties, and he voiced what other racers felt when he was disdainful of the roadsters and doubtful about their times, feeling that their

Virgil and Steve Hergert began building this '29 A-V8 roadster in 1951 as a track car, but by the time they got it finished the track racing days were over, so they drove it on the street.

During the winter of 1949-50, Collins and Jim Soukup built a complete big car body for the track-roadster chassis, forming the panels from aluminum at Judd Fuller's shop, and it was a beautiful job. So his roadster evolved into a race car, but it was still a hot rod under that smooth skin. Collins recalled, "They built a half-mile dirt track for us at the (Portland) Meadows. The first time we ran there and qualified we had fast time and set the track record. The PA system was kind of lousy, just the PA system they used for the horse race track, and I didn't hear what the hell time we got. Howard Osborne was driving. Just then Scovell happened to be walking by and I said, Hey, Bob, did you hear what time Howard got? Oh yeah, he said, fast, and just kept walking. But that shut him up right there. He never again called me a hot rodder or told me how the clocks were hopped-up. Never. It was just like you turned off a faucet!"

Track roadster racing really began in 1946 and it ended around 1954. By 1951 drag racing was well-established in many parts of the country, and while straight-line racing drew

clocks were inaccurate.

"Us hot rodders!" Collins recalled. "Scovell used to cuss at us, he used to tell us how Nick's got the clocks all hopped-up for us, and say you guys ain't going that fast. You guys ain't got no racing motors because it's got to have overhead camshafts in it to be a racing motor, blah blah blah! He had a HAL at that time.

"In 1948 I wanted to run my roadster as a big car, to run that Salem race. I asked Scovell if I could run the roadster if I had a tail on it. He said, sure. So I got hold of Les Anderson and asked if I could borrow the tail from his Maserati, and he said okay. I borrowed that tail, put it on my track roadster and we ran it down at Salem.

"That's when old Scovell slipped me a Mickey. We won the heat race, qualified eighth, but it was running kind of hot. I was pitted next to Scovell, and he

said, why don't you put some alcohol in it? I said, will it mix? He said, sure, just dump it in. He said, I'll even give you five gallons. So I dumped five gallons of alcohol in the tank and got in the main event. Hell, it only ran about a half dozen laps and it just fried the engine. That was the end of that!"

The Hergert car today is owned by Mark "Briz" Brislawn, who rebuilt car when he got it 23 years ago. Still has big flathead V-8, lots of 'Fifties details; note V-style windshield, tubular V8-60 axle.

Track roadster styling strongly influenced street-driven hot rods. In 1948 Stan Blinco zoomed around Portland in this 1927 T-V8 roadster. Grille shell and hood were adapted from a Franklin car.

some racers and spectators away, it was really circle-track racing that killed track roadsters: like Collins' roadster, they got converted into big cars! An early issue of *Honk!* attributes the beginning of the end to Walt James, a member of the California Roadster Association, who simply wanted to race his roadster more often than once or twice a week. He got an old big-car body, a set of Dayton knock-off wheels, and adapted both to his T-bodied track roadster. He'd race in the roadster races, then tow the car home, pull off the roadster body, bolt on the big-car body and wheels, and race the next night as a big car. Others soon caught on and disguised hot rods began appearing at big-car meets all over Southern California. Rolla Vollstedt did the same thing with his track

Track roadster racing was amateur racing, which explains part of its appeal.

Jim Martin in Story roadster and Don Moore in Reamer roadster, neck and neck at Portland Speedway.

roadster, also running it as a big car with merely a body change.

There's a strong irony here, since big-car people had long looked down on the circle-track hot rodders. The race car purists objected, but hot rodders pointed out that the roadsters *cum* big cars were more than holding their own. Finally the CRA scheduled a series of open races with big cars and hot rods running together on the same program at Corona, a half-mile dirt track.

This was a compromise, but it tipped the scales in favor of big cars; one by one track roadsters were made into big cars and by the mid-'Fifties the track roadster had gone the way of the dinosaur. The California Roadster Association became the California Racing Association, and the roaring roadsters were history.

Rolla Vollstedt's roadster/big car (or sprint car) was typical of the body swapping that permitted owners to run more races. In 1956 this big car, driven by Len Sutton, grabbed 12 firsts and two seconds, finishing all of the races. Car was GMC-motivated with Horning/Fisher aluminum 12-port racing head.

Track roadsters were intended to be functional, not necessarily beautiful. This '29 roadster uses a four-carb intake manifold—probably a Schnell— made in Portland as early as 1945 and generally regarded as the first cast intake to mount four carbs.

Traditional vs. Non-Traditional

If they had not been aesthetically pleasing they would never have become traditional hot rods.

Although hot rodding has always been an activity where a person could exercise his individuality, it has from the beginning followed two basic approaches: the traditional and the non-traditional.

Someone decided 'way back when that a fenderless Model T, a '29 Ford roadster on '32 rails, and a '32 Ford were good-looking machines, and people have been building them for 50 years. There were reasons other than appearance, of course. Those cars were fast in stock form, had great potential when hopped up, had a wide variety of speed equipment available for them, they were plentiful and cheap, etc. But if they had not been aesthetically pleasing they would never have become traditional hot rods.

When I built my first roadster in 1951, I knew I wanted a 1939-1948 Ford or Mercury flathead V-8 engine—not only because of its racing history but because I liked the way it looked. I liked the shape of the heads, generator, water pumps, Stromberg carburetor, and the

I shot this unusual '27 T-V8 at the Expo Show in Portland, February 1952, but the car came from California. The '39 Chrysler front end and skirted motorcycle fenders on all four wheels make the car distinctive.

Les Connor drove from Portland to the 1952 Bonneville meet in his 1932 DeSoto roadster. Windshield was chopped, spare tire cut down, grille filled, full hubcaps, metallic-blue paint, white-Naugahyde interior. Engine was hopped-up and very detailed Chrysler six.

combination fuel-pump stand and oil filler—most of all I liked the balanced effect the two long water hoses gave to the engine (and I still do!). I was sorely disappointed when my father arranged to get me a 1949 Ford engine whose heads, with front-mounted hose inlets, resembled the old 1932-36 Ford V-8 engines! I actually *hated* the shape of the 8BA heads, and strongly disliked the new Holley carb, the bulky generator, and the oil-inlet pipe (even though it was more accessible and practical than the design of the pipe on the 1932-48 engines). (My feelings about the 8BA and 8CM engines have mellowed some.) My concern was for the engine's appearance rather than its performance: I wanted that traditional hot-rod look. I gazed at hundreds of cars in *Hot Rod Magazine* and found only one that used the later model flathead: Bill Likes' full-fendered '32 roadster, and that engine did not have a speck of chrome. No wonder he ran a

Jack Woolfs' '27 Ford T roadster pickup was built on Willys chassis, used a Jeep engine. Red, with black-Naugahyde interior, and everything to make it street legal. I took this photo at 1952 "Speed-O-Rama" show in Portland. Car is still in town, unchanged except it now has Chev II four-banger engine.

Julian Bankhead built this unusual street roadster in 1949. '27 T body was nearly flat in back, with outside spare tire. Suicide front end used Ford parts, but almost everything else came from a wrecked 1941 Pontiac, including the straight-eight engine. It was painted chartreuse, with purple cycle fenders, had folding top, all road equipment. I saw car on street often during 1950-51, and it reminded me of MG-TC from rear. I took this photo at Scappoose drags, 1952 or 1953.

hood—that engine was unattractive!

For that same reason I knew I wanted a '32 grille shell and '39 Ford taillights, touches I'd seen on cars in *Hot Rod Magazine*. I got both items but we really had to search for the '39 taillights and along the way my father—ever the improviser—tried to talk me into using 1939 Plymouth taillights. They are teardrop shaped and resemble the Ford light, but they're fatter and have the Plymouth ship motif on the lens. They are *not* the same!

'39 Ford taillights

It's hard to say why a particular item has such an appeal, why it remains popular year after year, why it becomes a tradition. I have a photograph taken in 1932 or 1933 of a '30 Ford gow job with a brand-new '32 grille shell, and another taken in 1939 showing a '29 roadster with a pair of '39 taillights; in other words, those two items were instantly popular and became traditional touches for the

traditional hot rod. They still are. Perhaps 90% of the 1927-32 model street rods being built today, unless the builder opts for the pure repro look, use 1939 Ford taillights.

On the other hand, there were hot rodders who out of ignorance, disdain, preference, or a sense of individuality chose to work outside tradition. They had a vision that extended beyond the limitations of the traditional rod builder; they marched to a different drummer. The result might be a '29 Ford roadster body mounted on a massive truck frame, which had been beefed to accommodate a Duesenberg engine. Or a Marmon or a Cadillac V-16. When I first read *Hot Rod Magazine* I coveted the traditional rods like Allborn's A-V8 and Bob McGee's '32 roadster, but I also greatly admired—and certainly never forgot—cars that were non-traditional, like Bill Carash's special with a 1936 Plymouth chassis, a stock Cadillac V-16 engine, and a hand-made aluminum roadster body.

I remember, for example, seeing in Portland a 1932 Plymouth PB roadster, stock-bodied, full-fendered, with a stock Cadillac flathead V-8 and early Hydra-Matic. Actually, I seem to remember two such cars—not enough to create a tradition, however. The Plymouth roadster body was fairly attractive—not as nice as the Ford body of the same year, most people would agree—and I'm sure that the car was a kick to drive. I'd love to own that car right now, but I can't imagine anyone building a similar car today as a period piece.

1930 Durant roadster

Another fairly attractive odd-rod in my old neighborhood was

There were hot rodders who out of ignorance, disdain, preference, or a sense of individuality—chose to work outside tradition.

a 1930 Durant roadster which had the front fenders and running boards removed and the engine and running gear replaced with that from a Ford V-8. I can't recall ever having seen or read about another Durant that had been reworked, so that one still seems unusual. I know who built it, and if he were still alive I'd like to ask why he chose a Durant roadster in a world filled with Fords?

I'm not surprised that he chose to put a Ford flathead V-8 in his Durant, as they showed up in all kinds of cars, from '37 Chevy sedans to Jeeps to MG-TDs. I recall seeing a beautiful Cord convertible in California with a full-race Merc flathead; the car retained its front-wheel drive, which meant building an adapter as well as complex shifting linkage. Dee Wescott, the man who builds the glass repro bodies, has a Bantam coupe with a V8-60 engine; the conversion was done in the early 'Fifties. The installation of a flathead V-8 in a non-Ford was perhaps a tradition within the non-traditional mode.

Sometimes a non-traditional machine was built because the various parts were available or because they somehow recommended themselves to the builder. I recall a '27 T roadster body built on a shortened later-model chassis. The engine was a Buick straight eight with dual carbs, and the instrument panel was from a 1941 Buick. Thinking about the car years later, I decided that the builder must have used most of a 1941 Buick as the basis for the rod and that he had perhaps chosen that particular car because it came equipped with a factory-installed dual-carb setup. That is, I'm betting that he built the entire car

1939 Plymouth taillight (top) was similar to 1939 Ford taillight, but never became popular.

on the strength of that dual manifold.

Then there was Bud Sargent's 1942 Studebaker custom. It was a four-door, a model unpopular with customizers, and it was a Studebaker! What in the world could you do to a Studebaker four-door? Sargent, a body man, took the radical approach: he removed the roof and posts, discarded them, but left the windshield; then he strengthened the body so the doors would

function properly. This gave him a convertible sedan. Then he lowered the body, installed dual exhausts with brass extensions, skirts, whitewalls, nosed and decked it, and filled all body seams with lead. I don't think he ever got around to painting it, but even in primer this odd-ball custom looked good.

'29 A-Willys Roadster

Thinking about that car, I realize how cheap things were 45 years ago.

I got my first ticket in a hot rod. The wonder is that I didn't get it sooner and that the penalty wasn't higher. There was plenty missing on that car. Maybe that alone says something about the attitude of the law toward hot rods in the early 'Fifties. And thinking about that car, I recall how cheap things were 45 years ago—that's one reason they're called the "good old days." I bought the car in question, a running hot rod, for only $25!

That was in February 1952. A year earlier I'd bought a '29 A-V8 roadster, and with my father's help had gotten it into decent shape by June 1951. I'd driven it all summer and into the fall, when I had a stupid accident that wiped out the reworked '42 Merc axle, radius rods and the right side exhaust. It could have been fixed during a long weekend, but of course I decided to completely dismantle the car, channel it, put in a new dropped axle, and a hundred other things which

This was a $25 hot rod in 1952! 1929 Ford roadster body was mounted on 1937 Willys chassis, used a four-cylinder Jeep engine. Car had bobbed '29 A fenders, '32-style grille. Chassis had stock mechanical brakes, four semi-elliptic springs, four tube shocks, rode well and stopped okay. Car also had top, wipers, radio and heater.

Same '29 A-Willys after a Saturday of work: I removed grille, hood, top, lights, fenders and windshield. Now, I thought, the car's beginning to look like a real California hot rod!

meant that it was laid up for the better part of a year. I was a junior in high school, I had no money, the car was at my father's gas station some 30 miles away from home—in other words, everything was conspiring against my getting that car back together.

Odd, but interesting

One day a friend, Larry Deyoe, stopped by and told me about a hot rod sitting in the yard beside his house. He thought it was for sale, and, because I was nuts about hot rods, I had to go take a look.

The car was odd, but interesting—it was someone's idea of unusual daily transportation, a low-budget sports car.

It was a super-straight 1929 Model A roadster body mounted on a 1937 Willys chassis, and the two seemed to mate with ease. It had a grille shell that resembled a '32 Ford, but wider. As I lifted the one-piece hood, feeling again the excitement of checking out a mysterious modified car, I saw that the power plant was a bone-stock Willys Jeep engine.

All the parts seemed to fit together fairly well. And it had been built to be a daily driver. It had bobbed front fenders, a folding top—both necessary in rainy Oregon—windshield wipers, hood, lights and all road equipment. It even had a heater and an under-dash Arvin radio.

It could be something really *neat!*

Even though I'd hoped it'd be basically Ford, with a hot V-8, I was interested. I knew of two other hot rods in Portland that used a Willys frame and a Jeep engine; one was a '27 T, the other a '29 A. Already my mind was clicking, thinking how this rod could be made into something really *neat!*

We talked to the woman of the house. Turned out that the car belonged to her son, who was in the army in Korea, where the war was dragging on, and she was tired of looking at the car. I could have it for $25! I was always broke, but somehow I got $25 and a few nights later I got my father to go with me and drag the '29 from the mud with his big '42 Lincoln Zephyr.

In study hall I drew pictures of the car. It would be a fenderless roadster with a race car nose, powered by a full-race Jeep engine (speed equipment was readily available). Or it would be a full-fendered hot rod, nicely finished, something I could drive to school while working on my '29 A-V8. Or it would be a drag car or a show car.

On paper it became all those things. In fact, what it became in a single afternoon was a stripped-down hot rod. I removed the top, hood, radio, heater, grille, headlights, fenders and, sometimes, the windshield. Hey, the car looked great!

And it ran well—once I got it started. We'd tow the car for two or three miles before it'd run smoothly. I had five gallons of paint thinner, and to prime the car I'd shoot a few slugs of thinner into the carb. When I now think of that car I recall the distinctive odor of exhaust tinged with thinner, as if it had left an irrevocable stain on the engine.

Don't shut it off!

Of course, once the car was running I didn't want to shut it off. I drove around for hours, cruising the back streets. I loved the way it handled. It had the basic Willys suspension—four semi-elliptical springs and four airplane-type shocks (as opposed to my A-V8, which had two buggy springs and no shocks). The car was low, and would take a city corner at 40 mph. It would take highway curves at full speed, riding flat, without a tendency to slide. I drove it hard, figuring I had nothing to lose.

One afternoon I'd been driving around the neighborhood for a couple hours, and I kept telling myself to go home and park the damn thing before I got into trouble. I'd seen a cop car several blocks away, but I wasn't too worried. The neighborhood was quiet, with lots of empty land, and the road on which I lived was unpaved just beyond my house so there was almost no through traffic. I went past the house, bounced over the bumpy dirt road and floored the gas, zooming around the corner. One more time, I told myself, then I'd park it. As I again passed the house I thought, what the heck, just one more time. I *loved* to drive that car!

Before I got to the corner, a cop car came around it. I didn't need a siren or flashing lights to know what to do; I stopped. The cop slowly got out, looked it over, and said that they'd had complaints. Could he see my license? I didn't have it with me! I'd been driving my '29 A-V8 for several months, and a good part of that time I did not have a license. I'd never been stopped! I said wait a minute, and ran home to get my driver's license from my room.

When I returned he was already writing. He pointed out that the car lacked some essential equipment, such as lights, wiper, horn and windshield. It lacked the required four fenders. The plates were expired and the car was not insured. I'm sure I was shaking. I knew the fine for missing fenders was $10 a wheel, and I realized that this could add up. He only ticketed me for not having my driver's license in my pocket, a traffic-court offense, and told me he never wanted to see that car on the street again.

I believed him. Rather than follow my dreams and make the car into a sharp—or at least legal—machine, I pirated the windshield, headlights and Gemmer steering for my '29 A-V8 (they're still on it today) and traded the car for a complete 1930 American Austin. By a rare fluke of good sense I immediately sold that car to a used car dealer, who mounted it on the roof of his building, and I concentrated on finishing my very traditional '29 A-V8 which I hoped would look like all the '29 A-V8s I had seen in magazines.

And it ran well—once I got it started. We'd tow the car for two or three miles before it'd run smoothly.

CUSTOM GRILLES AND BARS!
FORD • CHEVROLET • MERCURY • PLYMOUTH
BEAUTIFY YOUR CAR WITH ONE OF THESE GRILLES, BARS, CONVERSION KITS. ALL GUARANTEED.

1954 FORD CUSTOM GRILLE

Replaces center spinner on all 1954 FORDS. Gives your grille NEW SMOOTH LINES. Comes in two piece sets for upper and lower bars. Piece for lower bar is designed to match perfectly with original offsets. Bolt-on features. NO ALTERATIONS. Beautiful highly polished triple chrome plate. **No. F-54-C Guaranteed—$6.45 set (2 pcs.)**

GRILLE CONVERSION KIT

To fit 1949-50 FORD

This kit enables you to customize a FORD 1949 or 1950 WITHOUT removing original hood moulding. Kit consists of: (1) Chrome plated center moulding. (2) Unpainted hood fill-in piece. (3) Hood safety release latch.

No. FMK-95. Price $7.95 set (3 pieces)
Note: For a complete Grille conversion this kit can be purchased together with our F-49-B, F-50-B, FBS-49 or FBS-50. Please give year of car when ordering KIT and BAR.

EXCLUSIVE! The "Style-Liner"

This 14½-inch BAR is designed to replace the center spinner on ALL FORD 1949-50 WITHOUT removing your original right and left grille bars. It gives your grille the appearance of ONE massive single bar. Amazingly easy installation. NO drilling, cutting or alterations. Highly polished excellent chrome plate.

No. FBS-49 for 1949 FORD
No. FBS-50 for 1950 FORD
Guaranteed . . . Price $9.50 each

CUSTOM STYLED TO MEET POPULAR DEMAND

FORD CUSTOM GRILLE

To Fit 1946-47-48 Fords

Now you can customize your Ford 1946-47-48 with this beautiful highly polished grille. It replaces the three original horizontal bars and is engineered for easy installation with only minor alteration. Comes in left and right sections with all instructions. F-46-CG—Guaranteed $14.95 Pair.

CUSTOM CENTER BAR

To Fit Your 1952 Ford

This 7½" bar will replace the original spinner on ALL FORD 1952. It is deep enough to match perfectly with the original right & left bars. Perfect fit. No drilling, cutting or alterations. Quality chrome. Guaranteed . . . No. F-52-CB, price $8.00 each.

CUSTOM-LINER GRILLE

To Fit 1949-50-51 Fords

This custom grille is designed to replace the original grille on all FORD 1949-50-51. Constructed of heavy gauge steel. Its gleaming chrome finish and massive appearance will beautify any FORD. Precision engineered for perfect fit and easy installation. Guaranteed. No. FCL-49 . . . Price $21.00 each.

CUSTOM GRILLE BARS

Customize your FORD, MERC or PLYMOUTH with one of these beautiful highly polished chrome plated grille bars. With trim across the center.
Ford 1949—Stock No. F-49-B..............$17.50 each
Ford 1950—Stock No. F-50-B.............. 17.50 each
Ford 1951—Stock No. F-51-B.............. 17.50 each
Ford 1952—Stock No. F-52-CGB.......... 19.75 each
Mercury 1949-50—Stock No. M-249.... 19.75 each
Mercury 1951—Stock No. M-251........ 19.75 each
Plymouth 1953—Stock No. PL-53-CB.. 19.75 each

CUSTOM CENTER BAR

To Fit Your 1953 Ford

Installed in a few minutes. No cutting or drilling. This highly polished chrome plated bar replaces the center bowl on the FORD 1953. It is 16" long to extend outward to cover the black striping and match perfectly with the original right & left bars. It gives your grille the appearance of ONE massive single bar. Guaranteed. No. F-53-CB, price . . . $7.50 each.

MERCURY CUSTOM GRILLE

To Fit 1946-47-48 Mercury

Customize your 1946-47-48 Mercury with this beautiful, highly polished custom grille. This grille replaces the original right and left upper and center grilles. Styled and engineered for very easy installation. M-246—Guaranteed $14.95 Each.

M-46-CG
1946-7-8
$4.95 Ea.

M-49-CG
1949-50
$5.95 Ea.

MERCURY CUSTOM CENTER GRILLES

Replaces the original center piece on your Mercury. Blends perfectly with the original right and left grilles. Gives your grille a beautiful massive look. No holes to drill. Easily and quickly installed. Excellent chrome plated finish. Guaranteed. Please mention car year when ordering.

CHEVROLET CUSTOM GRILLE

To Fit CHEVROLET 1951-1952

This well designed custom grille will fit exactly to the contour of the original upper moulding and parking light frames on all CHEVROLET 1951-52. Easy installation. Beautiful chrome plate. No. CH-51-CG. Price $17.50 pair.

We can supply replacement FORD 1951 PARKING LIGHT FRAMES AND HOOD MOULDING. Both parking light frames and hood moulding are necessary when installing our FCL-49 on a 1949 Ford. Only the hood moulding is necessary for a 1950 Ford. Parking light frames—Stock No. F-51-PKL are $10.00 pair. Hood mouldings—stock No. F-51-RLC are $9.00 a set. We produce many other custom and stock grilles in our own factory. ORDER DIRECT if your dealer cannot supply. DEALER INQUIRIES INVITED. NOTE: All orders MUST be accompanied by at least 20% deposit. Balance COD, FOB Detroit.

DETROIT GRILLE MFG. CO.
258 E. Vernor • Dept. HR • Detroit 1, Michigan

Detroit Grille Manufacturing Co. ad from December 1954 issue of Hot Rod Magazine.

Study Hall Mechanix

I spent hours daydreaming on paper about the cars I would build.

While other high-school students covered their notebooks with clever sayings and the names of friends, my Pee-Chee portfolio was covered with drawings of stripped-down cars, Stromberg carbs, and naked racing engines. Inside was always the current issue of *Hot Rod Magazine*, my text book in those days. During study hall when I should have been study-ing, I spent hours daydreaming on paper about the cars I would build. High school wasn't un-pleasant, it was simply a barrier to the things I preferred; as a consequence I wasn't a good student, and during my sopho-more year I missed many days of school while at my father's service station working on my roadster. When at school I probably spent more time

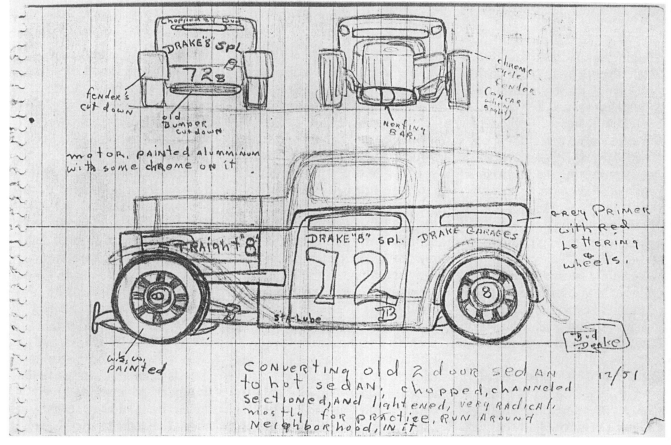

My plan for converting "an old two-door sedan" into a rod. Faint lines show original car, darker lines indicate my plans. It was based on a neighbor's Dodge or Plymouth, about a 1928. The main problem was that in 1951 the neighbor was still driving the car!

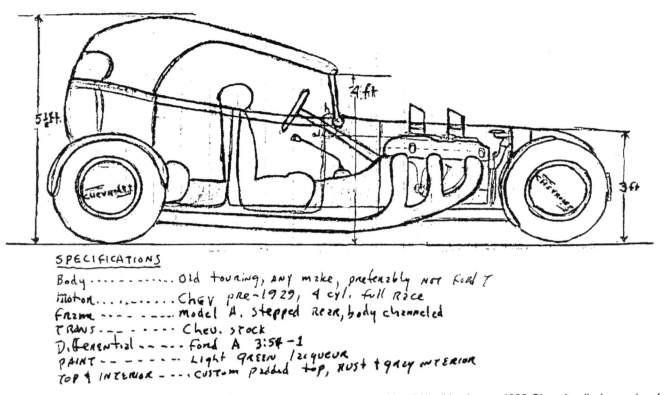

SPECIFICATIONS

Body............Old touring, any make, preferably not Ford T
Motor............Chev pre-1929, 4 cyl, full race
Frame............model A. stepped rear, body channeled
Trans............Chev. stock
Differential............Ford A 3:54-1
Paint............Light green lacquer
Top & Interior............custom padded top, rust & grey interior

Nutty touring was going to be really different, with odd-ball body, pre-1929 Chev 4-cylinder engine. I think I hoped to win AMBR trophy at Oakland Roadster Show!

thinking about cars than I did about algebra and Shakespeare.

Some of those youthful activities were vaguely literary. I wrote, but never mailed, letters to various people, including one to Will Moyes, *Oregon Journal* writer, protesting his indiscriminate use of the term "hot rod." I wrote to the editor of *Hot Rod Magazine*, asking a technical question and urging that they start a parts for sale column (which they later did) and to the editor of *Motor Trend* saying that I wanted to correspond with a teenager in California who was interested in dry lake racing.

Free catalogs and decals

I made a long list of businesses that offered free catalogs and decals—wish I had sent for more of them!—and a long list of old cars I could get for little or nothing. An example of the

latter: "'*32 Ford 4-door, V8 motor, stock '32. Bent front axle. Very poor 18" tires. Good body and interior. Rushman's Grocery, 106th and Harold. $30.*" I remember that car and, poor tires aside, it was a darn good 18-year-old Ford! But it was to my drawings I turned when the pressures of school became too great, when I was impossibly behind on my homework, when my clothes seemed uncool, when the girl I thought I mutely liked ignored me, when the minute hand on the clock seemed stuck at 2:45 p.m., when I longed to be in the cool, quiet of the garage. I was constantly making drawings of cars; some were simply doodles, some were intricate, detailed drawings. To escape from school I entered into the drawings as surely as if the cars were real, with doors that I could open and close behind me. The

drawings were of cars that I usually intended to build, and since I did not have enough money to build my '29 A-V8 the way I wanted, the paperwork allowed me to build a fleet of cars.

Early drawings were either traced from or influenced by car ads in magazines, i.e., a 1940 Packard or a 1948 Lincoln sedan. The drawings have lots of detail and shading, and are quite realistic. Another kind of early drawing was influenced by *Dyke's Motor Manual* which I used to read at the branch library. These were often cutaway drawings, showing the chassis details. I'd draw a realistic Model T chassis, and then, via dotted lines, add a speedster-type body. The detailed chassis came from an authoritative source, and from that basis I was able to fantasize.

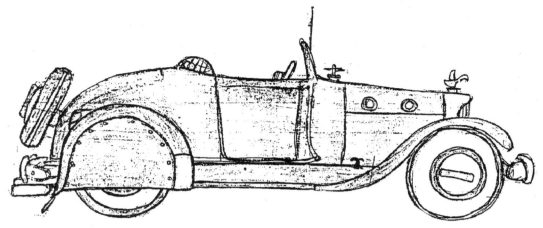

This '29 Model A roadster was simply "dolled up" on a budget. Lots of accessories; note sheet-metal skirts!

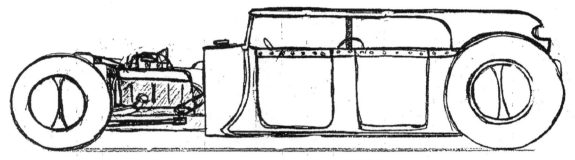

My idea of what to do with a '29 phaeton. Car was radical in design, but used Model A engine, running gear.

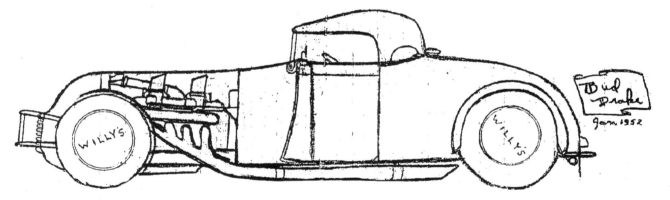

This track-style '29 Ford was based on a roadster I owned, which mounted the '29 body on a '37 Willys chassis, with Jeep engine.

Then there are those drawings influenced by—and sometimes plagiarized from—Tom Medley, who drew the Stroker McGurk cartoons in *Hot Rod Magazine*. My character was called *Big Bore Bud*, but he was really Stroker thinly disguised. Medley was from Oregon, too!

Low-budget machines

Mostly I drew hot rods, and the drawings fall into three categories: 1) low-budget machines; 2) odd-ball machines; 3) pure fantasy. An example of a car in the first category is a sweet little Model A roadster with bolt-on stuff; chrome ashtray on dash, dual mirrors, spare-tire kit, home-made skirts and solid side panels, curb feelers, mudflaps, etc. It also had some things I had taken from my own roadster, such as the front and rear bumpers and the '39 Ford speedometer. I envisioned the car as having painted white sidewall tires and a black paint job done with a brush. I was being

I made numerous drawings of competiton machines— drag cars and circle-track racers—with *Drake Garage* written on them.

High school weirdness! My idea of whacking the heck out of a 1936 Plymouth sedan and thus becoming a lunch hour hero.

realistic! But in 1950 one could find a Model A roadster for very little money, and it was certainly possible to do the modest changes I had outlined.

Another example of a low-budget machine sounds like fantasy but I was serious: "Car I actually plan to fix this way for 1952 drag season. Made from '34 coupe I get from Hal Miller for money he owes me." The coupe was radically chopped and channeled, something I guess I figured that I could do at no cost. It was otherwise essentially stock, with mechanical brakes ("rear only") and "ribbed tires" on the rear which I intended to rib by hand. I intended to rebuild the engine for racing; my price list was within the realm of possibility—adding a few bucks for gaskets and rings—but I don't know how well the engine would have run nor for how long.

3 or 4 carb manifold—used .... $?
Milled (stock) aluminum
   heads, 9 to 1 .... 10.00
Open exhausts 0.00
12-lb. flywheel (balanced) .. 5.00
Super mushroom cam 30.00
Adjustable tappets 8.00
TOTAL $53.00

I also noted that it "burns methanol (my own formula)"—wonder what that was? (Also wonder whether I got my money back from Hal Miller; I sure never got the coupe.)

Before and after drawings

Often the paper project would be the result of a car that I regularly saw, the 1930 Model A cabriolet parked near the bus stop, the two-cylinder 1939 Crosley parked in a neighbor's backyard. I'd study them, thinking what I could do with that machine if I had it. One car I built on paper was probably inspired

by Mr. Stone's 1928 Dodge sedan, a car he drove for over 25 years and that I was ready to chop up. "Converting old 2-door sedan to hot sedan. Chopped, channeled, sectioned, and lightened, very radical. Mostly for practice. Run around neighborhood in it." The drawing of the car "before" was done lightly, and the drawing "after" was done in dark pencil. It was low, with cut-down stock rear fenders, and the rear bumper cut down like a push bar. It still had the old wooden-spoke wheels and, again, painted whitewalls. I wonder what some of these cars would have looked like if they had been built, with painted whitewalls, "black-brush paint job," and "front end, engine, outside headers painted aluminum." But I have to remember that many rods built in the early 'Fifties were not fancy, and most drag rods were strictly business.

Although I was deadly serious about these projects I was probably trying to see what the cars might look like, and I had to make the drawing to visualize the car. An example was a "Custom 1934 Ford sedan I am going to build for street use." This car had a slightly modified Mercury engine, with the emphasis on reliability. It was to be used for street so it had nice appointments like radio and heater, '49 Plymouth bumpers, a spare tire, leather interior, chrome garnish moldings, and four tires of equal size! But the body was something else. It was "sectioned three inches, chopped four inches front, three inches rear, with a LaSalle grille." On another sheet I had a complete description of the car down to the chrome cigarette lighter, windshield decal, and a big three-bolt Buick Stromberg carburetor.

Few traditional rods

There are only a few drawings of traditional hot rods—a '32 or '29 coupe or roadster. Instead I seemed to lean toward the odd-ball. I planned a sports-type roadster with a Packard straight-eight engine, a sectioned 1936 Plymouth sedan, a Willys street roadster, a '32 Plymouth roadster with late-model Plymouth running gear, etc. I'm not sure why I had a penchant for the unusual; perhaps it had to do with cost or availability, but then early model Fords were available at modest prices.

I must have had something in mind. In a letter I wrote to the editor at *Hot Rod Magazine* I asked: "I would like to know if it is necessary to have a roadster to win 'Most Beautiful Roadster' (Oakland) prize? How about a touring car body?" On another sheet I followed through with that same idea: "Suggestions on completely different rod I plan to build. Frame: Willys rails and rear end. Front end Ford suicide suspension, all chromed. Body: Chevy or other odd touring car body. Channeled. Shorten body two inches. Motor: Studebaker V8, DeSoto V8, Pontiac 6, Nash Rambler, Ford 6, automatic transmission. Color: Frame and all running gear bright orange, motor, trans, rear end bright orange. Wheels bright orange. Body—metallic blue. Upholstery is blue gray outer, orange inner. Accessories: Willys steering, '37 Buick steering wheel, '48 Packard or '41 Hudson taillights. Chrome dash panel (Auburn, Packard). All body seams leaded in. Hood and side panels one piece. Model T chrome radiator shell, big old radiator cap ornament."

Even when I did a traditional car, like a '32 Ford coupe, I did the unusual. I have drawings of a wild '32 Ford 5-window and a hip-high '29 A phaeton; both have full race Model B engines, an engine that had become obsolete.

I drew a slick '29 A roadster with a chopped Carson top, beautiful race car nose, outside headers—and a Willys engine! It looks lovely, but who would spend time and money on a roadster powered by a Jeep engine? Well, I had a '29 A roadster mounted on a 1937 Willys chassis with a Jeep engine that I had bought for $25. I saw the possibility of fulfilling this vision.

Pure fantasy cars

The third category dealt with the realm of pure fantasy, although I may not have realized that at the time. I made numerous drawings of competition machines—drag cars and circle-track racers-with *Drake Garage* written on them. My fantasy involved owning a garage, making a living with it, and building winning machines. I'd be at the top, like Barney Navarro, Lou Baney and Vic Edelbrock, building my own equipment and blowing the doors off the competition. Soon, I thought, the words *Drake Garage* would be on everyone's lips. Sometimes I'd share the glory—I have a drawing of a T-type competition rig with *Drake Spl.* written on the hood and above, in smaller letters, *Weiand Experimental 4 carb manifold*. Another drawing of a Ford flathead has the caption: "Drake Built Competition Engine Breaks Class B Record by 7 M.P.H.!!" That engine, running Offenhauser heads and some kind of finned manifold, is notable for at least two reasons: it's running only two carbs (usually my paper engines had four carbs) and the record was set in a stock height '32 Ford coupe (usually my cars were lower than low). Finally I graduated to engines with my

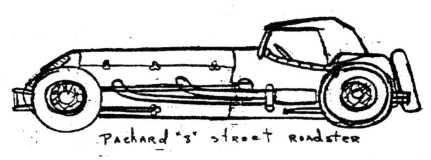

Packard "8" street roadster

own equipment. "Drake Custom Built Engines. Drake 4 carb manifold and overhead valves on a 200 cu. in. Ford block. 3-1/16" bore by 1/8" destroke. Ported and relieved. Dual ignition, headers. Howard mushroom cam and roller tappetts (sic). Magnesium (fly)wheel. 210 h.p. at 5000 (rpm). 14:1 compression. Drake theory: short-stroke, big bore, lots of carbs, good breathing, big cam." Sounds OK. From somewhere I got an interesting idea for the distributor mounting—it ran off the cam but via beveled gears so the distributor was in an upright position.

The grand fantasy was a drawing of Drake's Speed Shop, overhead view; this was obviously inspired by the world of Clint Curtis, boy hot rodder. There's a primitive machine shop, some racing engines, a hot cycle and a super-low sedan for sale outside, a two-car "parking lot," one place occupied by my own '29 A-V8 which, it says, "took 1st prize in 1952 roadster show," a room full of goodies removed from cars, a small wrecking yard, and a scrap pile. Inside are three rods and a cycle with a sidecar; I owned the cycle and two of the cars, of course, and I guess I figured I could make enough money on that one car to keep this establishment going.

The problem of wanting to own numerous hot rods is one that still afflicts me—I currently have three underway but none finished. Probably I should finish the A-V8 and build the other two on paper.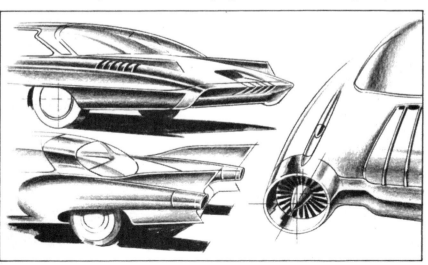

Ad from November, 1956 issue of Motor Trend, *promoting enrollment for the Fisher Body Craftsman's Guild styling and model car building competition.*

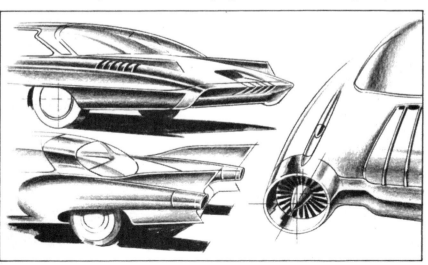

Street Racing

It was time to go street racing...they'd been practicing in the family sedan.

You sat in the drive-in sipping a Coke, trying to see in the restaurant's big window the reflection of your car. The white sidewalls were scrubbed until they shone with a guiltless innocence; the full-disc hubcaps glowed in the gentle light. Around back, out of sight, you knew the twin echo cans had the power of cannon barrels. The radio was off because the battery was sometimes undependable at night, but as you sank back against the new imitation-leatherette seat covers you felt utter contentment.

Because your car was spotless and so cool, everything was right in the world. You found it impossible to think about the next day—let alone next year—a job, family, what you would do with your life. There was only this long moment, the banjo wheel your hands rested on, the speedometer, the polished hood, the bullnose strip that replaced the hood ornament, and glowing like a mirage in the window, the

reflection of *the perfect car*.

Then a car pulled in from the street and crossed the parking lot and you heard that engine: aachuck, aachuck, aachuck. The '40 Ford coupe moved smoothly across the blacktop and the exhaust was muffled. But the noise didn't emerge from the dual pipes; it came from under the hood, as if there was a noise generator where there should have been an engine. And it wasn't bearing noise. The engine staggered, jerked, bucked, loped—even though the car moved smoothly—and the driver stabbed the gas to clear what you supposed were at least three or four carburetors.

All eyes were on the coupe as it passed, the driver looking straight ahead, his elbow cocked over the window edge. Then, slowly, his head turned, and he looked straight at you. He stabbed the gas, once, and left by the other entrance.

Later, when the parking lot had fewer cars, he returned and backed into the space beside you, driver's window to driver's window. He looked your car over carefully and asked with a sneer, "Whatya got?"

Wanna run it?

Conversation was difficult with the noise of that Potvin Eliminator lifting valves higher than anyone thought possible and holding them open forever, but you answered: "A stocker."

He hesitated, looked the car over from front to back, and curled his lip in disbelief. "Wanna run it?" He didn't believe you, but if you were running a stock engine he had you anyway.

"Naw," you answered. Second gear sounded a little rough lately—you can't afford

another VBR (Violation of the Basic Rule); and anyway, what was the point? "I guess not."

He gave you a bad look, put the shift lever into low, and rolled away without a word—seconds later, from the street, there came the sound of tires spinning lightly on pavement, like fine silk being torn.

When the ice from your second Coke had melted you started your engine (listening, trying to determine whether the battery sounded weak), turned on the radio, turned on your lights for the carhop, and counted your change. You cruised toward the street, the radio crooning *We Three* by the Ink Spots, and over the sound of the music you heard the pleasant burble of the duals. In the eastern sky there was a full moon, no sign of rain, which meant that the car would stay clean for another day or two without a wash job. You sighed contentedly; life was perfect.

Empty street

You moved slowly down the street, staying in low gear at a steady 20 mph until the sound of the exhausts built to a crescendo; then fell when you shifted to second. The street as far as you could see was empty of cars; there was just you, the burbling pipes, and the full moon.

Sleeper!

As you waited at the first stop light a dingy '37 Chevy pulled alongside in the right lane: a trail of mud on the door, a bent fender, the driver's window cracked. But it could be a "sleeper"—some rodders had begun to build hot cars that *appeared* stock. Stock chrome on the hood and trunk, stock hubcaps, blackwall tires, duals

without chrome extensions. Under the hood was a big load; you could pull up to a light, barely notice the car beside you, but when the light changed, look out! A doggie Ford might have a full-race Merc engine, an old Chev like the one beside you might have a hot 270 GMC. And there were more than a couple guys in town with Olds 88 engines in nondescript cars. A sleeper could be a lot of fun—for the owner—because it denied that it was hot.

This one turned right before the signal changed, and in its place appeared the same '40 Ford coupe you'd seen earlier. The driver looked at you, and you knew it was a race.

Scanning the road ahead, behind, and for as far as you could see along the cross street, you decided—you hoped—it was free of cops. You turned off the radio to be able to hear the engine; revved it a bit, released the clutch partway, tried to get it to roll forward as the light changed. You glanced at the coupe's driver, who sat half-turned, his back to you, one arm draped limply over the wheel as if he were bored.

Not this time

The light changed to green, you felt rather than heard the rear tires breaking loose, heard the exhaust roar. From the corner of your eye you saw the coupe's front fender beside your own and, for a second, felt optimistic. As you drove the clutch pedal to the floor and shoved the lever

It was exactly the kind of driving that our fathers had refused to engage in, the kind that they had warned us against.

into second you saw the coupe pull ahead by a car length. As he shifted the coupe's rear end dropped a foot, the nose lifted, and then it pulled away, the gap an impossible distance as you let up on the gas and lazily shifted into high. His taillights were barely visible in the distance and then the road was again empty.

It could have been worse. You still have all gears and axles intact. You could have had a fiver bet on the race, or even the car's title. You could have gotten a ticket, been arrested, taken to jail. You turned on the radio and settled back, easing the car to a speed five miles below the limit, content once again. But still there was that gnawing question: could you have kept up with him if you had had, say, a light flywheel?

For most young people in the early 'Fifties a set of dual pipes on a car meant it was time to go street racing, something they had been practicing in the family sedan. It was illegal, of course, but it wasn't as risky as it is today simply because there were far fewer cars on the street. The city where I grew up went to bed around eight o'clock, and the streets after that time were almost empty of traffic. Even during the day there were few cars, and if you were the first car at the light a long, clear stretch of road lay ahead of you. It was difficult to pull up to a light on a four-lane city street and not "dig out" with the car beside you.

Everyone wanted to race. When the city's first freeway was built in 1954 the paved sections of the unfinished road attracted crowds of young people who put on midnight drags complete with flagmen.

There was something terrifically exciting about two cars at a stoplight, rapping their pipes, the sound growing like an invisible power, and then clutches were popped, tires screamed, engines revved and wound tight; then the shift—it was exactly the kind of driving that our fathers had refused to engage in, the kind

There was something terrifically exciting about two cars at a stop light, rapping their pipes...

"Part of the well-stocked display offered to speed enthusiatsts by Newhouse Automotive Industries, Los Angeles, one of the leading equipment distributors" from Hot Rod Handbook *129, 1951.*

that they had warned us against.

Speed shift

If you wanted to race you had to perfect the "speed shift." Because almost all cars had manual transmissions, you had to get from one gear to another in a hurry; a race could be lost in the split-second it took to shift gears. Going from second to high gear required only a straight movement, but going from low to second was difficult, and it was a crucial shift; many a drag (or transmission) was lost on that one.

Some cars were inherently easier to shift quickly. All Fords, whether the lever was on the floor or on the column, shifted nicely. Most MoPars, and some cars like Studebakers, had floor-shift transmissions with a lot of play; the shift rod could be moved around freely, making it difficult to know what gear you were in. In fact, as Bill Fisher once told me, he owned a couple of 1937 Chevrolets with a "whippy" floor-shift lever that would move forward so far it'd hit the key in the dash, turning off the ignition!

Chevrolets of the 'Forties used a vacuum-assisted column shift that was really a slow nuisance. Automatic transmissions like Fluid Drive or even three-speed HydraMatics suffered from slippage. Even a car like the 1951 Chrysler V-8, with 180 hp, had a transmission that seemed to take a full minute to change gears.

There were different approaches to speed shifting. There were two basic philosophies concerning a floor shift: some drivers wanted the shift rod cut off a few inches from the floor, with the belief that it saved excess motion; others added two feet of pipe to the shift rod, with the belief that a long rod gave one additional leverage.

The approaches to speed shifting with a column shift also varied. One driver might hug the steering wheel and gently but swiftly move the lever with two fingers, a delicate movement, while another driver might sit far back, arm stiff, and, using pure muscle, ram the shift lever forward and up in a single motion, almost breaking the windshield.

A neat trick adopted by some was to reverse the shifting pattern on column-shift Fords. This was done by knocking out the pins that held the shifting tube to the steering column and flipping it over. This meant that you shifted with your left hand. To shift from low to second you pulled the lever toward you, and some claimed that this motion was easier and faster than pushing it away. Perhaps, but it's certain that this arrangement was more convenient for non-racers when out on a date, as it allowed the driver more room and let him steer and shift with his left hand while his right hand was busy elsewhere.

Girl-type shifter

One guy in my town was legendary. He had a 1939 Chrysler Royal coupe with a full-race Chrysler straight-eight engine. Not the most promising machine, perhaps, but it was fast. He'd leave the Jim Dandy drive-in and drag up and down Sandy Boulevard, taking on anybody, whether they had a roadster or a chair car. He kept both hands on the wheel, worked the brake, clutch and gas, while his girlfriend did the speed shifting! She sat in the middle of the front seat, gripped the lever, and when he yelled "now" she'd throw her weight against the lever!

Missed shift = broken trans

Occasionally you'd "miss a shift," meaning that you either shifted too slowly or the lever didn't go into gear. The next step was disaster: to "lose" or "knock out a trans." The transmission and rear axles were the weak points on early Fords, and the teeth seemed to fall like dandruff. It was common to get a ride with someone whose car had that distinctive clunk-clunk-clunk of a missing tooth; he'd start off in second gear if low was out, or shift directly from low to high if second was out. Another test that took a terrible toll was trying to shift into low gear at 30 mph; you had to rev the engine and feel with the gear shift until the unwilling gears seemed willing to mesh.

It was usually cheaper to buy an entire transmission than it was to rebuild a box. I remember knocking out three (3!) transmissions in just over a week, and paying only $3 for one. I threw the busted gearboxes away; everyone did, and if all the transmixers had been put in a pile it would have reached to the sky. But that was part of the price one had to pay for the sport of street racing.

Your car was spotless and *so* cool, everything was right in the world.

The Day They Broke 100 at Scappoose

**There was a barrier—
perhaps psychological—
perhaps dependent upon
the laws of physics.**

In the early 'Fifties, when drag racing was in its infancy, the chance of a car breaking the magic speed of 100 mph in the quarter mile seemed as impossible as a man running the mile on foot in under four minutes. There was a barrier—perhaps psychological, perhaps dependent upon the laws of physics—that would not allow a person to reach 100 mph in such a short space. It was reminiscent of the belief held by some doctors at the turn of the century that if a person traveled over 8 mph in a motor car his blood would boil!

Well, no one was that superstitious or naive, but as the 1952 drag season rolled around some of us had our doubts that it was possible to motate to a hundred in the quarter. I had been at the last two drag meets of 1951 at Eugene, and I had seen the fastest roadsters turning only 88-90 mph. At the final meet of

Harold Davis built this lightweight '25 T bucket and scooted through the clocks at 101 mph. Stepped frame, suicide front end, channeled body gets it down. Big Merc engine ran early four-carb intake manifold. Pair of aluminum aircraft bucket seats were army surplus.

that year the two fastest machines—Willy Wagner's '29 and Larry Eave's '32, both with hot flatheads—had had to run off *three* times because they consistently tied. Three times they came to the line, engines revving, and were flagged; I recall vividly the noise, smoke, the cars fishtailing like mad, the engines winding through the gears, and—as I recall—three times they crossed the finish line wheel-to-wheel. They were going like hell but the speed was slightly under 90 mph—and it's a long way between 88 and 100!

High-buck machines

These weren't junkyard dogs with dual carbs—they were machines capable of high top-end speeds. Eave's car was timed at 125 mph at Bonneville, and Wes Strohecker's '27 T with the race car nose turned 128.82 mph at the same meet in street form. Ron DeLong ran his full-fendered street roadster at Bonneville in 1952 and turned 119.24 mph. In spite of experimenting with cams, multiple carburetion, gearing and tires, none of these cars could do better than 90 mph in the quarter.

To make things worse, and reinforce the belief that a car couldn't break 100 mph, heavy sedans were turning in the high 70s and low 80s. A 1948 Cadillac fastback with a hot Cad engine—a *chair car,* for crying out loud!—turned over 75 mph in the quarter. Some of the hot drag machines in the lower classes were turning speeds close to the hotter, lighter machines in the higher classes. It looked like pretty soon everyone would be turning 90 mph!

Drag racing was pretty simple in the early 'Fifties, and classes were determined by a combination of weight and engine displacement; you divided the car's weight by cubic inches and that figure put you in a class. A light car with a big engine was in A class, a heavier car with the same size engine might be in B class, and so on. A person could bore to the water jacket, then play around by adding or reducing weight to get to the upper limit of a class, but all in all this method of classifying cars made things fairly equal. The clocks used to time the cars gave a speed but didn't record the elapsed time. In fact, at the first drag races I attended at Eugene the winner was determined by a flagman at the finish; I had that job a few times at the far end of the quarter at Scappoose, and it was pretty hairy to stand on the strip and flag a pair of screaming machines as they blasted past only feet away.

119.36 mph in California!

The 1952 drag season in Oregon opened with good weather and plenty of hope. In California the 100-mph barrier had been broken. By the spring of 1952 a new record was set at Paradise Mesa by Otto Ryssman: 119.36 mph. This was broken within a month by Art Chrisman in the Miller Crankshaft Special, which turned 121.95 mph at the same strip, and then by the Howard Cams Special which turned 122.95 mph. If the California boys could do it, why couldn't we?

But at that first Scappoose meet the fastest time of the day was set by Larry Eave in his hot, super-low '32 roadster. This machine had everything: Kinmont disc brakes, a Norden center-steering assembly, the best Stewart-Warner dash, etc. It had a trick engine too: small bore and stroke, with a Norden 180-degree crank and cam, a Harman and Collins magneto, Edelbrock heads, and numerous intake manifolds—a two-carb, a three-carb, a four-carb, and a dual manifold that mounted two '49-'50 Mercury Holley carburetors. Top speed that day—93.16 mph! Later in the season he turned 96.77 mph, but he never did break the century mark.

The second race of the 1952 season was held on June 8, and expectations were rising that the magic mark could be surpassed. Or perhaps someone would finally hit 95 mph. Mile by mile the speeds would increase, until someone would slip past the Big One.

Stripped bucket with an engine

At this race there was a new car, a '25 T roadster built by a kid named Davis of the Gremlins Club of Portland. Simply a stripped-down bucket with an engine, it looked terribly fast. I don't know why someone hadn't built a car like this earlier, or, for that matter, why someone hadn't dumped a big OHV engine in a light frame and covered it with the skimpiest of sheet metal. Down in Los Angeles, where most of the automotive trends seem to begin, a young fellow named Dick Kraft had built some

Drag racing was pretty simple in the early 'Fifties, and classes were determined by a combination of weight and engine displacement; you divided the car's weight by cubic inches and that figure put you in a class.

beautiful rods. In this case he took the body off an early car, built a cowl, strapped on a three-gallon gas can, named the machine "The Bug," and went like hell.

Davis' roadster was simply a stripped '25 T body on a set of Model A rails; it had a pair of airplane bucket seats, but no street equipment. The engine was a 296-CID Mercury flathead with Weiand heads and four-carb manifold, Wico dual magnetos, and big outside headers. It was low, with the frame stepped several inches in the rear and a suicide front end. It had a Halibrand quick-change, and a pressure fuel system. On the other hand, it had absolutely no chrome or adornment—it didn't even have paint, unless you consider racing gray primer rubbed with engine oil a paint job! This car was built with one purpose in mind, and that was to get to the end of the quarter mile as quickly as possible. In that respect, it was one of the first dragsters built.

Along about mid-morning, after fooling with gearing, Davis fired up that mother. His crew had to push-start the car in the pits; when it fired everyone turned at the sound and when Davis rolled to the starting line we could see flames coming from the ends of the headers. Then the odor of something—alky or nitro, we couldn't tell—it was the odor of the exhaust of a hundred model-airplane engines.

101 mph at Scapoose

Davis pulled down his goggles—he had no crash helmet, no roll bar, no fire-control system—and nodded at the starter. The flag went up, and we all held our breath. Then the voice over the PA system an-nounced that a plane intended to land. Damn! But this was an airfield we were using as a drag strip, and planes had priority. Davis waited impatiently, revving the engine to keep the four carbs from flooding the cylinders with torrents of whatever in the world he was burning, trying to keep the plugs from fouling. Then the word came that the plane appeared to have changed its plans and had gone off toward Vernonia to cruise timber.

Again the flag went up, and when it fell Davis tromped the throttle. He was running regular passenger-car tires—they were fairly tall, probably 7.00 X 16, but also fairly narrow and without any special adhesive qualities—and the rear skins spun in a cloud of smoke. The engine rose, fell, the car fishtailed, got right, and then Davis was gone.

In the pits there was silence. In the distance we could hear the diminishing sound of Davis' engine as he backed off and braked. We waited, no one speaking for fear that he would miss the reported time. Then the voice over the PA system: 101 mph! A cheer went up. It had been done: in a feat comparable to Chuck Yeager's breaking the sound barrier or Roger Bannister's four-minute mile, someone in our neck of the woods had gone over 100 mph in the quarter. We all went home happy that day.

Of course, now that someone had broken the barrier, it was not a barrier for others. Something had been lifted that allowed others to pass through. Before the 1952 season was over three cars had broken 100, and Monte Rowland ran his *full-fendered* '33 Ford coupe through at the century mark. The following year he removed the fenders, channeled the car, put on a streamlined nose, and, with the same Mercury engine, got up to 110 mph. Before the season was over there were half a dozen bona fide dragsters running at Scappoose.

But to be the *first!* That was really something. Davis was a hero—the center of attention. When I think about the event now I think of the opening lines of Housman's poem, "To an Athlete Dying Young": "The time you won your town the race/ We chaired you through the market place." Two days after he had broken the barrier, on Tuesday evening, he was at Bill's Steak House in Parkrose, a favorite hangout for Portland rodders. He was driving a '32 Ford roadster that he had been trying to sell, and as he was drinking coffee and accepting the congratulations of all, someone said he wanted to buy the '32. Davis fired it up and drove east on Sandy, into the open countryside; at 160th and Sandy the road curves, but Davis missed the curve, traveling much too fast, thinking perhaps even as the roadster went off the road and tumbled end over end across the field, killing him, that he was flying through the traps at Scappoose. Perhaps Housman had his finger on the truth when he wrote: "Smart lad, to slip betimes away/ From fields where glory does not stay...Eyes the shady night has shut/ Cannot see the record cut..."

Addendum:

I love the way I remembered that story, but now I have to admit it's not quite accurate. In 1991, several years after I wrote it, a guy sidled up to me at the first CTA reunion and whispered: "I'm not dead!" He was Harold

Davis, the guy who built the T bucket and who cracked the 100-mph mark. But it was another rodder, Jack Miller, who left Bill's Steak House in his '32 roadster and had the unfortunate accident that took his life.

Honk! magazine May 1953.

The "Minnesota Missle" from Cars and Clubs, *May 1958.*

Top dragster from Idaho and Utah Regional Drag Meets, Hot Rod Magazine, *December 1954.*

1953 — The Year of the Dragster

We accept the idea of a dragster because they've been around 40 years.

Legalized drag racing began simply, with cars pairing off and going through the gears, much as they had done during illegal street drags. But within two years drag racing became more sophisticated as racers realized ways to get to the end of the quarter mile more quickly. First there was the street machine, then the lightweight, gutted coupe or roadster, then the dragster. The dragster, built for the sole purpose of covering the quarter mile as quickly as possible, is a unique type of machine, purely American in concept. It owes nothing to the tradition of auto racing, whether grand prix, sports car, circle track, Indy, NASCAR, or even land speed record cars.

We accept the idea of a dragster because they've been around 40 years. But when I thought about the origins of the dragster I realized what a big jump it represented in the history of the sport. I began to wonder how it happened, and why it hadn't happened earlier. Why

Dick Wall built this simple, attractive dragster using a full-race four-cylinder Model B engine. Over next several years car had variety of four bangers—flathead, Cragar, even a HAL DO engine.

hadn't someone stripped the body from a new 1950 Olds 88 and simply raced the chassis? Perhaps someone somewhere did, but they didn't do it in my neck of the woods, and I've never seen a magazine photograph of such an attempt. In fact, the dragster came about through evolution, as shown by Dick Kraft's, "The Bug." The pattern in most cases was that the person was racing a coupe or roadster with a hot engine, and when he had wrung the maximum speed out of that combination he built a lightweight chassis, installed the hot engine, and made the jump to an all-out quarter-mile racer.

In Oregon, 1953 was the year of the dragster. The previous year a gutted '25 T with a big flathead V-8 had broken the magical 100-mph barrier. At least two other lightweight T buckets were nudging the century mark. One, owned by Bob Eayrs, was powered by a 292 GMC engine with five carbs. Essentially a street roadster with chrome front end, headlights and rear fenders, it went like the devil. Before the 1952 season was over Eayrs had built a single-person chassis, covered it with a crude, semi-streamlined body, and installed the hot GMC engine from the roadster. He competed at the final drag of the season, and his primitive dragster encouraged others to build their own versions over the long, wet winter.

First double-tube frame

In the fall of 1952 a Portland speed-shop owner and Indy 500 mechanic, Blackie Blackburn, his son, Jim, and an employee, Eddie Krebs, began work on a dragster. Jim remembers that it was Kreb's idea. "Eddie was a California boy, and he had picked up the style (of the dragster) in California some time before he came up here. He developed a tubular frame, with double-tube construction—the first guy to do this so far as I know—and mounted the engine to the rear end with a stub driveshaft."

Krebs built the chassis and the Blackburns built the hot flathead V-8 powerplant. Jim said, "The engine was a full stroker that ended up about 304

Bob Eayrs' dragster evolved from his street roadster. He built a '27 T modified for street and strip. It used a six-cylinder 292 GMC engine with a five-carb manifold, magneto, etc. By 1952 it went over 100 mph in the quarter.

In 1953 Eayrs removed '27 T body, used same front and rear suspension, but stretched the frame by welding in sections from another frame. He used engine from the earlier car, welded a roll bar, ran it without a body and turned 118 mph in the quarter. For 1954 season he teamed up with Chuck Blanchard, who owned a big Jimmy six, and they built a new dragster.

cubic inches. Dad (Blackie) had the idea of going for the full stroke for leverage. Of course, piston speed changes like crazy, but we had a special set of pistons made up by Jahns, had Winfield grind us a cam, had a Hilborn injection system and a Harman and Collins magneto. That engine would run 8,000 rpm with no strain or pain.

"We took a 1/4-inch Merc shaft, welded it all up and reground the centers. Dad was heavily into crankshaft balancing and so, with additional counterweighting, we were able to get the engine to run extremely smooth. It ended up being a very neat engine that produced lots of torque—that was what gave us all the trouble off the line."

There were problems—not with the engine—but with clutches, flywheels and gearboxes. The best clutch available was the Velvetouch and Jim remembers, "We'd just cook 'em!" Those problems occurred in spite of the lack of traction. They finally agreed that the best way to run the dragster through the quarter was to simply start out in high gear.

125 mph in the quarter

In spite of the problems, the machine hauled—it was the first car in the Northwest to top 125 mph in the quarter. Primary drivers were Blackie Blackburn and Monte Shelton, now a sports car driver, but Jim drove it occasionally. He remembers "It had enough power to scare you. I made a mess of it one time at the (unauthorized) drags at the shipyards. I got it into a situation and put the thing around a pole! It tore the rear end right out from underneath the car. It was a close call!"

This was the first Northwest dragster to get national attention when it was featured in *Hot Rod Magazine* (July 1955). That super flathead engine went on to greater feats when the dragster was garaged after the second season; it was sold to Johnnie Hart who put it in a '25 T street machine, won everything in the Northwest and cleaned up at the NHRA Nationals.

In the fall of 1952 Ray Van Dorn also began to build a dragster. He had been influenced by Eayrs' dragster and by machines he'd seen in California. "Mostly I was influenced by the Bean Bandit, down in California. I was down there with my ('50 Ford) coupe, that was where I had the engine built, and when the Bean Bandit came out I was really impressed with that." In a transitional stage Van Dorn put his big flathead in Bud Parham's neat '23 T-V8 pickup and working together they campaigned that machine during the 1952 drag season.

Van Dorn's dragster was much more sophisticated than the Bean Bandit. He got Don "Duck" Collins, the noted race car builder, to construct the chassis and it employed a good deal of race car technology—the tube frame, tubular radius rods, center steering, quick-change rear end, etc. "It was patterned after a sprint car actually," Ray said. "But it was early stuff. They hadn't even (designed them) with the driver over the

In 1955 the Drag Safari came to Oregon; this was first NHRA-sanctioned drag race here. Ray Van Dorn's dragster is running Don Ellis' blown Studebaker V-8 in Open Gas class; on far side is Clarence Fish in his '25 T roadster. Van Dorn won, small Studebaker turned 137 mph on gas.

rear end then—I mean *down* over the rear end. We were well *above* the rear end."

In its first race the car ran without a body, but new rules required some kind of covering so Ray built a body from an old airplane belly tank that he bought for $2.50. This gave the car an appearance that resembled a longer, more streamlined version of the Bean Bandit.

What was it like?

What was it like to drive one of the first dragsters? "That was the first one I ever drove," Ray recalled. "I just jumped out of the roadster into the dragster. It was fun. Handled really well. Duck Collins set it up to handle right— it didn't wander, it went really straight. Even at Madras it handled really well—up there (running the half mile) we went 153 mph."

Another Portland dragster, this one built by the father-son team of Earl and Monte Rowland, was remarkable because it was probably the first rear-engine dragster in the country. Again, this dragster evolved from the owners' previous machines. In 1950 they raced a 1950 Mercury coupe with a hot flathead. The following year they built a '33 Ford coupe which became the first *full-fendered* car in the Northwest to break 100 mph in the quarter. In 1952 they removed the fenders, channeled the body, and built a race car nose; their best time with the car in this form was 110 mph.

In the fall of 1953 they began work on a dragster. They originally intended to use a 500-cubic-inch Hispano-Suiza engine. But when they were told that the car would have to have an American-made engine they used the Merc flathead from the '33 coupe—which they mounted in the rear. This was a full two years before Don Garlits built his rear-engine rail. Monte Rowland recalled how they got the idea of building a dragster. "It was one of my father's ideas. We wanted to get in a class where we wouldn't have to be worried about who's cheating whom. We wanted to go a little faster too, so we thought we'd go to a dragster. There were only one or two

around then..."

Earl had lived in California, built midget race cars during the 'Thirties and 'Forties and had had a lot of hot rod experience. They made a radical departure from orthodox construction by putting the engine in the rear. "My dad got the idea of getting the weight over the rear wheels, get the motor back there and get a long wheelbase—I think that ours was 112 inches—now they are up to 250 inches!" They built the dragster in the basement of their house during the winter. "We had everything drawn on the basement floor so we could keep it in line, made our own jigs. We didn't put the roll cage in, then we just carried the frame up the stairs and pushed it through the big window of this old house."

Fast & clean

This super-sanitary machine handled very well; the 284-cubic-inch Merc flathead eventually pushed the car to a top speed of 129 mph on nitro. Monte recalled what it was like to drive: "It felt like somebody put a floor

In 1953 Ray Van Dorn had race car builder Don "Duck" Collins build a dragster chassis, into which Van Dorn put his big Merc flathead. Here he's working on carburetors, Reed Fleener wearing an early crash helmet

At first Van Dorn raced dragster without a body, but by 1954 he'd built a body, using part of a surplus belly tank for the nose. Car was orange, with black interior and trim, and was first drag machine in Portland area to have a sponsor. Still has Merc flathead, and Van Dorn said the car ran around 128 mph. Pits at Scappoose strip in background.

jack under the front end—there was nothing there. Also you didn't have any sensation of where the rear end was. Scappoose (drag strip) was kind of sandy and your rear end would slide over. We didn't have the wide tires they have today—I think the widest tire you could get was a Banzer cap which was eight inches. We got the Banzer out of 'Frisco. They weren't the best (tire), sometimes they (the cap) would fly off, but they were the best at the time. We had real traction problems. We didn't have the compounds that they have now, nor the wrinkle-wall tires running about five pounds they have now."

Soon other dragsters began to show up. Ron Gorans came down from Longview, Washington, with a tall, unsubtle dragster running a six-cylinder Chevrolet engine. Clarence Everett, who

campaigned at Bonneville, came up from Salem with a frame using a flathead and Ford running gear. When they refused to let him run until he put a body on the chassis he got a metal sign board, cut it up, built flat sides for a body, and they let him run. Don Fancher built a simple but streamlined body for his dragster by putting together four pieces of flat aluminum so they came to a point.

Hot Jimmy

And the hot cars got hotter. Bob Eayrs teamed up with Chuck Blanchard; they built a new chassis to house the 292 GMC, the first of several engines in that machine. In 1954 Ray Van Dorn yanked the flathead, then teamed up with Don Ellis, who had a supercharged Studebaker V-8. Later Earl Rowland teamed up with Bill Bonebrake, and used

an injected Studebaker V-8 in the Rowland machine. The next year Earl and Monte Rowland built a 392 Chrysler Hemi for their dragster, and with this combination they were competitive into the early 'Sixties. But by that time the dragster had become an active part of the history of hot rodding, attaining speeds that those first dragster builders could not have imagined, not even in their most wildly accelerating fantasies.

When Del McClure wrecked his circle-track car, someone got the idea of using the big DeSoto V-8 engine, front end, Halibrand rear end and knock-off wire wheels, center steering, etc., to build a dragster. McClure, Gale and Wayne Morris, other members of Pacers club worked a solid week to get car ready for drag strip.

I tend to remember the sunny days of hot rodding, when the red-leather seat was warmed and the chromed engine reflected the sun—when driving a rod without front fenders was not a problem. In Oregon it rains a lot. I have strong memories of driving a fenderless roadster in the rain—the naked tire throwing water on my shoulder and arms, the vacuum windshield wiper moving slowly across the glass, the dampness that would turn to mildew before it would go away.

Rain

I could imagine the layers of mud the open front wheels would throw across the sides of that splendid body.

Wet memories

Before that there were years of walking or riding my bicycle in the rain—not necessarily unpleasant memories—simply wet ones where your shoes, pants cuffs and hair are just plain wet. I had stripped off my bicycle's front and rear fenders, and the tires would send a line of muddy water up my front and backsides until I was drenched. After a half-hour of riding in the rain nothing seemed to matter because one can get only so wet.

Eddie Duhon's 1939 Ford four-door convertible featured custom body work, fender skirts, dual spotlights and full-race flathead V-8.

'48 Ford convertible.

Even after I got a car I sometimes had to ride my bike. I'd get up on a Saturday morning, eat oatmeal and jump on my bike for a quick survey of the neighborhood, even after I felt I was too old to be riding a bike. Then I would ride beyond the neighborhoods, my eyes open for any old car in a field or at the rear of a yard that ought to be investigated. I'd ride around for hours, soaking wet—my faded Levis and army-surplus Eisenhower jacket dark with rain. Once I rode my bike to Johnson Ford Specialty—a wrecking yard about four miles from my house, and bought a perfect 1932 Ford grille and shell for $7.50. I carried it back on my bike, but I didn't go straight home. I was so charged up with this purchase that I rode to the Fred Meyer auto parts store and perused the stuff there, carrying my grille, slopping water on the floor.

Why did I remove the front fenders?

The subtext of my desire to own a car was a desire to be dry. Why then, did I buy a roadster, and why did I remove the front fenders? The first question is easy to answer: in those days a hot rod was a *roadster*. Any other body style was something that your father might drive. I know why I removed the fenders, even after I was told not to. I was following the examples I had seen in *Hot Rod Magazine*, which featured cars that, almost without exception, were fenderless. I don't suppose I even thought that those rods were running around the streets of So-Cal, where rain is infrequent. Even if I had thought about the nature of weather, I think I still would have removed the car's front fenders, because, although I knew little about cars, I loved that look! My father and I got the car running in June, and we enjoyed the good weather of summer and early fall.

Speed lines of mud

When the rains began my enthusiasm was only slightly diminished, not by the rain that came in through the open places but by the mud thrown across the sides of the body. It was impossible to keep the body clean, let alone the chassis and the chromed pieces on the front end. Whatever visions I had of my roadster as a magazine feature or a show car rapidly disappeared when I looked at the speed lines of mud on the doors and quarters, and the mud buildup on the front of the rear fenders. The residue of muddy water stained the chrome generator, oil filter and air cleaners, stained the red paint on the block and heads. The oil pan—well, it was almost as dirty as the one on my father's Lincoln.

My whole life might have been different

In spite of the rain and the mess, I rarely longed for a full-fendered car, and never for a closed car—not at that point in my life. Years later I thought that the best car for me in high school would have been some kind of sedan, say a 1936 Plymouth with skirts, duals and nifty seat covers. If I had had such a car I would've blossomed in other ways: I would've had friends; I could've double-dated; gone to the school dances and football games; driven a bunch of school chums to the beach or mountains, where we would ski, swim, dance, have group sing-a-long sessions, roast wieners and marshmallows late at night around a bonfire—my whole life might have been different. I could have participated in such things in a roadster, at least in a marginal way, with one girl rather than a group—a girl who didn't mind sitting on a wet leather seat or having water thrown in her face from that fenderless front tire. The problem was that an attitude came with the car. I now realize I was far too serious about being a roadster jockey. Being a hot rodder, I thought, *was serious business.* You couldn't motate down the road in a red-and-chrome (and muddy) roadster the same way you could in, say, a '36 Plymouth sedan.

Phaetons impressed

An obvious compromise would have been an open car with fenders that could accommodate several people. For example, a 1935-36 Ford phaeton, a body style I have always loved and occasionally lusted after. The first car from Oregon featured in *Hot Rod Magazine* was Wayne Mahaffey's 1935 Ford phaeton, which I had seen at the Eugene drag races during the summer of 1951. Also outstanding was Mid Barbour's 1936 Ford phaeton that I had seen at "Speed Cycles," Portland's first hot rod show, held in March 1951. Both cars were lowered, black, with long, low, padded white tops, beautiful custom interiors and customized bodies. Early on I was impressed by this kind of machinery. This was the type of car I drew on the cover of my Pee-Chee notebook in high school. These were low, sleek, idealized custom forms of rolling sculpture.

Although those phaetons were only 15 years old at the time, they were rare. I saw or heard of a few other 1935-36 Ford phaetons, but I can actually remember only two—plus a 1936 Ford four-door convertible that a friend built, and which I owned most of during the mid-'Fifties. But there must have been a hundred hot roadsters for every fixed-up phaeton, maybe more.

I thought that the best car for me in high school would have been some kind of sedan, say a 1936 Plymouth with skirts, duals and nifty seat covers.

Wayne Mahaffey's 1935 Ford Phaeton. Shot in 1952 at the Scappoose Drags.

Also, it cost considerably more to build a phaeton than a roadster because they were bigger—there was that large top, the bigger interior and more body to prepare and paint. But, done right they looked so good—if you happened to see one. Fortunately, there was one at my high school, at least for a short time. Owned by Joe Tarkington, a guy my age, it had been built a few years earlier in the late 'Forties, perhaps by Joe's older brother. He turned it over to Joe when he got drafted. It was a daily driver but it looked awfully good. It was maroon, with all the good stuff: it was lowered, had whitewalls, full hub caps, skirts, solid side panels, dual pipes and 1937 DeSoto bumpers. The top was chopped but not padded; it probably folded down. In those days people seemed to know exactly how to build a graceful top—even an unpadded top would have a lovely curve, especially at the rear where the last top bow always seemed too high in stock form.

The phaeton was usually parked on Woodward, a side street beside the school. I remember standing in the rain, looking through the isinglass side curtains, seeing the flat brown-leather interior, which may have been original, the column shift, the chromed '36 dashboard. Even now I can see it clearly in my mind—that sweeping piece that curved around the back of the front seat and served to stiffen the body. As the rain ran down my hair and my cheeks, dampening the clothes I would have to wear in classes for the next few hours, I studied that phaeton and knew if I owned it I would have friends, go on social activities and that I would be dry!

Horrified at what the owner planned

I saw Joe's phaeton only a few more times and then it disappeared. Although Joe and I shared a Social Studies class I don't remember discussing the car with him. I didn't see it again until two years later, shortly after we had graduated, when it was parked in the spectator area at the Scappoose drags. The hood, grille, front fenders and running boards had been removed, and the car's natural elegance was gone. I spoke with the new owner and the notes I made at that time indicated he planned to channel the car, put cycle fenders on the front and build a "Novi grille" (his words). While I was in favor of modifying almost any car in those days, I was horrified at what the owner planned for the phaeton. It had had an elegance, a custom with echoes of the true classic car. I could not imagine a 1936 Ford phaeton with a race car style grille, regardless of how nicely it was shaped, but I could well imagine the layers of mud the open front wheels would throw across the sides of that splendid body.

Bill Page's '40 Ford convertible featured in May 1953 issue of Honk! *magazine.*

What We Read: Magazines

I can remember the sense of wonder, excitement and pleasure I felt when I first saw a copy of *Hot Rod*.

In the years following the end of World War II, a great deal of interest grew in car activities of all kinds: new cars, sports cars, race cars and hot rods. Before 1948 there was not a single mass-circulation magazine aimed at the hot rodder, and only one aimed at the race car enthusiast. Within three years, almost a dozen new magazines catered to the interests of these groups.

These magazines were important to the growth of the sport not only because of their editorial and car features, but also because of their "how-to" information which was absorbed by would-be builders who wanted to build the cars they had been dreaming about.

I can remember the sense of wonder, excitement and pleasure I felt when I first saw a copy of *Hot Rod Magazine*. I was 14 and just getting interested in cars. There was something about the open-wheeled machines tooling down wide palm-tree-lined Los Angeles streets that I found fascinating—a fascination that hasn't waned during the 45 years I've been involved with hot rods. What follows is a brief description of the car magazines, some notable, some obscure, that we read at mid-century.

Hot Rod Magazine

The first issue was published in January 1948 and it has come out monthly ever since. The founders, publishers and associate editors were Robert Lindsay and Robert Petersen. Petersen soon bought out Lindsay and used *Hot Rod Magazine* as the basis for building his publishing empire (finally sold in 1997).

Before the advent of *Hot Rod*, only three publications were aimed at the hot rodders: *SCTA Racing News, Throttle,* and Veda Orr's newsletter. All were short-lived and had extremely limited circulation. The first issues of *Hot Rod* were done in press runs of 5,000 and the two Bobs sold copies at the drags and at El Mirage Dry Lake. The magazine quickly caught on and has inspired and informed hot rodders ever since.

In the beginning, *Hot Rod Magazine* was 36 pages in length and sold for only a quarter. It had excellent photos, detailed cutaway drawings and well-written stories. It established high standards for builders by featuring fine hot rods; this was at a time when a lot of junk was on the streets, and builders were searching for models of excellence.

In fact, the term "hot rod" was considered derogatory—a label applied to almost anything by journalists. Petersen and Lindsay knew they would have to showcase the finest examples

HOT ROD OF THE MONTH

Sitting in the driver's seat is Eddie Hulse, who, a few moments after this picture was taken, drove number 668, to set a new SCTA record for Class C roadsters. Hulse, a native Californian, nosed out Randy Shinn, a long-time top honor holder for the RC Class. Shinn's old record was 129.40 in a channeled Mercury T.

Keeping the Car Out Front by George Riley—Page 10

Hot Rod Magazine, first issue dated January 1948. So few people saw one of the 5,000 copies printed many thought the magazine began in July 1948, which was when the early issue order list began. The first issues have recently been reprinted at an affordable price.

of hot rods if they hoped to overcome the stigma with that title.

Motor Trend

Begun in September 1949, this was the second magazine published by the Lindsay-Petersen team. The first editor was Walt Woron, and the staff included some members who went on to make a name for themselves, including Albert Issacs and Thomas J. Medley.

From 1949-55 it featured many custom cars including exciting radical customs out of So-Cal, being careful not to conflict with *Hot Rod Magazine* which stuck strictly to rods. There was also an emphasis on new cars and sports cars—in fact, their discussion on the comparative vices and virtues of American vs. foreign machines lasted for years!

Speed Age

An eastern magazine, *Speed Age* caught the interest of the race enthusiasts. It featured the entire spectrum of racing activities: midgets, hardtops, sprint cars, Indy, NASCAR and occasional coverage of sports car and motorcycle events. It contained hard-core racing articles, with great concern for accuracy and technical information. Articles about the board tracks, grand prix racing, etc., were also highlighted.

The magazine changed its format in 1951, and in addition to a larger page count, it dropped the old black-and-white cover photo for a somewhat garish color cover. It continued at least until the late 'Fifties, at which time it had new editors and a new "Hot Rod Department." The name was revived in late 1969 when *Drag Strip* became *Speed Age*.

Road & Track

This magazine first appeared in June 1947. It has always been edited from Southern California and always focused on sports cars. The founder was Oliver Billingsley, and the technical editor was John R. Bond, who became the editor in 1955 and eventually its publisher. Bond shaped its content for over 30 years. The photographs treat the cars as art objects, showing a configuration that wouldn't even occur to many people and the race coverage and technical features were great. Besides, many sports cars are really hot rods with a spare tire!

Motorsport

First published in January 1949, *Motorsport* was an east-coast publication. Occasionally there were well-written articles on sports cars or race coverage. But it was generally lacking in any editorial viewpoint, zap or

Rod & Custom **is probably the magazine most street rodders think of when they recall publications of the 'Fifties.**

Another terrific pocket-size magazine was Rods and Customs; *this first issue came out May 1953. Subsequent issues were titled* Rod & Custom.

Motorsport *was an east-coast magazine with coverage of rods, customs, sports cars, boat racing, etc. The customized 1940 Mercury convertible on the cover of the June 1951 issue is unusual.*

On the cover of June 1950 Road and Track was Chet Miller in the Novi Indy car. This mag has been coming out for 50 years!

The first issue of Hot Rod's companion magazine, Motor Trend, appeared September 1949. Cover car is Muntz Road Jet, a stretched version of Kurtis sports car.

pizzazz. That awful pulp paper didn't help either. The one thing I did enjoy was a monthly two-page feature entitled "Bodies Beautiful and Bizarre." The magazine wanted to be another *Road & Track*, but the difference between the two was as great as the distance across this country.

Speed Mechanics

This regular-size magazine sold for a quarter. It first appeared in January 1953, and continued until at least October of 1961. It was published and edited by the east-coast editors of *Motorsport*; if that magazine wanted to be another *R&T*, then *Speed Mechanics* wanted to be another *Hot Rod*. No way!

During the 'Fifties, there were two definite kinds of rods and customs: the East Coast and the West Coast. The East Coast machines were generally kind of goofy, I thought, with extra chrome or exhaust pipes protruding through various places. If someone built a fairly nice car he'd manage to goof it up (i.e., a channeled '39 Merc convertible with a '50 Nash grille!).

There were also two definite kinds of magazines, and they followed that same division. *Speed Mechanics* was an east-coast magazine. Its pulp paper seemed to yellow as soon as it hit the stands. It often had paintings rather than photographs on the cover, with figures who stood stiffly in baggy pants. The magazine continued for several years, so I guess there was an audience for it. Part of its

success was no doubt due to the two west coast editors, Griffith Borgeson and Eugene Jaderquist, who also wrote for other auto magazines at the same time.

Auto Sport Review

Another east-coast magazine using pulp paper. The first issue came out in January 1952, and issues followed monthly for a

These magazines were important to the growth of the sport because of their "how-to" information which was absorbed by would-be builders who wanted to build the cars they had been dreaming about.

year or so. Editorially it was kind of a mixed bag: sports cars, Indy cars, cycles, etc. It also had a series called "How To Make A Hot Rod" by Ed Almquist.

Honk!

This pocket-size magazine appeared in May 1953 and had as its motto "The Voice of a Motoring World." It has become a somewhat famous publication, especially when one considers that it appeared for only six issues.

The publisher, the editor, the managing editor, and the photo editor were all *Hot Rod* staff members. In the first issue editor Wally Parks declared the reason for *Honk!* "It is our belief that the car enthusiasts, motorists and just plain folks of the U.S. and neighboring countries want

a small-size magazine loaded-to-the-hat with information concerning the machinery the other fellow is building and running. Basically, the format will be COOL CUSTOMS AND HOT RODS…"

The magazine featured superb rods and customs, but it also had a penchant for interesting odd-ball cars such as a chopped and channeled '38 Ford tudor with a Lincoln V-12 engine. They were odd-ball, all right, but they were neat cars. *Honk!* did not feature any cars from the east coast that issue and only one from the midwest. *Honk!* lasted for six issues and then became *Car Craft*.

Car Craft

This magazine, a continuation of *Honk!* used the same

staff, page size and numbering system. It continued to feature superb rods and customs, as well as an occasional odd-ball. By April 1954, it had become "The Show How Magazine," emphasizing detailed "how-to" articles for the builder. In June 1959, *Car Craft* went to a full-size format.

HOP UP

This pocket-size magazine was published by the crew of *Road & Track*. As the editor said in the first issue, "As publishers of ROAD & TRACK Magazine, which is editorially directed toward sports car activities and road racing, we have had many requests to include material of other activities such as hot rods, custom cars (American), motorcycles, speed boats, and various forms of American speedway

Speed Age *was started in 1947, and had editorial offices in Washington, DC. It had excellent coverage of auto racing. Photo on August 1950 issue shows Johnny Parsons and wife after he won Indy 500.*

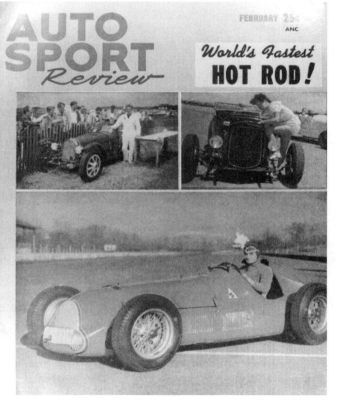

Another east coast publication was Auto Sport Review, *which covered various automotive interests during its short life.*

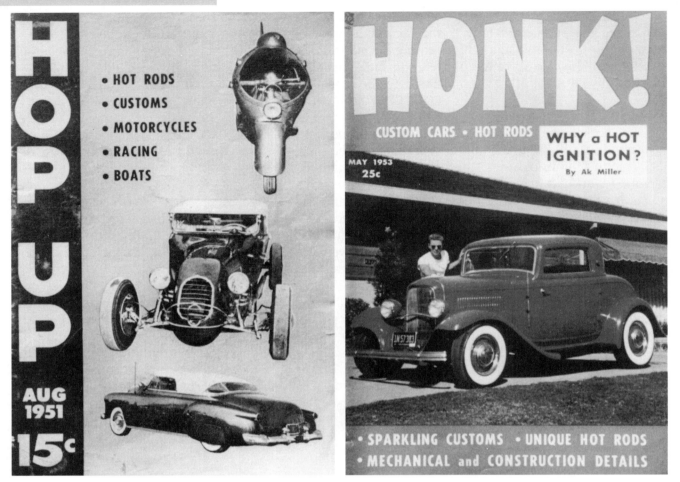

Pocket-size Hop Up *began in August 1951, and after a year it went full-size format. It had brief articles and rod features, but it was awfully satisfying.*

This first issue of Honk! *appeared May 1953. It lasted only for six issues, but it was an exciting mag.*

racing. Now, with HOP UP, we can cover all of these deserving subjects, without varying the policy of ROAD and TRACK. Also, recognizing that many of HOP UP's potential readers may be of a young age group, we have decided on a smaller page size and an fifteen-cent price. Subscriptions will only be $1.50 for 12 issues." Its subtitle was "If it can be hopped up, it'll be in HOP UP."

The first issue, cover dated August 1951, showed the gamut: stories on the new Kurtis 3000 series Indy car, a record-setting Lambretta motor scooter, the Catalina Grand National motorcycle race, a visit to Auto Acces-

sories, etc. But the main emphasis was on hot rods and custom cars.

After a year the magazine went from pocket-size to full-size, which allowed more coverage of hot rods and longer articles. In October 1953, the magazine became *Hop Up and Motor Life* but with none of the life of the original *Hop Up.* By that time, the magazine was owned by William Quinn's Quinn Publications. Quinn had been the advertising manager at Enthusiasts' Publications, Inc., publishers of *Road & Track* and the original *Hop Up.*

Rod & Custom

The pocket-size *Rod & Custom* is probably the magazine most street rodders think of when they recall publications of the 'Fifties; it is the name most often talked about today, and it had an impact back then. It was born out of *Hop Up* when that magazine went to a larger format, due, we're told, to readers' reaction against the change.

The first issue came out in May 1953. The publisher was W.S. Quinn, and the editor was Spencer Murray, a bonafide hot rodder who edited the magazine

Continued on page 126

Cover Story

Motorsport photograph came out first on April 1951 issue. Ray Brown (left) owned the '32 roadster that's being worked on

The photograph became a rendering on cover of Speed Mechanics January 1953.

I wondered why it would use essentially the same illustration on two issues

I'd been looking at these two magazine covers for 45 years, and I'd long recognized that they were variations on a theme. In my mind the two versions had appeared on the same magazine, and I wondered why it would use essentially the same illustration on two issues. It wasn't until recently that I realized they

were different titles, although both were from the same publisher, Hobby Publications. And it wasn't until my friend, Stan Ochs, commented on them that I realized that they were of more than passing interest.

I bought the issue of *Motorsport* when it came out in April 1951. It had a neat cover, with guys, girls *and* a '32 Ford roadster. I was living and breathing that world, and I could put myself in the scene. Later the only thing I really remembered about it was that smooth left front tire, and, although my own

roadster had some smooth tires back then, that detail really bothered me.

The rendering on the *Speed Mechanics* cover came out on the January 1953 issue, and it was based on the earlier photograph. That was issue number one, but because it had the same publisher as *Motorsport* I assumed they had the original photo in their files. One thing I always thought odd was that in the rendering the car still has that smooth

Continued on page 126

Cover Story continued

left front tire, because it would've been almost no work for the artist to paint in some tread.

Stan Ochs saw the magazines several years after they were published; he thinks he saw the *Motorsport* cover first, and found it memorable. The first thing he pointed out was the device on the end of the camshaft. "Years later I saw one. It's got a little wheel inside that turns, with numbers on it; there's a window on top and it shows you which cylinder's up on compression so you can adjust the valves."

The photo credit was to I. Willinger Shostall, which meant nothing to me then nor does it now. Because the magazines were published in Maryland, I assumed that the roadster was an east-coast car. Stan shed light on that, and he may be the only person in the world who knows the identity of the car. "I considered those covers to be of some significance. Many years after I'd first seen them I was studying the photographs in one of Don Montgomery's books, and I noticed one photo of a '32 Ford roadster with a passenger-side headlight support bent in an odd way, just like the support in both magazine covers. I still think it's strange that the artist would paint a crooked headlight support when he made the painting. The color used in both covers helped to confirm my suspicions—kind of a Buick green. Then, when I looked at the photo, I realized who the guy on the left was, the guy in the Road Runners T-shirt—it's a youthful Ray Brown! That's his '32 roadster!" Ray Brown, incidentally, was one of the first people to offer seat belts for fitting into cars—no stock ones had them at the time.

The Ray Brown '32 roadster ran at El Mirage immediately after WW II, and was sold in 1948 to Bob Hutchinson, who took the car to Pennsylvania; therefore, the photo was taken between 1946 and 1948. In 1973 Hutchinson moved to Las Vegas, Nevada, and took the car with him. At some point over the years the car got fenders. In 1991 he sold the roadster to Kirk White, who had it restored to its post-WW II configuration. The car is easily recognized by the distinctive louver pattern on the hood, but that's removed on the cover shots, and Stan may be the only person who could identify the car. Incidentally, both headlight supports are nicely curved on the restored roadster.

What We Read: Magazines continued

for many years. No explanations were given for the slight name change, from *Rods and Customs* to *Rod & Custom*, with the second issue.

From the beginning, *Rod & Custom* had spirit. It featured rods and customs, of course, and car shows and drag races. It ran an occasional piece about the good old days (at that time they were the 'Forties!) and, surprisingly, there was some cheesecake, usually three or four per issue, always tastefully done. Numerous technical articles also appeared..

The small-size format continued until July 1961, when it became a full-size magazine.

"New large size and still only 25¢." Like the others, it covered the car-show circuit, the booming drag-racing scene, and club activities as well as having feature cars and "how-to" information. It had a personal sense, as if the reader really mattered, and part of that feeling came across because the editors were involved in the sport. The editors participated at Bonneville, and built the *R&C* "Dream Truck" as a magazine project. The editors even presented plans for building a roadster that would cost a dollar a pound, and some readers did, in fact, build the car. There were contests, one of which was won by Neal East (whose '32 roadster was later featured as a cover car).

From Hot Rod Magazine *January 1948.*

Regional Rodding Magazines

Enterprising individuals felt a regional rodding magazine could be a success.

As proof of the way the sport was growing, by the mid-'Fifties less than ten years after *Hot Rod Magazine* appeared, regional rodding magazines began to be published. It takes a certain number of subscribers and advertisers to get a specialized, limited-circulation magazine to the break-even point. It also takes time—usually two to three years—to get it solidly in the black. But with the rapid increase in rods and customs and their related clubs, there were enterprising individuals who felt a regional rodding magazine could be a success.

Northwest Rods

An example of such a publication is *Northwest Rods*, which first appeared in October 1957. A tastefully done pocket-size 36-page magazine, it sold for 25¢. Editor Peter Sukalac was a professional photographer who had been selling feature stories

Interior of the Rhythm Rods' 15-car garage, featured in the May 1958 issue of Cars and Clubs. *The club had a closed membership of fifteen, with dues of $137 per year!*

to *Hot Rod Magazine* and other automotive magazines since the early 'Fifties. He continued with that work until the mid-'Eighties. Over a period of three decades he put northwest rod and custom activities on the national map. Apparently in the mid-'Fifties he realized the northwest was not getting the attention it deserved. In his editorial in the first issue he cited the hot rodding history of the area and noted the "...fellas have not received the publicity they should have... However, no national magazine devoted to 'The Sport' can commit all of its space to any one geographical area... No one has attempted a regional magazine before, but since we're of pioneer stock we would like to try."

He went on to say that the magazine would "cover cars and events in the area stretching from Northern California to Canada..." and it extended to Idaho, Montana and Wyoming. Sukalac traveled extensively in Oregon and Washington, so most of the coverage was devoted to these two states. For example, in the first issue there was a three-page feature on the Oregon Championship Drags held the month before at Aurora, and the recent Northwest Championship Drag Races at Shelton, Washington. It was proof that a regional magazine could cover a local event that a major magazine might ignore, and that it could scoop a major magazine by months. The cover car, also featured inside, was Jim Miller's Dodge roadster with an Ardun, a show car finished a year earlier. Also featured was a full-fendered 1932 Ford roadster owned by Geno Ames from Washington and built by Wayne Miller of Portland. It was a beautiful traditional roadster built for the

Cars and Clubs, *issue number one, October 1957.*

street, featured in shows and now, with tremendous interest in drag racing, used on the strip. It appears here without hub caps for that racing look!

In the first editorial Sukalac promised *Northwest Rods* would feature a wide variety of machinery, including sports cars, race cars, boats, motorcycles and even quarter midgets, which were beginning to be very popular. In this first issue there's a nice feature on Larry Eave's fiberglass-bodied sports car. Eaves was a serious hot rodder who had money to realize his dreams. With the help of Orville Withey, a top-notch machinist, they built a

beautiful tube-frame chassis with torsion-bar suspension, Bendix front brakes, Dayton knock-off wire wheels and a Halibrand quick-change. And, because Eave worked for General Motors, it had a brand-new Chev V-8 engine. The kind of car that deserved attention, it showed what Northwest rodders were capable of doing.

In a limited time, *Northwest Rods* covered lots of material. There was a feature on a customized 1954 Pontiac convertible from Spokane, a piece on a supercharged 1956 Corvette from California (photographed when it came to Jim Flanagan's shop in

Portland), an article on how to gap valves, a feature on quarter midgets, drawings by Doug Nicoli on how to restyle the '57 Plymouth. (40 years later Doug is building a two-person A. J. Watson type car for the street.) There was a report on the first Everett, Washington rod and custom show, announcements for the Seattle Autorama and the second Portland Roadster Show, plus ads from many of the area's major specialty auto shops.

Only four issues

Four issues were published, with the last two titled *Northwest*

Rods and Sports Cars. It stuck to its bimonthly schedule, with the final issue published in March 1958. It was an attractive publication that I bought and read with real interest. Years later I was told that the magazine had money problems and that there were personal tiffs among certain people connected with the magazine, It's hard to know which was the greater problem. Sukalac told me that, in addition to doing the photography and most of the writing, he also contributed a good deal of money which he lost when it folded. An interesting sidelight, and one we

readers could not have known was that, as Sukalac found later, Petersen Publishing was buying up various magazines. One fellow associated with *Northwest Rods* had put all of his energies into developing the magazine up to the point where it could be sold profitably. I bought my copies off the newsstand, but Paul Smith subscribed and he recently told me that when *Northwest Rods* folded he received copies of *Rod & Custom* until his subscription ran out.

Cars and Clubs

Another regional rodding magazine was *Cars and Clubs*, subtitled "The Midwest's Own Hotrod Magazine." The first issue came out in May 1958, and it was smaller than most magazines at 5-1/2 x 7 inches; it was 32 pages long and sold for 25¢. Like *Northwest Rods*, the photos were black and white. The cover let the reader know that this magazine was "Owned and Operated by Hotrodders." Publisher John Hall lived in Bloomington, Minnesota and editor Ron Johnson lived in Minneapolis. Their plan was to feature cars and events in their area and beyond, because they felt coverage in national magazines was lacking. As they wrote in their editorial in the first issue, "As you all know, the Upper Midwest is not yet an area of renown in the hot rod world. There are certain centers in the southern states such as Cordova, Omaha, and Sioux City where there is really quite an amount of action, but if it is reported at all it is done so, somewhat grudgingly by the east or west coast publications." A sense of being neglected is perhaps one of the strongest motives for publishing a regional magazine. These guys

The Oregon Championship Drags, Aurora, Oregon, held in September 1957, and featured in Northwest Rods, October 1957.

read *Hot Rod Magazine, Rod & Custom, Car Craft* and others and noticed very few rods from their area, the Upper Midwest. Yet they saw neat rods and customs every weekend at the drive-in and felt those cars should get some attention, just to let the world know that all rodding didn't take place on the two coasts. "This is where we come in. We will be on the spot, or in contact at drag strips, car shows and all the other activities that make up hot rodding. We will be reporting nothing but cars and activities from this area." Their plans were, of course, extensive: cars, club activities, action at the drag strips, technical articles, stories on engine swaps, a directory of clubs and associations, etc.

Inspired editors

That first issue gives a good idea of what inspired the editors. There are features on a reworked 1958 Olds with J-2, a nice chopped and flamed 1932 Ford tudor, a customized '40 Ford pickup and the "Minnesota Missile," the Cassidy-Anthony Chrysler-powered dragster. These were all good-looking machines, especially the dragster, described as "the first real dragster to be built in Minnesota." The car had not yet been driven in competition, so no time (or speed) was available. There was also a feature on a club, the Rhythm Rods, with several pages of photos taken in the club's 15-car garage in Minneapolis. A history of Gopher State Timing Association mentioned that it started in 1954 and included 25 Minnesota hot rod clubs. The association's activities reads like the birth of hot rodding: the first reliability run held in spring 1955; the first car show in September 1956, in a

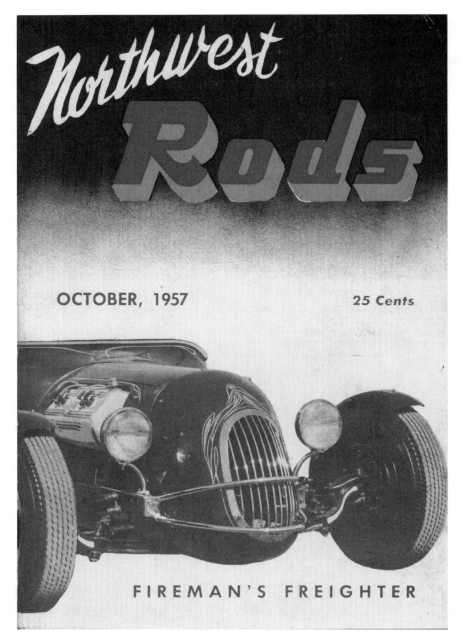

OCTOBER, 1957   25 Cents

FIREMAN'S FREIGHTER

Northwest Rods, *issue number one, October 1957.*

parking lot and the first indoor show held in the Minneapolis Armory in 1957. Lacking a drag strip, the association did circle-track racing on the ice during the winter. There was also overage of the 1958 Chicago Car Show, which featured several Minnesota cars.

I'm not certain how many issues of *Cars and Clubs* were published; I've seen several and know the coverage extended over to Michigan. One hopes it had a

long and profitable life. But even if it only lasted a few issues, it no doubt did a lot of good in making people in that area aware of rods and customs. Today Minnesota is a very progressive state in terms of hot rodding, and I've heard it called the center of street rodding in the United States. Some of these positive things might be due to the early issues of *Cars and Clubs.*

In 1949, about the time I got interested in cars, I discovered Floyd Clymer and his publications. His first titles were the *Historical Motor Scrapbooks.* He did the first one in 1943, pasting together old auto advertisements and, the wartime shortage of paper aside, printing it at his own expense. It's funny to think that the automobile was only about 40 years old and already there was a sense of nostalgia about it. But, as Clymer pointed out, already some 2,200 different makes of cars and 300 different makes of motorcycles had been built in the United States. Many were short-lived, and apparently there was a fair amount of interest in those names that had quickly passed from the scene.

What We Read: The Clymer Books

His first titles were the
Historical Motor Scrapbooks

HOW TO BUILD A RACING CAR

Here is a book that everyone planning a midget or dirt-track racing car should have. It gives complete car-building data for drivers and mechanics . . . gives rules and regulations of AAA, CSRA, and URA, the three famous racing organizations. It gives safety requirements, dimensions, tips, short-cuts, and many sound, fundamental and well-tried building principles. Cam data, superchargers, compression information, etc., clearly explained. 60 photos, charts, drawings. 48 information-packed pages. Postpaid........................ $2.00

HOT ROD PICTORIAL

The newly revised 1949 edition contains 100 PHOTOS, ILLUSTRATIONS of famous record breaking winners used on Muroc and other California dry lakes, and also speedways. PERFORMANCE RECORDS OF EACH CAR . . . many valuable "hot-rod" tips . . . Specifications of many winners . . . Close-ups and action shots . . . Streamlined bodies . . . Overhead and stroked Fords, Chevrolets, others. A unique and historical book of the California "Hot Rods." Postpaid $1.50

Motor Racing with MERCEDES-BENZ

Written solely about GRAND PRIX RACING. 176 pages, 100 full size illustrations. Illustrates and describes such famous race cars as Auto-Union, Mercedes-Benz, Alfa-Romeo, Bugatti, Maserati, many others. Tells the exploits of such famous drivers as Caracciola, Fagioli, Chiron, Rosemeyer, Brauchitsch, Mays, Lang, Nuvolari, Stuck, Seaman, others. Describes Grand Prix races at all famous European tracks, also Vanderbilt Cup Race at Long Island, N.Y. Postpaid $2.00
De Luxe Cloth-Bound................................. $3.00

MOTORACES

128 pages, over 100 fine photos. Photos of such world-renowned drivers as Caracciola, Nuvolari, Seaman, Rosemeyer, Eyston, Von Delius, Brivio, Chiron, Farina, Lang, Straight, Von Brauchitsch, Count Trossi, Benoist, Bourlier, Varzi, Divo, Dreyfus, Lehoux, Wimille, Mays, Howe and many others. World-famous cars shown include Maserati, Alfa-Romeo, E.R.A., Auto-Union, Mercedes-Benz, De Lage, Bugatti, La Gonda, Bentley, M-G and others. Articles by Earl Howe and the late Richard Seaman.

Postpaid, $2.00   De Luxe cloth-bound, $3.00

"THE SALT OF THE EARTH"

The personal story of Ab Jenkins, former Mayor of Salt Lake City, greatest long distance driver the world has ever known—no other person has ever traveled so far, so fast on land. The history of the Bonneville Salt Flats. Jenkins' record runs described in detail. The MORMON METEOR, Ab's streamlined racing monster, and other racing machines, illustrated and described. The record runs of Campbell, Eyston and Cobb. Profusely illustrated.

Postpaid	De Luxe Cloth Bound
$1.50	$2.50

FASTEST ON EARTH

By Capt. Geo. Eyston. 175 pages, 75 photos. Gives complete history of every land speed record ever made. Famous cars, racers, tracks illustrated and described.

Postpaid	De Luxe Cloth Bound
$2.00	$3.00

AUTOMOBILE RACING BOOKS cont'd

"SPEED ON SALT"

by Captain G. E. T. Eyston, author of "Fastest on Earth" and other racing books. Here is the full story of racing at Bonneville Salt Flats as told by a former speed record holder. History of the Salt Flats is told in detail, with graphic accounts of all the important speed events held on this, the world's finest natural speed course. Well illustrated. Postpaid, $2.00; De Luxe Cloth-bound, $3.00.

Postpaid	Cloth Bound
$2.00	$3.00

DICK SEAMAN — Racing Motorist

The Only Englishman to become a member of the Mercedes-Benz racing team, Dick Seaman was regarded as England's greatest road race driver. This book gives details of Grand Prix and other races and outstanding victories on European tracks. Contains full list of all Seaman's long distance races, with names of tracks, cars driven and his position at finish, including the Roosevelt Vanderbilt Cup Race in 1937. Fine halftone action photographs. Complete biography from birth to death.
Here indeed is an important contribution to the world's motoring literature. 190 pages.
Postpaid, $2.00   Cloth-bound De Luxe, $3.00

BOOKS on MODERN U.S. CARS

CATALOG OF U. S. AUTOMOBILES

NEW! DIFFERENT! A book of ALL MODELS and MAKES of U.S. Cars Between the pages of ONE BOOK you can compare specifications, photos and other data on all U.S. built cars. NOTHING LIKE THIS NEW BOOK! See and read about EVERY G-M, FORD, CHRYSLER and all INDEPENDENT Makes . . . including unusual Del Mar, Tucker, Playboy, Keller, Hoppenstand, Gregory, Davis 3-Wheeler and the NEW KURTIS SPORTS CAR . . . with all SPECIFICATIONS . . .
AUTOMATIC TRANSMISSIONS of ALL makes shown . . . COMPRESSION RATIO COMPARISON CHART . . . WHEELBASE CHART . . . OTHER SPECIFIC DATA AND SPECIFICATIONS OF ALL CARS.
120 PHOTOS . . . CHARTS . . . 72 LARGE PAGES
ONLY . . . . $2.00 POSTPAID

THE FORD OWNER'S COMPLETE HANDBOOK

of Repair and Maintenance — Complete V8 and 6 Information Contains everything that the Ford owner wants to know about his car. Charts, drawings, pictures, tables of clearances and adjustments. The most complete maintenance and repair book on Fords ever published. Covers ALL Fords from 1932 to the new 1950 models, inclusive, including the Ford SIX! Nowhere can this information be duplicated. Changes in models indicated. Improvements throughout the years noted. The only COMPLETE Ford repair book on the market. Whether you adjust windshield wipers or overhaul transmissions, you should have this book. Ask for FORD OWNER'S HANDBOOK. Postpaid $1.50

MODEL "A" FORD REPAIR MANUAL

With 35 Charts and Drawings
By Victor W. Page

This complete book on care and operation of the Model A Ford tells everything you want to know . . . Fine cut-away drawings on every part . . . chassis, engine, brakes, ignition, transmission, differential, electrical units . . . in fact EVERY essential service for "A" owners is included. POSTPAID $1.00

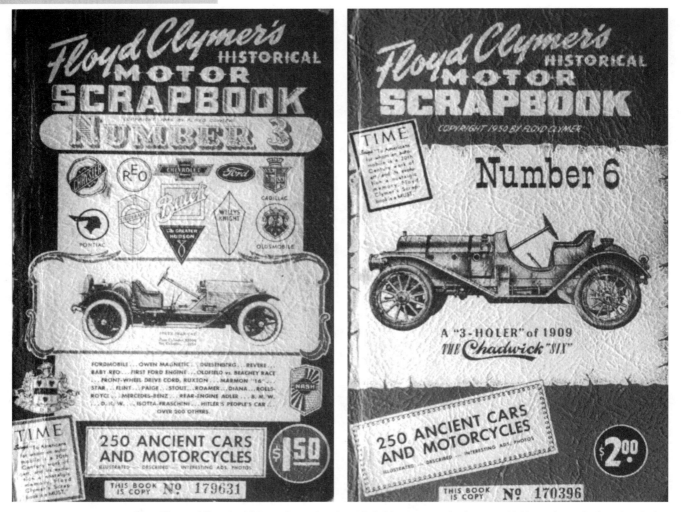

Two Clymer Historical Motor Scrapbooks. #3 (left) came out in January 1946, and was in fourth printing in 1950, while #6 came out that year. Note that each copy was numbered on cover, an unusual touch.

Clymer estimated it would require 10 or 12 volumes to illustrate and describe at least one model of every make. He eventually did eight volumes, and they were quite popular.

Interesting guy

Floyd Clymer was an interesting guy. Born in Colorado in 1895, the son of a physician, he learned to drive at age 7 in his father's new 1902 curved-dash Oldsmobile. When he was 11 he established a dealership for Reo, Maxwell and Cadillac in Berthoud, Colorado. By the time he was 14 he had a Flanders dealership. As a way of promoting the car, he and his brother, age 11, attempted to drive across

the roadless west in a 1910 Flanders Model 20. The grueling journey was from Denver to Spokane, Washington, and, after many breakdowns, the car was eventually shipped to Spokane by train.

During the 'Teens he was an Excelsior and Harley-Davidson dealer in Greeley, Colorado, and to promote these machines he began racing them on fairground tracks. In 1916 he won the prestigious Pike's Peak race, competing against the country's big-name racers. During the early 'Twenties he competed several times at the Capistrano hillclimb in California, with great success. From 1922 to 1925 he raced an early midget powered

by two 61-CID Indian motorcycle engines, competing against full-size race cars.

Stock-car records and "easy money"

In 1925 Floyd decided to quit car and cycle racing and set his sights on breaking established stock car records. Those were the days when speed and endurance sold cars, and manufacturers were eager to back record-setting attempts. Drivers like the famed "Cannonball" Baker made their reputations by driving on the road the way they drove on the track—fast. In many places there was no speed limit and no highway patrol, and it was possible to drive flat out on what then passed for a highway.

In 1924, when he was a distributor for Indian cycles and Dort cars, Clymer drove a new Dort touring car 34 times over Lookout Mountain during a 24-hour period. To make this feat more meaningful to the manufacturer, the car's transmission was sealed in high gear and the radiator was also sealed; no shifting was done going up and down the mountain and no water was added during the 437 miles driven. He also carried 187 passengers, five or six at a time. In 1925 he drove a stock Oldsmobile six up Pike's Peak to set a new stock car record. Oldsmobile paid Floyd $1,000 to make the trip, which he described as "the easiest money I ever made." He continued this kind of driving through the 'Thirties, setting records between numerous cities, such as the Chicago-to-Detroit record.

Inventor

Clymer was an enterprising fellow, obviously. The auto was in its infancy and he saw things that were needed. He invented and patented the Clymer spotlight, which attached directly to the flat glass of the windshield. (One fellow who cut the hole to mount the spotlight was another Denver lad, Bill Kenz. Years later, when Kenz ran his streamliner at Bonneville, Clymer was his primary sponsor.) Clymer's spotlight was a great success and he made money.

Another invention, the Clymer Automatic Air Gauge, designed to measure tire pressure, cost too much to manufacture and it lost money. He also invented a headlight control, sort of a dimmer switch that was operated from the steering wheel to dim the headlights gradually.

Soon after, state laws dictated the use of high and low beam only and that invention also lost money.

Publishing success

But Clymer's publishing ventures were a great success, and by 1949 he had 70 titles in print. They covered everything from the history of steam cars (over 125 different makes produced) to the life of famed auto racer Ted Horn. Clymer also reprinted folders and catalogs on Cord, Duesenberg, etc. Clymer publications were the only source of automotive books in North America during that period, and they filled a need, When Veda Orr compiled her *Dry Lakes Pictorial* in 1947—a year before *Hot Rod Magazine* started— Clymer published it, and kept it in print for many years. As hot rodding grew by leaps and

Clymer's publishing ventures were a great success...by 1949 he had 70 titles in print.

Bantams had a four-cylinder water-cooled engine.

I was a couple of years away from getting my driver's license, but I yearned for mobility. Floyd Clymer was driving at age 7, and here I was, twice that, still riding my Western Flyer. All I wanted was to be able to go 10 or 15 miles an hour without effort, as if I were always going downhill on my bike.

Looking at the early motorcycles in the Clymer albums, I thought it seemed possible to mount a small engine on my bike. I had two paper routes, and I told my father I could use a powered bike to deliver papers with. It made sense to me. My father, like Clymer, had cars, motorcycles and even a homemade snowmobile when he was a teenager, but now he muttered something about a driver's license, a license plate and insurance. I tried to imagine what Clymer's life would have been like if his father had given him similar advice, and thought about how awful it was that the times had to change.

Publisher's Note:

When I started California Bill books in 1947, I was given lots of encouragement by W. Everett Miller of Eagle Rock, California. Miller, a close personal friend, owned the Library of Vehicles, one of the largest collections of automobile literature ever assembled. It was always a sore point with him that Floyd Clymer created his first scrapbooks from dozens of catalogs and magazines from the Miller collection. Said materials were "borrowed," cut up and used to make the scrapbooks—and never returned. To make matters worse, the source for the materials was not mentioned in the scrapbooks.

bounds during the early 'Fifties, Clymer published books like Roger Huntington's *Souping the Stock Engine, How to Hop Up Ford & Mercury V-8 Engines* and *How to Hop Up Chevrolet & GMC*. About 1954 he also purchased Bill Fisher's "California Bill" Ford and Chevy speed manuals and continued to publish them for many years..

I was terribly interested in the books themselves, of course, because I wanted to know all about cars built before I was born. But in 1949 there were still plenty of cars from the 'Thirties and even from the 'Twenties on the road. An elderly couple came to church every Sunday in a primo 1926 Model T Ford coupe. There was a Franklin sedan down at the welding shop with a busted cylinder, and an old Rolls-Royce parked behind the bank. My interest was in hot rods, and although I never wanted to own what has become a classic or antique car, I wanted to look at them, sit in them, and think what I could do with the parts. Oh, there were a few I wanted, like the 1939 Bantam convertible in a neighbor's yard with its little two-cylinder air-cooled engine; it seemed like a toy, and I thought a kid could drive that on the sidewalk! Incidentally, some

In addition to the growing number of magazines that appeared in the late 'Forties and early 'Fifties to cover the hot rod scene, there were also books and one-shot publications. Rodders and would-be rodders hungered for information. Some of these books supplied it in detail, while others were pretty superficial; all are interesting today from an historical perspective.

Hot Rods

Wally Parks and Walt Woron, editors. Trend Book No. 102, 1951.

I love this book. I bought it in 1951, I lived with it, read it repeatedly, practically memorized parts of it and I continue to read it. Assembled by the editors of *Hot Rod Magazine* and *Motor Trend*, this book gave me an introduction to and a sense of perspective on the sport. It came out when hot rodding was really just getting going, and it gave a good survey of rodding. There's a brief history of hot rodding, and a chapter that discusses the future of the sport. In between there are chapters on lowering cars, raising compression ratios, building dual exhaust systems and doing engine conversions. There are also chapters on competition engines and racing at Bonneville (hot rodders had been holding speed trials at

What We Read: Books

Books gave us a sense of perspective on the sport.

BILL BURKE'S 'WING TANK' STREAMLINER

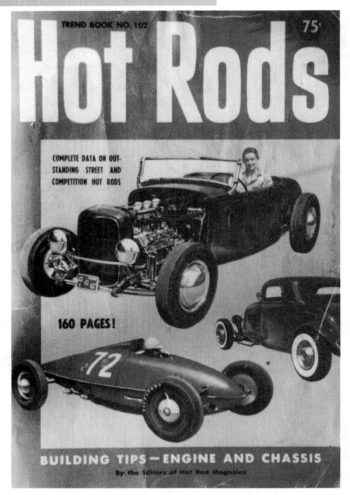

I've almost worn out my copy of Hot Rods *(1951). It's loaded with car features and technical articles, most culled from 1948-51 issues of* Hot Rod Magazine.

Roger Huntington had a self-taught engineering background, so his How to Hop Up Ford & Mercury V-8 Engines *had lots of slide-rule stuff. This and two other Huntington books from the 'Fifties have been reprinted by Fisher Books:* Souping the Stock Engine, *and* How to Hop Up Chevrolet and GMC Engines.

Bonneville for only two years).

But the chapter that knocked me out was called *Types of Hot Rods*. Ninety pages of this 160-page book are devoted to photos and brief descriptions of all kinds of hot rods: roadsters, coupes, sedans, competition rigs, all gorgeous. Even today, as I flip the pages, the book drives me crazy! There must be 200—300 rods pictured—'32 roadsters, ground-hugging Model As, stripped T buckets, belly tanks, the Pierson brothers' radical '34 coupe, chopped pickups, Art Chrisman's sleek customized '36

Ford four-door, Jack Calori's even sleeker '36 Ford 3-window, Lynn Yakel's chopped and channeled '32 5-window, and on and on, a bevy of Bonneville streamliners, a Cord with a Merc flathead, a lakester with a Pontiac 6, etc. All this material was new to me, and I must have spent a hundred hours of study hall reading this book, until I could see right into the cars, just like a Rex Burnett drawing. I don't know what a used copy of this book sells for, but I wouldn't take $500 for mine.

How to Hop Up Ford & Mercury V-8

by Roger Huntington.
Floyd Clymer, 1951.

I bought this book by mail when it was first published and I still own that same dog-eared copy. I can't recall *using* it in a specific way but I must have read it a dozen times and I know I absorbed a good deal of information about souping the only engine I care to work on.

This book, 160 pages in length, was the first to present a solid, comprehensive procedure for souping the flathead V-8, the most popular engine of the era. There was very little information available about reworking the flathead V-8 outside of an occasional article in *Hot Rod Magazine*. But here was everything we wanted to know, presented in clear, readable prose. There were chapters on the basics—compression ratios, multiple carburetion, ignition systems—as well as things that seemed more exotic, such as porting and relieving and supercharging. And, because Huntington was an engineer, there were many pages of graphs and charts.

The book emphasizes the need to be systematic. Too many rodders were bolting high-compression heads and three-carb manifolds on stock—and sometimes worn-out—blocks, with disappointing if not disastrous results. The author created a character, Leadfoot Louie, "the moron hot rodder" (who, for example, grinds his own high-performance cam with a hand file), and it is in contrast to Leadfoot's stupidity that the author can instruct on how to build an engine correctly. Reprints of this book, as well as two of Huntington's other books *Souping the Stock Engine* and *How to Hop Up Chevrolet* and

GMC 6 cylinder Engines were brought back by Fisher Books in 1997.

Ford Speed Manual
Fred W. "Bill" Fisher. 1952.

This book, written and originally published by "California Bill," (now one of the owners of Fisher Books) is similar to Huntington's book in that it covers the various approaches to hopping up the Ford flathead V-8, but it's different enough so an engine builder might want both books.

Huntington's book is more theoretical, while Fisher gives hands-on information. It also

Guys were crying for information on how to hop up the Ford Flathead V-8 in early 'Fifties. "California Bill" Fisher's 1952 book also had info on Ford four, six, Lincoln V-12, etc. It's recently been reprinted, along with his speed manual on the Chevrolet/GMC six and Buick straight-8 engines.

This 1950 Fawcett book, Sports Cars and Hot Rods, was long on sports cars, but that was OK; we never saw the sports cars and we wanted to read about them!

covers the Ford Model A and B, Ford 6, and Lincoln V-12 engines. In addition there are chapters on how to channel an early car, install hydraulic brakes and column shift, how to put a V-8 in a Model A, etc. This information was eagerly sought by an army of shade-tree mechanics.

Ford Speed Manual has been reprinted by Fisher Books.

Bill Fisher went on to produce books on how to hop up Chevrolet and GMC engines. Although he started HPBooks with automotive titles, this publishing house subsequently expanded into photography, health, gardening, home improvements and cooking. He and his wife Helen and son Howard operate their current company, Fisher Books, the publisher of this book.

Sports Cars and Hot Rods
Fred Horsley, Editor.
Fawcett Book #109, 1950.

This book has articles by excellent writers, among them Ken Purdy, John Bentley and Tom McCahill. But from the title on you could easily tell where the emphasis was: Sports Cars was in large letters while Hot Rods was in much smaller letters, and of the book's 144 pages less than 35 pages deal with hot rods. But this was an east-coast publication, and in 1950 in New York City MGs must have out-numbered hot rods by 20 to 1.

But there are some good pieces—taken from the pages of *True*, a Fawcett publication—such as "Don't Call it a Hot Rod" and an account by Tom McCahill, America's first road test driver-writer, about a track roadster he drove. Of course, he had to go to Los Angeles to do the test! There was a nice piece on the second Bonneville Nationals, and a rundown on the ten hottest rods (all from So-Cal).

A piece I liked very much, and which I re-read often, was called *Hot Rod Heaven.* Heaven was Lou Baney's garage in Hollywood; just a two-bit Golden Eagle service station, but the small lot was filled with terrific roadsters. The photos evoked an ideal situation, a community of rodders, and I knew the place would look just the way it did in the photos if I could just get there to *see* it.

Best Hot Rods
Number 1, Arthur Unger, Editor.
Fawcett, 1952.

Another Fawcett publication, this time via the editors of *Mechanics Illustrated, Best Hot Rods was* a more exciting publication than it might seem. This was because of its large size, which allowed room for more photographs, and because 90% of its material came from the west coast. The first issue had articles on the dry lakes and Bonneville, NHRA activities, and an extensive survey of the best

Best Hot Rods (1953) was aptly named, loaded with info on drags, Bonneville, dry lakes, rods built for sports car racing, etc.

The first edition of Hot Rod Pictorial came out in 1947; this is updated 1949 edition. Primarily a collection of photographs of dry lake cars, with captions, it's of interest because it pre-dates Hot Rod Magazine. Veda Orr was a regular at the dry lakes, and only woman to run there for decades.

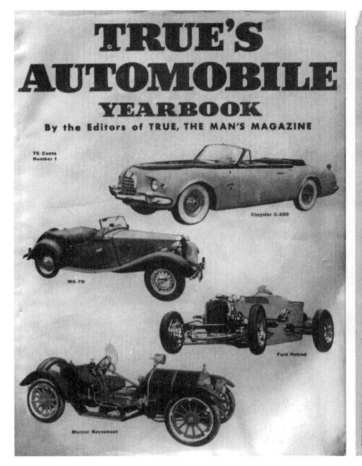

True was a popular magazine aimed at male readers; along with articles about hunting, fishing, adventure, food and clothes, it ran pieces on classic and sports cars. Its editor, Ken Purdy, loved fine cars, and squeezed in an article on hot rods occasionally.

Hot Rod Handbook is not dated, but it must have come out in 1951, as I recall. It is a hodgepodge of material, but interesting. Although published by Fawcett, and got information from Motorsport, it contains much in the way of west coast cars and events.

rods. There were also four articles by Ed Almquist on hot rodding, including one that had the title "Build a $300 Street Roadster" but showed in detail a car that could not have been built for less than $1,500. His article was absolutely useless to anyone who was actually trying to *build* a hot rod. Ed was automatically suspect in my book because he always wore a bow tie while working on engines!

I think that there were only three issues of *Best Hot Rods*. The second, largely written by Eugene Jaderquist, was published in 1955. It featured drag racing, the NHRA Drag Safari, dry lakes racing and articles on

acceleration and using gasoline as a fuel. A third, published in 1957, was edited (and perhaps mostly written, as well!) by Griffith Borgeson. The third issue surveyed drag racing, Bonneville, and what is now called *Street Rodding*. By 1957 material in the magazine came from all parts of the United States.

Hot Rod Pictorial
Veda Orr.
Floyd Clymer, 1949.

This book focuses on dry lake racing during the years 1946-49, although it also has pages on earlier dry lake cars and track roadsters. There are many photos, but the text is

limited to photo captions; there are also eight drawings by Dick Teague, then a student at the Los Angeles Design Center and later a styling executive at American Motors.

This book pre-dates *Hot Rod Magazine*, and its primary purpose was to inform people about dry lake racing. Veda Orr, for many years the only woman who was a member of SCTA, had begun a newsletter that she wrote and mailed to SCTA members who were scattered all over the world during WW II, and in a way this book is an extension of that activity.

True's Automobile Yearbook

No. 1, Charles Barnard, Editor.
Fawcett, 1952.

It's hard to realize how exciting *True* magazine was during the 'Forties and 'Fifties. It was billed as *the* man's magazine, and it was; *Esquire* seemed effete beside it. *True's emphasis* was on hunting, fishing, camping, drinking and, occasionally, women. And automobiles. Before *Road & Track* and *Hot Rod Magazine* began publishing, a car nut had to read *True* to learn about the Golden Age of Grand Prix racing and about the great American classics. But of course *True's* editor Ken Purdy was the first interesting, knowledgeable and literate American automotive writer.

I don't know how many *True* *Automobile Yearbooks* were published—I have two, 1952 and 1953. There's very little in them about hot rods—albeit a nice article by Dean Batchelor in the first volume—but there is much about automotive history and a survey of the then-new American cars by the dean of automotive road testers, Tom McCahill.

Hot Rod Handbook

Peter Bowman, Editor.
Fawcett Book #129, 1951.

This book is less a survey of hot rodding and more of a hodge-podge, but an interesting one: Some historical stuff, some track roadsters, Bonneville, drags, hot rodding in Florida, etc., etc. I suspect Fawcett Book #109 sold well to a hot rod hungry public and that the publishers threw this collection together to make a few bucks.

How to Build Hot Rods

Bill Czygan, Editor.
Fawcett Book #156, 1952.

A pattern emerges: From Fawcett Book #109, which emphasized sports cars, to #129, which combined a hodgepodge of material but all aimed at the hot rodder, to this book, #156, which is better edited, has nicer photos and is more cohesive. Although there are articles about buying a used hot rod and about various tools found in a machine shop, the book does cover the kinds of subjects one would want to know about to build a hot rod. It's useful, and interesting.

That's Louis Senter, of Ansen Automotive, left, and Lou Baney putting a hot flathead in a neat roadster. How to Build Hot Rods *(1952) had abundance of technical information.*

What We Read: Henry Gregor Felsen

Felsen captured what it was like to be a teenager during this period.

In 1984, when I wrote this essay, I assumed Henry Gregor Felsen was dead. I'd searched for him the year before without success. If he were still alive he'd faded into obscurity, and no one talked about him or his books. In 1985, shortly after this essay was published, a mutual friend told me Felsen was living in Vermont. I called him from Oregon and later interviewed him over the phone. The following year we were both living in Michigan. We met, the first of several meetings over a period of years, and I continued the interview.

A delightful person, Felsen loved to talk, primarily about writing and literature. I don't think we ever talked about cars, except as they figured in his own books. During the last years of

"SHOCKING . . .
TRUE-TO-FACT"
N.Y. Times

his life there was a Felsen revival; several of his books were reprinted, his fiction began to appear in a rodding magazine and he was a celebrated guest at various automotive events, where he met many fans. I like to think that this essay helped to promote the new interest in Felsen and his books.

During the 'Fifties, Henry Gregor Felsen wrote four novels about a new phenomenon called hot rodding: *Hot Rod, Street Rod, Crash Club* and *Rag Top*. Better than anyone else, Felsen captured what it was like to be a teenager during this period. Especially if you lived in a small town in the midwest and were

being told by everyone over 21 that the desire for a stripped-down, hopped-up machine was madness. The reading audience, teenagers yearning for mobility, empathized with the youthful characters found in these books.

Not great literature, the books were well-written, published by major publishing houses and sold through numerous printings both in hardback and paperback editions. *Hot Rod* is still in print years later. The books offered the reader what he wanted: a strong plot line, lots of action, a character who overcomes adversity and a world that was recognizable.

What makes them stand out

from later books about hot rodding is that Felsen was first—he established the conventions of the genre. Hot rodding was just getting started in most parts of the United States when Felsen wrote *Hot Rod*. He saw, and helped others see, that something was going on with kids and cars, and the relationship would not simply end; rather, it had to be developed in a constructive manner. Parents had to see that a boy who built a hot rod was not automatically headed for a fiery crash on the highway or for a prison cell, but that his technical abilities might someday help to build a rocket that would place men on the moon. All this

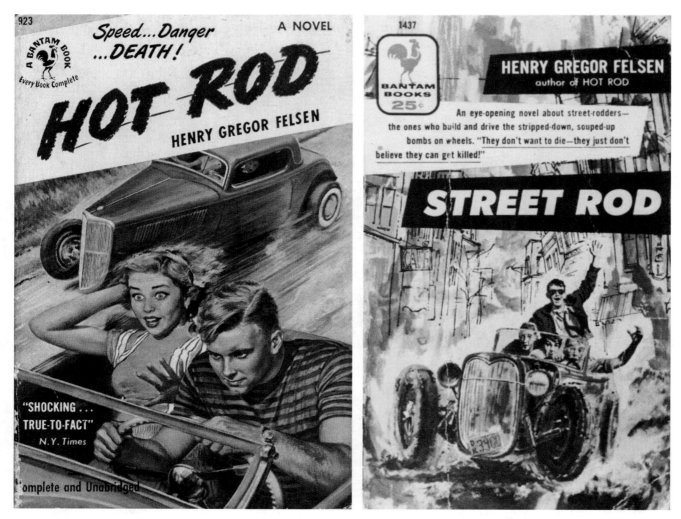

Cover of the first paperback edition of Hot Rod.

Paperback cover of Street Rod. *Hardback edition came out in 1953; was that the earliest use of term "street rod"?*

Dramatic Crash Club *cover involves new Corvette.*

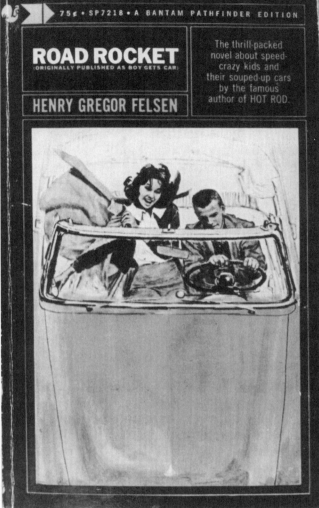

Road Rocket *was originally published as* Boy Gets Car. *The price of paperbacks had tripled since* Hot Rod.

sounds old hat now, but it hadn't been said then. To some degree, the books anticipated the mood of youthful America during the next 30 years.

Meet Bud Crayne

The main character of *Hot Rod* is Bud Crayne. He's 17, a high-school student (although we never see him in class), easily recognizable by the old fedora he wears, the brim turned up and held in place with a large safety pin. But what makes him stand out in a small town like Avondale is his car. "The body had come off an old Ford coupe, was

sanded down and repainted with a dull-red primer. Three inches was chopped from the top of the body, the windshield streamlined and fenders from another Ford added."

The coupe had a full-race flathead V-8. In the book's opening chapter we see Bud pushing the coupe from 50 mph to 110 mph in 10-mph increments and jotting down notes about the coupe's performance on a clipboard strapped to his leg. It shows adults that speeding isn't simply a youthful foible, but is instead a meaningful activity! That's the kind of serious driving

that interested me when I was 17!

Bud Crayne has his coupe, his girlfriend, LaVerne Shuler, whom he hopes to marry, and a part-time job in Jake Clymer's garage, which he hopes to buy someday. Bud already has his life planned. I wonder how many young men who read this book

The books offered the reader what he wanted: a strong plot line, lots of action, a character who overcomes adversity and a world that was recognizable.

shared that view of the future? Thousands, I'll bet—I know I did!

There's a paradox here, because although Bud claims that he wants to settle down, everything he says and does indicates that he wants to escape. The book's setting is Iowa, and the flatness of the landscape reflects the flatness of the people's lives. The picture projected to the reader was that small town life was repressive. Most of the characters dream of leaving Avondale. LaVerne dreams of going to Hollywood. Others, like Chuck Liddell, dream of going away to college. Bud's dream of escape is fulfilled when he makes his daily speed run in the coupe.

The devil's handiwork

In a world governed by the puritan work ethic, a car like Bud's coupe, with its chromed engine and loud exhausts, is seen by adults as the devil's handiwork. The younger people however, appreciate it for its power, gaudiness and beauty. The coupe represents something joyful in their otherwise flat world. In fact, the garage where Bud works becomes a light in the darkness. A clean, well-lit place where young people congregate to drink a Coke and hang out.

In the first chapter, we are told about the Trenton Speed Run. Bud asserts that he can drive from Avondale to Trenton, a distance of 40 miles, in 30 minutes. At stake is a 10-dollar bet and more importantly to Bud, his reputation and the fact that he has been challenged. He not only makes the run, with LaVerne as a passenger, but he makes the return trip, evading numerous police cars. As a punishment he agrees to garage the coupe and to enter the

upcoming Teen-Age Roadeo.

The local highway patrolman, Ted O'Day, grooms Chuck (Chicken) Liddell for the Roadeo, emphasizing caution. Meanwhile, two grade-school boys steal a new Buick and go for a joy ride; using Bud's driving philosophy ("power") they wreck the car and are killed. Bud realizes he's indirectly responsible for their deaths, but he doesn't change his driving habits. At the Roadeo the winner is Chuck, with Bud as the runner-up. Bud Crayne has been whipped in a driving contest by a beginner! Bud, who has devoted all his life to skillful driving, was whipped by Chicken Liddell! Returning home, he takes the coupe out for a speed run, but soon realizes that the old pleasure is gone.

In the final chapter the teenagers are playing chicken, and when the cars crash head-on, only Chuck survives. Ted O'Day orders Bud to drive Chuck to the Trenton hospital; he balks, but make the necessary speed run with the siren and the police car's lights flashing. He makes it in 27 minutes, and more importantly realizes that he hasn't lost his touch at the wheel. With Chuck in the hospital, Bud goes to the state Roadeo and, thinking a bit more about caution, wins.

Same material, different book

Another novel, *Street Rod*, published in 1953, takes similar material and presents it very differently. The book's plot is oddly complicated and digressive. Ricky Madison is 16 and lives in Dellville (Dullville), Iowa; it's the kind of town where the drugstore has a screen door, the old men smoke their pipes while sitting on the park bench, and one's father might walk home for

lunch. Bud Crayne was an orphan and largely unrestricted, but Ricky Madison has parents and they tell him that he cannot have a car. (The book, like many books and movies of the 'Fifties, refers to psychology texts to argue why a young man should not own a car.) However, Ricky takes $75 out of the bank, and, without telling his parents, buys a 1939 Ford coupe that he probably could have had for $20. His parents are unhappy about his purchase, but allow him to keep it. His only true friend seems to be Merle Connor, the shoddy mechanic and wheeler-dealer who sold him the car. Together, Ricky believes, they'll design their own cars, the Connor-Madison, and sell them. But before that idea gets off the ground, Merle loses his business and becomes a drunk. Once again, Ricky is scorned by his peers.

Ricky's father suggests that he and his friends form a timing association and start work on a drag strip. They immediately form the Dellville Timing Association with Ricky as the president. Unfortunately, the town council turns down the proposal for a drag strip and the hot rodders take off for Des Moines where they raise a little hell. When Ricky returns, he and his father talk about the drag strip again. Ricky says he's going to get the club back together to work towards getting the drag strip (to reduce highway deaths). Ricky also thinks about going into business with Merle, and opening a custom shop. He feels there's a big future in new kinds of plastic bodies, but doesn't know enough about the materials, which means he will need to go to college to get better knowledge of mechanics and business

Henry Gregor Felsen (left) and Albert Drake (1990).

procedures. Whew! When I first read this novel, I identified with Ricky, and perhaps my mind was full of big ideas too. Now I identify—and sympathize—with Ricky's father!

On his next trip to Des Moines, Ricky is stopped by Ted O'Day but this time his attitude is a bit more respectful because of the DTA sticker on the window of Ricky's car. Ricky realizes that he has an image to uphold and when he refuses to horse around on the road he gets in a fight with a club member named Link. Link has been bucking with Ricky for the leadership of the group for a long time. Ricky loses his title to Link and once again, feels slighted by his friends.

Ricky's father and a friend named Sharon help make a show car out of his '39 Ford. Local businessmen offer support and the entire town shows up to give him a send off before the car show.

Ricky has built a super coupe, has won the respect and admiration of his parents and of the town. He wins first prize at the Des Moines car show and receives a dozen or so offers from people who either want to buy his car, or have him build a body for their own cars.

As if to say that all this is too much for a kid like Ricky to handle—after all he's only 16— on the way back from Des Moines, while racing Link, he goes into the river at 110 mph killing himself and Sharon. That ending has always bothered me. What kind of statement was Felsen making? I always thought that the point of this type of book was to show a character moving from being irresponsible to being responsible. From owning a junky car to building a sanitary set of wheels. Ricky seemed to follow the rules and he got knocked off.

Perhaps the ending of the book was imposed by the author because he wanted something more dramatic, more exciting, more memorable. Perhaps he found the original ending too full of sweetness and light, and felt that it needed an image of the darkness that was just under the surface during the entire decade.

Perhaps he found the original ending too full of sweetness and light, and felt that it needed an image of the darkness that was just under the surface during the entire decade.

Tom Medley cartoons from June and July 1949 issues of Hot Rod Magazine.

What We Read: Hot Rod Comics

Hot Rod Comics treated the subject in a fairly serious way and the quality of the illustrations was high.

I can remember being terribly impressed with the first issue I saw of *Hot Rod Comics.* It was an early summer day in 1952 and perfect for a ride in a roadster. The problem was that mine was in about a thousand pieces. I'd channeled the body, installed a dropped axle and pulled the valves in anticipation of the Smith and Jones 266 cam I was going to install. The only difficulties I had encountered were little time and no money. I was pondering my sad state of affairs when I walked into the Rexall Drug Store and found that issue of *Hot Rod Comics.*

Of the many comic books about rodding that came out in the 'Fifties and 'Sixties, only one, *Hot Rod Comics,* interested me. Most comics had shallow characters, mediocre plots and, most of all, badly drawn cars. *Hot Rod Comics* treated the subject in a fairly serious way and the quality of the illustrations was high. This was even more astonishing, to my mind, because the books were published on the east coast, not a bastion of hot rodding in the early 'Fifties. But the editors must have had contact with west

Although Hot Rod Comics *was published on the east coast, the editors must've read* Hot Rod Magazine *because the Road Knights' cars look suspiciously like the real So-Cal Speed Shop team. Low '32 with headrest is Clint's rod.*

Hot Rod Comics *debuted November 1951, and six issues were published by Fawcett. Number 6, shown here, put Clint Curtis in a track roadster to do some hill-climbing.*

coast rodders or else they read the California magazines carefully. Or maybe the artist lived in California. Issue five, for example, had cars closely resembling the famous So-Cal racing team. The editorial content was high, the conflicts strong, and the characters fairly well developed. Moreover, the technical information was accurate, although occasionally strained.

But I liked the comics because I closely identified with the characters and their situation. Like myself, the rodders were high-school students. The main character, Clint Curtis, was a young upstanding rodder and a good student. I know I wanted to live my life the way Clint lived his; he seemed to exist in a nearly perfect world. He lived in Mid City, somewhere in the eastern United States, and it was the typical, idyllic small city I'd seen in movies.

The Road Knights

Clint was a born leader, so it's natural that he was the president of his local hot rod club, the Road Knights. He had the required girlfriend, Rusty, who was usually an integral part of the story, as were his two close friends, Pete, and Alexander Mazda Beddison. The girls were frequently used in subordinate roles throughout the stories. In one case, Rusty had her own A-V8 roadster and her girlfriend drove a Siata Spyder. But in the driving contests, the cars were driven by their boyfriends, Clint and Alex.

Clint and his Road Knight buddies seem to be the center of the community, whether it has to do with complaints about speeding or praise for a benefit the club has sponsored. These comic books came out in the early 'Fifties, a time when hot rod

I liked the comics because I closely identified with the characters and their situation.

clubs were being formed all over the country to better the public's image of hot rodding, and the Road Knights are constantly trying to impress upon the community their sense of responsibility. The club is also important at school. The Road Knights are respected by their peers and many of the school's activities revolve around cars. Now that's the kind of world I envisioned when I was 16, a member of a hot rod club, a hot rodder, but I found a very different kind of reaction.

The Beast

We ought to note that the members of the Road Knights are sensible young men and appear to have a fair amount of money. Clint drives a '32 Ford roadster with a '27 T windshield, and it's nice. The car's most distinctive feature is the molded headrest, an east-coast touch, I always thought. His name for the car is "The Beast," and he has no qualms about cutting it up. One story was concerned with hill climbs, and young Clint revamped his rod, severely altering the frame, locating the engine in the rear and streamlining the front sheet metal. This took him two weeks, with help from some of the guys in the club. I ached to be a guy like Clint—I tore my roadster down and it was down all winter.

Always a lesson learned

Each issue of *Hot Rod Comics* could be counted on to have a moral of some type. Whether it was getting a good education or gaining respect, there was always a lesson to be learned. Perhaps a closer look at the plot elements of one story will reveal how complicated and interesting these stories are and how they affect the reader.

A story in issue six, titled "Clint Curtis Drags Hizzoner," describing the Road Knights' efforts to obtain a drag strip, reveals typical plot elements. The story opens with the Road Knights meeting in the front room of the Curtis house. The local judiciary, Judge Temple, arrives to tell Mr. Curtis that the neighbors are up in arms about the boys' driving, and that they want to circulate a petition banning hot rods. The judge seems to be on both sides, and asks Clint to see him the next day. In the office Clint learns that the Road Knights will have to stop driving their rods for two weeks.

The members use this time to rebuild their rods, and to install fenders and mufflers as per the judge's orders (this coincides with the 1952 California fender law). Once again what seems a penalty becomes a benefit. Clint builds his fenders from fiberglass (or *plasticizer*, as it's called here) while another uses aluminum cycle fenders "that turn with the wheels." Once again a benefit is found: "At least our rods will stay clean."

After two weeks the club members are allowed to drive their cars, and the judge offers them a one-mile section of old highway for a drag strip. It's in terrible shape but the Road

Hot Rod Comics always make a distinction between right and wrong.

Knights, with the help of a local businessman, resurface it pulling rollers behind their rods.

The following Saturday morning a group of townspeople are at the site of the new drag strip, albeit begrudgingly. When Judge Temple arrives in his new Packard, he tells the townspeople that he can't ban the hot rods because they're now street-legal. But he promises that all the club's racing will be done on the new drag strip. To officially open the track, the judge challenges Clint to a drag race. The judge has secretly had his Packard straight-eight hopped up; he also knows that the ram tube set-up that Clint has devised will force gas back into the float chambers. As the green flag drops, the roadster quickly pulls ahead, but the engine bogs down and the Packard wins easily. The judge then retires from drag racing, saying "Spare the rod, spoil the rodder."

Moral fiction

Hot Rod Comics are moral fiction. They always made a distinction between right and wrong, and they always tried to teach a lesson. In 1953 a book entitled *The Seduction of the Innocents* said comic books led their readers toward the devil. No such charge could be made against *Hot Rod Comics*.

From April 1949 issue of Hot Rod Magazine.

Hot Rod Smashup
from January 1948 issue of
Hot Rod Magazine

When you're reading in the paper
That a fellow cut a caper
With a hopped-up cut-down Ford of '29
You'd better think about it
And perhaps you ought to doubt it
Or you may mislay the blame along the
  line
Now the caption say it's "hopped-up"
That's because the engine's propped up
To prevent its falling out into the road
There's the line that reads "it's speedy"
That's the truth, bud. Yes indeedy!
It made thirty miles per hour…
  without a load
And when it says the car is cut-down
Then the writers hit a rut down
At the local office of the Star Gazette
For the body's strictly stock
No more cut down than a clock
And I'll lay you odds on that for any
  bet
But the part that brings a gripe
Is where reporters add the tripe
That the "hot rod" driver thought he
  as so bold
When the car was really "junk"
And the driver just a punk
Only seventeen or eighteen summers old
Someday you'll read the story
Of the hot rods in their glory
When they're legal and accepted in their
  place
By then you'll have forgotten
All the items that were rotten (I mean
  written)
By the "hopped up" news reporters
  who've lost face.

Hot Rod King

The idea of straight-line racing is inconceivable.

Comic-book publishers are always looking for new readers, and they're willing to aim specific titles at various special interest groups. In the early 'Fifties hot rodding became a possible subject. The first issue of *Hot Rod Comics* was published November 1951, and a year later another company brought out a competing title, *"Hot Rod" King*. This is a truly rare, even obscure publication and I confess I only recently saw a copy.

The title is taken from the main character whose surname is King. It's hard to pin down who he is or even how old he is—in some stories he seems barely out of high school while in at least one other he seems older and more mature. It's also hard to imagine his occupation or how

he lives, although we are told that this young rodder "has driven everything on wheels." It's hard to guess where he lives or in what part(s) of the country these stories are taking place.

Fast-moving with plenty of action

These may be quibbles to some who insist comic books aim at young readers primarily interested in a fast-moving story with plenty of action. There's plenty of that in the four stories in issue one. In the first King drives an experimental auto for an owner with a "win-at-any-price" attitude, and must choose between winning a race or saving a life. In another, to promote a racetrack, the owner arranges to stage a race using antique cars, and King wins driving a Stanley Steamer. In the third episode, King wins another race against the daughter of a scalawag car owner who resembles Colonel Sanders. In the final story King twice helps capture a desperate criminal. In other words, there's the usual mixture of clichés and sensationalism, placed in the context of rodding activities. Unlike Clint Curtis' life in *Hot Rod Comics*, nothing here borders on the real world.

Writer/artist/editor didn't understand

The artwork by Frank Giacoia is more satisfying than the content, and is fairly sophisticated with realistic characters and interesting visual angles. Many of the cars are well-drawn, including the experimental car King drives in the opening story (it resembles the then-new Buick XP-800) and the antique cars in the second story. The artistic weakness has to do with the hot

Cover of "Hot Rod" King, #1.

rods, which makes it a central weakness. Giacoia had no idea of what a hot rod was! The publisher, Approved Comics, was located in Chicago. Fawcett, the publisher of *Hot Rod Comics* was in New York. Both were far removed from the California rodding scene. The editors and artists on *Hot Rod Comics* apparently did a lot of research. At the very least, they read *Hot Rod Magazine* and borrowed from it. The faulty concept of what a hot rod is extends beyond

some awkward artwork and into content. For example, all the racing takes place on circle tracks, whether it's the "200 mph" experimental cars of one story or the rods that compete together at a "dry lake" in another. It's not just that the writer/artist/editor doesn't understand the rules of dry lake competition, it's that the idea of straight-line racing is inconceivable.

The "Masked Driver" from "Hot Rod" King, #1.

Lasted only one issue

One could argue that since rodding was a new activity most readers wouldn't recognize the errors or distortions. Others might say that the kids who read *"Hot Rod" King* weren't looking for realism. I think even immature readers notice flaws, perhaps on the subconscious level. They're also attracted to flashes of inspiration. That's how one work develops a cult following, while others of the same genre disappear forever. So far as I can tell, and for whatever reasons, *"Hot Rod" King* lasted only one issue.

Ad from "Hot Rod" King, *#1.*

"F.O.B.–Junkyard" and "Baby Face" from "Hot Rod" King, *#1.*

The Good Old Bad Days

The '38 standard was some kind of styling mistake.

I tend to forget I once owned a 1938 Ford tudor, standard model. Perhaps that's because I owned it for only a short time, or because I don't have a single photo of the car. Most likely I'm repressing the memory because it was the *ugliest* car I've ever owned—uglier than the Terraplane or the '36 Buick Special I owned as a teenager, uglier than the '78 Nova winter-beater rustbucket that recently died, or the '79 Checker now sitting in my driveway.

Remember the '38 Ford standard? There aren't many around, thank God; maybe Ford didn't make many or they didn't sell, or they ended up in WW II scrap drives. I hasten to add that I love Fords of the 'Thirties. In the 'Fifties almost no one liked '37 Fords, but I owned a nice '37 coupe that I liked. I even like '38 deluxe/'39 standard models. But

This could have been author's old 1938 Ford Standard tudor 45 years later. If so, it's been improved considerably.

the '38 standard was some kind of styling mistake. The grille was a faceful of wrinkles that went clear back to the cowl. Ford added a couple pieces of stainless trim after seeing what it had created. The rest of the car was probably interchangeable with the '37, but somehow it was less interesting. The best feature was the single taillight—the '39 teardrop light that people forget came out in '38.

I bought this Ford from my friends, Jack and Jerry Burns. They were forever finding cherry machines, which they ran the wheels off. I remember a pristine 1930 Olds roadster they owned, and a gorgeous '46 Ford deluxe sedan, gray with red trim and, a short time later, a 1950 Mercury convertible. They were twins, pooled their funds to buy a car and used it to meet chicks. They were obsessed with meeting women, and they met lots, in part because there were two of them and they could be in two places at once. Although we were the same age they were light years ahead of me socially—they were meeting girls downtown for lunch when I was home in the hammock reading comic books. In addition to owning neat cars and being socially adept, the Burns twins were good-looking; they thought they looked like Peter Lawford or Stewart Granger, and there was a resemblance.

The '38 Ford was not an asset in meeting girls. It was not only uglified at the plant, the Burns brothers had primered it and, with blackwall tires, it was, well, gray. It had a dingy interior, and a ratty set of dual pipes (its second-best feature, after the taillight). I remember seeing it once at the intersection by Dick Wise's house, with Jack or Jerry

at the wheel, and there may have been a girl. What I remember is the sheen of white smoke that rose from under the hood, from under the car.

We bought the '38 for $20. I say we because my friend, Jimmy Graham, and I became partners. Neither of us had $20, but we each had $10. Jimmy may have had a car then, I can't remember. I had my '29 A-V8 roadster, torn apart, and a hundred-dollar '39 Merc convert that needed work. I think Jimmy and I saw the '38 Ford as instant transportation, something we could cruise around in and attract girls. Hey, if the car worked for the Burns brothers it ought to work for us we figured. They had bought a cherry 1934 Lafayette, a car almost as ugly as the '38 Ford, but with better paint and interior, and they always had a couple chicks with them. Why not us?

I'm almost certain we didn't have insurance on the '38—I didn't have any on my other cars!—and I think the license plates had expired. I know we didn't transfer the title. I also know that we parked the car in front of my house because Jimmy's father was a fascist dictator. My mother probably wasn't too happy about having the car out front either, but I don't remember any ultimatums. Not even when on Halloween someone wrote the f--- word on the trunk lid in wax. It permeated the primer and nothing short of sandpaper would remove it.

No love for the '38

Usually I have notions of modifying any car I own, but I had none in this case. We did nothing to the '38, not even an oil change. We just drove it— with diminishing enthusiasm— perhaps because it had not been

helpful in introducing us to girls.

I remember a Sunday afternoon in the fall, the air crisp, the sun bright with promise. Jimmy and I took our .22 rifles and drove out Foster Road in the '38. In those days anything beyond Damascus was the wilderness, back roads and lots of land that no one seemed to own. We plinked at cans for a couple of hours and then headed back. We were on a narrow gravel road and, goofing around, Jimmy began to swing the wheel to the right, then to the left. The steering was loose anyway, and soon the car was careening in one direction, then the other.

Suddenly, at about 40 mph, it went into a long slide. I thought: this is a wreck! Time was frozen; the car seemed to take forever to get to wherever it was headed. Probably a huge Douglas fir, I thought. I looked out the side window and realized I was looking at the road ahead. It probably took only a second, but it seemed to take minutes for the car to turn 180 degrees; then it suddenly and sharply slid off the road, and I heard a roar as my head hit something.

When I looked up the car had stopped, engine off, back on the road. Both doors had flown open; the hood was ajar. We got out, laughing, and surveyed the damage. Everything seemed to be looser—fenders, hood, the entire exhaust system—but nothing was hurt. I began to shut the hood and noticed that the battery had fallen from the firewall. I put it back, checked the cables, we got in and the car started up about as quickly as it ever had. Within a mile we noticed a strange odor. The battery had dumped some of its acid on the manifold heater, and the car was filled with the odor of hot cat pee! It was in the metal, and continued to permeate everything for the next month or two, until we got rid of the car.

Rainy Sunday night

A dominant memory of the '38 has to do with a rainy Sunday night in late fall. We were out driving around—why does it seem in memory to be the car's final outing?—and as usual trying to pick up girls. The night was cold; we wanted to get warm. We wanted to meet a couple of nice girls, talk, drink coffee at Flanagan's, maybe cuddle up later. We drove dark, wet streets almost devoid of traffic, and no pedestrians, for who would be out walking in a cold rain with the hope of a ride from two guys in a jerky car with an obscenity written on the trunk lid?

We cruised Foster, Powell, headed along 82nd. A bus stopped, an old man got off; we could see there were no girls on the bus. The '38 bucked, coughed, as if the plug wires were wet. We drove along an empty Division Street, turned on 122nd and headed toward home, our hopes shattered. All houses were dark; all decent people were asleep at 9:00 p.m. The car's backfire broke the silence, and it began to slow. The dash lights dimmed. Either we had developed a serious short or the battery was going dead. Jimmy revved the engine, trying to generate juice but the lights got progressively dimmer. When the engine developed a ragged chatter he had to kill the lights.

We drove slowly, jerkily, along the shoulder, not talking. Jimmy turned right on Harold without stopping for the sign. We wanted to coax a few more minutes from the battery, a few more feet from the dying car. It sputtered, stalled, then caught; it did this a hundred times, each time lurching ahead a few feet. Eventually it came to rest in front of my house, and died. We sat for a moment, and I became aware of the damp upholstery, my damp clothes, and the chill of the night air warmed only by our steaming breath and the odor of hot cat pee.

The "Tornado" powered by a 296-CID Merc reached 150 mph during test runs at El Mirage. From August 1949 issue of Hot Rod Magazine.

RESTYLING
A 1941 FORD CLUB COUPE

PAT LA NARZ

R. E. PETERSEN

ORIGINALLY, the '41 Ford in the photographs above was like any other production model, but by the clever use of welding torch, power hammer and other sheet metal working tools, the car has evolved into a distinctive custom car. Designed and built by Barris Kustom Shop for Jesse Lopez of Bell, California, the car has been chopped, channeled and sealed from bumper to bumper.

To obtain the overall height of 4 feet 11 inches, 6¼ inches were taken out of the top, a dropped front axle was installed, the body was channeled, and the frame was "kicked up" over the rear axle. The car is sealed from bumper to bumper — the fenders, the headlights, the doors, and the running board strip.

The fenders have been rolled to clear the tires, with the fender skirt being only four inches from the ground. The grille is from a '48 Cadillac. Plastic tail lights are built into the rear bumper guards.

The doors, hood, and deck lid are operated by electric push-buttons, the power source being a 21-plate battery, with cells separated by glass. Interior trim is all chrome, while the seat upholstery is green and white leather to match the dark green organic body paint.

This car is powered by a '41 V-8 three-quarter race engine, with Offenhauser heads and manifold, and a Weber cam.

From September 1949 issue of Motor Trend.

We Never Called Them Kemps

Language is in a state of constant flux. This is especially true of slang or idiomatic expressions.

Recently a group has been formed to celebrate custom cars of the 'Fifties. It's called the *Kustom Kemps*, and while I'm 100% in favor of the group's goal, its name sounds redundant. If, as they claim, *kemp* means a customized car, then why say a custom custom? But I have to admit that I never heard anyone during the 'Fifties call a car *kemp*.

Or a *low-rider*, a term on everyone's lips these days. Those terms are used today to describe cars of the 'Fifties but they weren't used then.

Language is in a state of constant flux. This is especially true of slang or idiomatic expressions, where new words appear and force old words out. That's what keeps the language alive. Perhaps it's time to resurrect the dead, and give currency in the 'Nineties to words that were popular in the 'Fifties. Here are some interesting words associated with period hot rodding that I recall:

A Bone: a modified Model A Ford.

Bathtub: a phaeton or touring car.

Binders: brakes.

Build-up: an engine that has been modified.

Burn Rubber: to spin your tires, to peel out.

C'd: cutting a radius in the frame rails so they will clear the rear axle on a car that has been radically lowered.

Cruise the Gut: driving up and down the main street(s).

Dago: a dropped front end, a dago axle.

Dig Out: to accelerate quickly from a standing start.

Echo Cans: large chrome-plated exhaust extensions.

Fadeaways: fenders that taper back into the body.

Fender Lizard: a car hop.

Four-Barrel: a four-cylinder engine, also four-banger.

Full House: an engine that has been completely modified.

Garbage: non-functional chrome accessories.

Gear Box: a transmission.

Goat: a car that performs badly (pre-GTO).

Goodies: chrome accessories.

Gook Wagon: a car loaded with garbage.

Gow: to accelerate, dig out (or as a noun, a gow job is a car).

Grand Prix Gray: gray primer.

Hop Up: a fast car (also a rod, a set of wheels, a cut-down).

Jimmy: a GMC inline 6-cylinder engine.

Jockey Box: the glove compartment.

Jugs: carburetors (also carbs and pots, as twin pots).

Juicers: hydraulic brakes.

Lead Sled: a somewhat pejorative term for a customized car.

Mill: an engine.

Moulded: body seams filled in (also paneled).

Nerf Bar: a tubular bumper, front or rear.

Nosed and Decked: chrome removed from the hood and trunk, the holes leaded in.

Pink Slip: the title to a car.

Piped: a leather interior with narrow, padded pleats.

Pipes: dual exhaust system.

Prune: to beat, or be beaten by, as in "pruned by a stocker."

Rolled and Pleated: a deluxe interior sewn with padded pleats.

Rink Rat: a person who hung around a roller-skating rink.

Sectioned: a car with a section of metal removed horizontally.

Shade Tree Garage: working on a car in the open. Also Pepper Tree Garage or Mechanic.

Shaved: removing the chrome trim, filling in the holes.

Shoe-stringing: the optical illusion experienced when you lean out the window at high speed; the road seems to weave.

Skid Lid: a crash helmet.

Skins: tires.

Slicks: tires purposely made with a flat, no-tread surface.

Speed Shift: to shift gears rapidly.

Squirrel: a reckless driver.

Stacks: carburetor velocity stacks.

Stepped: dropped frame with a vertical section welded-in.

Stick: a camshaft. Also bumpstick.

Stovebolt: An inline 6-cylinder Chevrolet.

Stroker: a crankshaft whose throw has been extended, increasing the engine displacement.

Sunken Plate: recessing the license plate within the body.

Three-Quarter Race: an engine hopped-up for street use.

Transmixer: a standard transmission, especially one with a gear knocked out.

Z'd: a frame stepped in the front or back or both.

Of course, some words from the past are not synonyms for words used today. In the 'Forties and 'Fifties we called an early model car that had been modified a *hot rod*; in the late 'Sixties it became known as a *street rod*, a term that rapidly gained usage in the early 'Seventies. This new term is appropriate, because it more accurately describes the machine, its purpose, and the nature of the sport. It's also a more respectable term. Hot rod suggests a noisy cut-down, painted racing gray and driven by a greasy squirrel, while street rod suggests a car capable of carrying the whole family for great distances in complete comfort. I guess I'm dated by my language, because I inadvertently continue to call them *hot rods*—which raises some eyebrows when I'm around a bunch of street rodders!

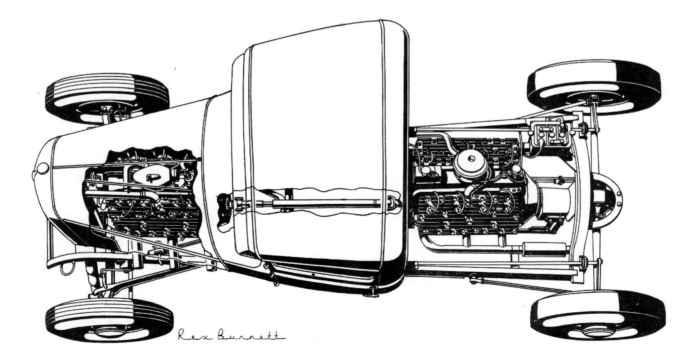

The original Kenz-Leslie twin-engined Model A from Hot Rod Magazine *July 1949.*

Textures of the 'Fifties

**Poetry of parts—
things taken off new
cars and used to
customize older cars.**

I've been interested in the cars of the 'Fifties since they first appeared on the street, but my interest then was largely theoretical.

While I appreciated various makes for their lowness, sleekness and speed, in my mind's eye I was constantly taking each car's best features and rearranging the parts into the *perfect* car. I liked the styling touches found on cars of the 'Fifties. They were bits of sculpture imbedded in the larger work. It was the last decade of automotive design when elements of a car could be removed and placed with relative ease on another make. It was *poetry of parts*—things taken off new cars and used to customize older cars.

Grilles

I've always loved 1949-51 Mercurys, but the cleanly designed grille cavity invited substitutes. A straight bar

My favorite grille was the 1949-53 Cadillac, which grew more massive each year, yet retained a classical simplicity.

complete with dual pods from a '54 Olds, or a '54-55 DeSoto bar with its delicate teeth and slim parking lights would hover beautifully in that space. Ditto for the 1951 Kaiser bar or the more massive 1951 Plymouth bar. Conversely, the Mercury grille cavity could be adapted, complete with grille, to other makes, and it looked right at home in cars as different as the 1949 Ford, 1951 Plymouth and the 1952 Studebaker.

My favorite grille was the 1948-53 Cadillac, which grew more massive each year, yet retained a classical simplicity. Also attractive was the 1954 Pontiac grille, which was easily adapted to the 1951 Ford opening. The free-standing 1953 DeSoto upright teeth looked good in a Mercury cavity, and the 1955 Plymouth grille looked good on 1949-54 Fords.

Even trucks had something to offer: the 1951 Ford pickup grille, chrome-plated, fit a Merc cavity, and a 1955 Chevrolet pickup grille looked nice in a 1942-52 Chevy car.

Taillights

Taillights were cleanly styled, and were easily transposed from one car to another. 1949-52 Pontiac taillights were favorite replacements on pre-war cars. 1949-50 Mercury lights fit the contour of earlier fenders and could be mounted in pairs, and 1950 Dodge taillights were made for '40 Ford fenders.

I disliked 1949-51 Ford taillights, and felt that replacing them with lights from a 1950 Chrysler or even a 1950 Plymouth was an improvement; these were mounted low on the fender after the stock light's wind-splitter had been flattened.

I loved, and still do, '50

Lincoln taillights, with their peace sign tri-part divider and tapered chrome rim; I mounted a pair on my 1947 Ford coupe in 1955, the first such installation I'd seen, and they fit the contour of the Ford fender perfectly.

1949 Buick lights, '52 Studebaker lights (which could be mounted vertically or horizontally), and '55 Chrysler Windsor lights were attractive. Cadillac taillights from 1948-53 were elegant, as were the entire rear fenders, with their sweeping French curve. Perhaps my favorite taillights of the decade were those on 1953-55 Lincolns or those on 1953-56 Packards. Both were heavy yet simple, and nicely hooded by the surrounding sheet metal.

Parts swapping for looks

Useful hardware was everywhere. The fluted bumper on the 1949 Plymouth recalled the rare 1937 DeSoto bumper, and was not too large for use on pre-war cars. The '49 Chevy offered a neat license plate guard that cost almost nothing new. The Kaiser guard was wider and had bullets at each end that offered themselves as tailpipe outlets.

The small scoops over the headlights on 1954 Pontiacs and the hood scoop on the 1954 Kaiser were easily adapted to other makes. Hooded headlights, as found on 1955 Chevrolets and Pontiacs, were grafted to sundry fenders. '53 Buick headlight rims were attractive. Although I have never seen a pair mounted on another make of car, I liked the massive 1950 Lincoln headlight with its tunneled, chromed bezel.

1950 Chevrolet Pickup.

1950 Buick Eight.

Buick portholes made neat exhaust outlets when mounted at the bottom edge of the fender.

Stars from the decklid of a 1950 Pontiac could be bolted elsewhere, as could the "teeth" from the rear fender of a 1954 Mercury. Buick portholes, especially the tear-drop shape portholes, made neat exhaust outlets when mounted at the bottom edge of the fender.

Today, when grilles are made of plastic and sheet metal is only slightly tougher, I enjoy going to swap meets and hefting the weight of an old car part. A taillight, say, with real pot metal and a real glass lens and a Made in America bulb. I don't anticipate owning a 1953-55 Lincoln or a 1954-57 Packard, but I'd love to have a pair of taillights from either of those cars. I'd mount them on my desk, as one would a piece of sculpture by Brancusi.

Ford pickup grilles were often used in Mercurys. This is a '52.

General Motors studio styling sketches from R. H. Gurr's Automobile Design; The Complete Styling Book *published by Post Publications, 1955.*

The Gook Wagon

For the owner who subscribed to the add-on school, accessories became an addiction.

When we think of a 'Fifties custom we think of an austere machine—nosed and decked, its panels void of trim. We rarely think of its counterpart, the *gook wagon*, where chrome trim and mechanical gizmos were everywhere. The former is an example of the take-it-off school of design, while the latter is an example of the add-it-on school. This is something no one talks about: the anti-custom, or another view of customizing—the add-on school.

The gook wagon was common in the late 'Forties and early 'Fifties. Because car production was curtailed during World War II, there was a shortage of cars until around 1953. New cars were expensive and old cars— well, they were available, but they were old! They had a body

① TWIN ANTENNAS WITH FOX TAILS ② VENETIAN BLIND IN REAR WINDOW ③ DUAL MIRRORS
④ DUAL SPOTLIGHTS ⑤ LEOPARD SKIN COVER ⑥ SQUIRREL KNOB ⑦ GILT INITIALS ⑧ MUDFLAPS
⑨ '41 BUICK CHROME ⑩ CURB FEELERS ⑪ HOOD ORNAMENT ⑫ ILLUMINATED FENDER MARKERS
⑬ DUAL CHROME TRUMPETS ⑭ HEADLIGHT EYEBROW ⑮ CHROME DEFLECTOR ⑯ PORTHOLES

It's difficult to find a photo of a "gook wagon," and when I needed one several years ago I made this drawing; I had in mind an old Ford coupe I'd seen many years earlier (it was a '35, not a '36). I tried to include accessories I'd seen, and sometimes admired until I learned better, such as fox tails, dual antennae, portholes, etc. The skirts and '41 Buick trim I still like!

A partial view of this '39 Ford deluxe sedan, shot only a few years ago, gives an idea of the owner's intentions: aftermarket chrome trim along lower fender edge, over-ride bar and extra guards on bumper, backup light, clearance light high on fender, extra trim strips, star, 1948 Ford trim strip on trunk, etc.

Rare 1932 Ford cabriolet with extra lights, non-functional intake and exhaust stacks, horse head hood ornament, horseshoes above license plate, a large driving light that appears to turn with the front wheels, etc.

style that seemed more than a decade old. In an age of rockets and fins, it was embarrassing to drive a car with pre-pontoon fenders! An easy way to update, and at the same time individualize, that old car was to go down to Bud's Auto Supply and buy an armful of bolt-on accessories.

For the owner who subscribed to the add-on school, accessories became an addiction. Probably most gook wagons were the outgrowth of a simple purchase, something like a squirrel knob and matching gearshift knob. A squirrel knob—or steering-wheel spinner, the salesman's term—clamped on the steering wheel rim and allowed the driver to get a good purchase by wrapping his fist around it; in this way he could cut a doughnut and leave his left arm crooked over the window molding.

"Moderne"

They came in a variety of shapes and colors, and were examples of the miracle of modern plastic. One line had the car's emblem mounted in the top;

another line had colorful rainbow designs; another had hand-carved roses floating in clear Lucite. There was the "Moderne" knob, with "concentric alternate circles of white and red, green, blue, or black for third dimensional effect." Then there was the "Sweetheart wheel spinner" which had one of "six lovely girls fetchingly posed and reproduced in natural colors." An added ploy was that the "Lucite lenses enhance lifelike pictures." The lens also magnified the photo of the girl who was, of course, nude.

From that start the sky was the limit. To continue with the interior the owner could quickly install a suction-cup thermometer, a Hull automobile compass and altimeter. He could get a steering-wheel cover in mohair, quilted plastic, tufted plastic or in a jungle pattern. If he chose the latter he could get leopard or zebra seat covers, which gave "your car that interesting, breathtaking luxury look." In those days, when dashboards were deeper, a favorite accessory was the car tray; this sat on top of the dash and was held there by magnets. You could get the Hollywood Kar-Tray as a set of two, for the left and the right; they were "good for eating, drinking, smoking," meaning that they held food, drinks and cigarettes. In the back window you could put a Noblo venetian blind—"one model fits all rear car windows."

Gadgets galore!

It was possible to cover every part of the car's exterior with a gadget of some sort, functional or nonfunctional. A Calvisor sun visor, "with iridescent hammertone baked-enamel finish," could be mounted over

the windshield to cut the sun's glare, or "Glare Shield," a transparent press-on green plastic, could be put on the inside of the windshield. If the elements posed a real problem, Kromvents could be installed; these were chrome-plated pieces of metal that fit like small awnings over the side windows on two- and four-door sedans. "The outstanding auto window ventilators…lets air in, keeps rain out." There were colorful plastic wind and rain deflectors that clipped to the vent windows. A bug deflector, in a matching color of plastic, attached to the hood ornament and deflected bugs over the roof of the car. The favorite style was the plow design, but there was a flat type with a chrome inlaid cap, and another design with a propeller that spun as the car moved.

Chrome

Chrome gravel guards protected the rear fenders, replacing the factory rubber guards, and for the front fenders

Continued on page 168

It was possible to adorn every part of the car's exterior with a gadget of some sort, functional or nonfunctional.

Survivor

Pete Bambao's '35 Ford 3-window was his daily driver through the 'Fifties and first half of the 'Sixties. I saw the car several times around 1953, always with the hood removed; it appears that the cowl-mounted horns make use of hood impossible. I count 5 horns, 5 front bumper guards and 2 hood ornaments! Merc flathead had heads, manifold, lots of chrome goodies.

Rear view is more sedate; note twin fox tails and checkered flags. Rare wheel covers over spoked area of '35 Ford wheels. 1956 Oregon license plate with '64 tags suggests car wasn't driven in the 30 years from '64 to '94, when Joe bought it.

About three years ago I got a call from Joe Ditschinger, a rodder in Seattle, asking whether I remembered seeing a 1935 Ford 3-window coupe around Portland back in the 'Fifties. I probably sighed—there were hundreds of '35 Ford coupes back then—but before he said one word to describe the car my mind focused on a particular coupe, green, loaded with doo-dads. I really don't know why I thought of that car, it wasn't remarkable, just different, and actually I couldn't remember whether it was a 3- or a 5-window. Ten years earlier I'd written an essay about "gook wagons" and, unable to find a photograph of one, I drew a picture of a '36 Ford 3-window adorned with accessories, but I'd had that '35 in mind.

"I'm thinking of one," I said, "kind of fixed-up, but there were so many…"

"Did it have lots of stuff on it?" he asked, and when I said yes, he said, "I've got it. It's still got all that stuff—horns, lights, about ten guards on each bumper."

I must've been on a psychic wavelength. I was amazed that, one, I would've thought of that particular car, and, two, that it still existed. The car and the whole experience were just too strange. Joe wanted to know the car's history, so I called a couple old timers in Gresham, where I'd seen the car in the 'Fifties. They vaguely remembered it, and said it'd been owned by a Filipino, who always wore a broad-brimmed hat and was a local character. They couldn't recall his name, but Joe pursued the quest and learned the owner, Pete Bambao, was born in the Philippines in 1898, which would've made him an exceptionally old hot rodder in the 'Fifties. He apparently had worked in a restaurant near the Burnside Bridge, and the coupe had been his daily driver. Apparently he'd quit driving the car in 1964, the last tag on the 1956 Oregon plate. When he died, years later, the car was taken to his sister's house in Seattle, where it was kept in the garage. When she died, Joe was able to buy it.

I told Joe that he should leave the car just the way he got it, an original gook wagon from the 'Fifties, but when I saw the photos he sent I had second thoughts. It's got a beautiful flathead engine, with all the speed goodies and lots of chrome, but beyond that Pete had strange ideas. The car is green, with red-and-blue rolled-and-pleated Naugahyde interior, and if that color combination doesn't set your teeth on edge there are those cowl-mounted horns, fox tail, the chrome trim on both edges of the doors, and a plethora of bumper guards.

Gook Wagon Continued

there were "Beautiflow shields." A large Cello guard could be mounted to the front and rear bumpers, for show as well as for protection. In the spaces that were left you could mount a "Ball Tenna" six-in-one aerial, jewel license fasteners ("modernistic style"), a "Country Gentleman" luggage carrier on the roof, and "Auto-Crest" frames on the door, showing the car's crest and your initials. Chrome-plated shields or eyebrows fit over the top half of the headlights (an illegal addition, a cop told me way back when). On the right side of the car behind the front and rear wheel openings were gadgets called *curb feelers;* these looked like Martian antennae and pinged against the curb so you wouldn't mar your lovely wide white sidewalls. The "Warn-O-Curb" and "Curb-D-Tektor" had a thin wire with a knob on the end but the "Curb-A-Line" had a coil spring that extended to curb height.

The owner of a gook wagon had a central thought—to get as much stuff as he could on a car—but he also hoped that his vehicle would look uniquely individual by his additions. If he yearned for the luxury appearance of the classic cars of the 'Thirties, he might mount large chrome-plated horns on the fenders or hood of his car. For example, the "Grover Organtone Air Horn," mounted singly or in pairs, were considered "the ultimate in luxurious equipment...spun-brass trombone type, as scientifically developed by Grover." If he yearned for novelty, he might choose a cattle-calling horn which "bellows like a bull on the road" or he might choose a Wolf Whistle which operated off the engine vacuum and gave a piercing whistle. Or, given the nature of a gook-wagon owner, he'd probably choose all three systems! And, of course, a Bermuda Bell!

Auto-Shocko

For the practical joker there was the "Auto-Shocko" device. "Have some REAL FUN with your car. With Auto-Shocko you can give anyone who touches the outside surface of your car a harmless but very effective shock."

To ease the conscience of the gook-wagon owner who felt he was being frivolous, auto-accessory houses offered the "Life Saver Automatic Warning Signal—The World's Most Advanced Warning Signal to Help Prevent Collisions!" This 8-inch device shaped like a traffic light was placed in your rear window (unless you had a venetian blind there!). This light "thinks for itself" the ads said. It had three bulbs: press the accelerator and the green light went on; release the accelerator and the yellow light went on; apply the brakes and the red light went on. The idea was that drivers behind you would be watching the mini-traffic signal and would know what you were doing. A variation on that idea was the winking cat whose eyes lit up.

Lights and Portholes

There were lights of all kinds: fog lights, dual spotlights, tear-shaped clearance lights, and the Hollywood license-plate light. One could also buy running lights mounted atop a rod that clipped to the front fenders; this was a device similar to an option offered by Pontiac.

Gook-wagon accessories evolved with the times, as if there was an army of designers anticipating what would be needed: by the early 'Fifties there were continental kits and "falsies" kits, giant dice and shrunken heads to hang from rear view mirrors, checkered racing flags to bolt on fenders and deck lids. By 1954 you could buy imitation Buick portholes to bolt to any flat surface—some people put half a dozen of these across the hood of their 'Forties car. Or you could get *real* Buick portholes at a dealer, and mount colored lights within the chrome opening. Cadillacs were popular, and you could buy imitation "Caddy touch" chrome headlight rims for other cars. There were Cadillac "El Dorado type" chrome hood ornaments, and there were painted or chrome fins that bolted on the rear fenders of GM cars—as well as 1953-54 Fords, whose fender line did not invite fins!—for that "El Dorado look."

Statements of Individuality

By the late 'Fifties the interest in gook wagons began to wane, but by then the manufacturers had taken up the cause and the new cars were swathed in chrome trim, had elaborate fins, and were loaded with accessories. Until then, gook wagons, although laughed at by many people, were found in abundance. They were statements attesting to the owner's individuality. A *lead sled* was a custom because all trace of the factory's imprint had been removed or modified. A *gook wagon* was a custom because the factory's imprint was overwhelmed with doo-dads, and the car certainly did not look like anything that had come from Detroit!

The 1953 Oakland Roadster Show

In those days, my life centered around hot rodding.

I seem to remember most vividly the quality of the light. The clear air of the Cascades, sun reflecting from the snow beside the road and the gloriously pink Merc as we cruised southward. And in Oakland the air was brilliant, slightly chilled, yet that entire week in early February was T-shirt weather. We left the grayness of Portland and entered the golden state where everything shimmered with the clarity of a mirage. In those days my life revolved around hot rodding, and California was the *center* of hot rodding. It was Mecca, a place where fenderless roadsters motored down wide streets lined with palm trees and kids hovered over chromed engines at every gas station. It was the place where all the cars featured in *Hot Rod Magazine* came from. It's hard to separate illusion from

Behind someone's '29 A-V8 are, from left to right: Al Rogers, Al Drake, Norm Cahill, wearing their Road Angels jackets.

169

Oakland was primarily a roadster show. This is Paul Dallmeir's '25 T-V8, which was entered in the competition class. Kurtis nose, hood and bellypan were hand-formed from aluminum. Maroon paint, cream-eggshell leather interior, louvered deck lid and much chrome. 305-CID Merc flathead-propelled 1,800-pound car. The question is: How come nobody builds cars like this now?

reality, romance from fact, but I'm sure California was a very different place 45 years ago: the sky was clear, unpolluted; traffic was not a problem; crime seemed insignificant; everything seemed possible. Was it California, or was it youth?

This trip, my first to California without my parents, began when Earl Beard decided to put his custom Merc in the Oakland Roadster Show. Earl and his younger brother Joe had moved to Portland from Los Angeles a year earlier, and they immediately established themselves as top-notch lead-slingers. I assumed that because they were from L.A. they knew customizing tricks unheard of in Portland, and perhaps they did. They Frenched lights, installed push-button doors, welded Mercury grille shells into all kinds of cars. They chopped and sectioned bodies and did beautiful paint jobs. From their shop came a

bevy of mild customs and a number of extensively modified cars, including a '32 Ford tudor that would later become the famous "Orange Crate." The Beard Brothers joined the Road Angels, a club I belonged to, and because their shop was only a short mile from home I was always hanging around, even if I had to walk there. The shop seemed to be open 24 hours a day—in the middle of the night someone would be banging away

with a body hammer or slapping lead. When another Road Angel, Chuck Blanchard, moved his upholstery shop from far-away Beaverton to the same building that the Beard brothers occupied, I knew that this was the center of customizing on the West Coast—north of 'Frisco, anyway.

Nosed, decked, lowered

In December, 1952 Earl finished a nice 1950 Chev Bel Air; it was a mild custom owned

Beard brothers' '49 Merc convertible with chopped, padded top, '51 Ford truck grille, Frenched headlights, '51 Merc rear fenders, etc. Took second in tough custom convertible class.

In the program this is Norman Damico's car, but it's clearly the Blackie Gejeian car. '27 T bucket was mounted on '34 Ford chassis, with everything but the body and frame rails chrome-plated. T body was deeply channeled, painted black with white-leather interior. 296-CID Merc had four carbs, turned 102 mph in the quarter. Work on car was begun in 1945, and it was damaged by fire around 1956. I believe Blackie still has the car.

by Ron Gotcher, a high-school student with bucks. It had Frenched headlights, leaded rear fender seams, electric doors, '50 Pontiac taillights, was nosed and decked and it was lowered. The paint was a deep maroon with a gray top. When Gotcher said he wanted to enter the car in the Oakland show Earl hit the ceiling. Not because he wasn't proud of his bodywork, he was, but if Gotcher was going to enter a mild custom in this most famous of shows then why shouldn't Earl enter his '49 Merc? The Merc was super-low, with cut springs, reversed spindles, a C'd frame and chopped top. It looked like a show winner—except it was horribly unfinished! It had no top, little interior, no grille or chrome. And it was painted 20 shades of colored primer, as if someone had cleaned the gun on the car.

True temperamental artist

But Earl was adamant and began to work like a man pos-

sessed. I should mention that he was a true temperamental artist. He was tall, wiry, dark and brooding, while his brother Joe was heavier, rounder, more easy-going—a stabilizing influence. If you believe in behavioral types, Earl was clearly Type A while Joe

I was living the life I'd imagined from magazines. There was a mystique about California, and it was all coming true.

Hank Vincent's 1932 Ford 5-window was built for street but had won nine drag trophies (note trophies in window shelf). It had a full-race 1941 Ford engine. The beautiful stock body was painted orange. The next year Hank made it into a drag car and cut holes in every body panel to lighten it! It looked like Swiss cheese—and we wonder where these cars went!

Clyde Kitchens and Mel Grisel, from Hayward, California, entered this bobbed job. It had a '27 T body, painted orange as I recall, mounted on 1931 Ford frame, with 6-inch step and shortened 6 inches. Engine was 239-CID Merc flathead. Bent Eights club.

was Type B. Both had long black hair swept back to a duck's ass, and they went around winter and summer with the top three buttons on their shirts undone. They differed in that Earl was a wild man, either ecstatic or maniacally depressed about his work. A rippled panel or the inferior Korean War chrome on a reworked bumper was enough to send him into a blind frenzy. He'd swear, scream, throw a ball-peen hammer across the shop—he was a true artist!

Now he got busy on the Merc, straightening panels, installing electric doors, replacing the dual exhausts and rebuilding a stock flathead engine. He reworked and chrome-plated a 1951 Ford truck grille to fit the Merc's cavity and it looked distinctive. Then he performed a minor miracle on the rear end. He grafted on a pair of '51 Merc fenders, which made the car five

Competition roadster owned by Richard Dederian of Berkeley, Calif. (Cal-Neva Roadster Association). It had a 260-CID Merc flathead, tube frame, center steering, full belly pan. Notable feature was nose from '39 Chrysler. Paint was white with purple flames. It sold at show for $75, less engine!

inches longer, Frenched-in 1952 Lincoln taillights and sectioned the lower part of the trunk lid so it was half its original size.

No sleep!

Earl worked around the clock, ignoring customers who wondered when their disassembled cars would be put back together again. He leaded seams and smoothed ripples and block-sanded until his hand was bloody and cursed and threw tools. And then, at perhaps 2 a.m., he'd come out of his funk and, in a better mood, he and Joe would jump in the Merc and drive two blocks to Flanagan's drive-in, laughing, pounding on the car door, honking for service because they'd left the car's headlights back in the shop.

27 coats of pink lacquer

Eventually the car got done. Earl painted it Caribbean Pink—27 coats topped with six coats of clear lacquer. It was gorgeous—like a big, brightly polished

Lewie Thompson's competition coupe from Hughson, California, used '32 Ford 5-window body with quarter windows filled in. Body was channeled 8 inches, chopped 3 inches, painted Gypsy green. 241-CID Merc engine used water-transfer tubes instead of radiator for drags.

fingernail! Then he had Chuck Blanchard build a chopped, padded top that omitted the quarter windows, and upholster the interior and headliner in red-and-white thinly pleated Naugahyde. There were still problems—he needed a set of tires, and he fumed over the

All during that drive, inspired by what I'd seen, I thought of what I would do to my '39 Merc during the coming year.

Frank Rose's '27 T-V8, from Oakland, Calif. This super-neat rod was the kind we knew we'd see in California. It had a tube frame, modified flathead engine moved back in chassis; Jack Hageman formed the fenders, belly-pan and hood. Painted black, with white pin-striping, two-tone blue-Naugahyde interior. Featured in Hot Rod Magazine, *June 1953.*

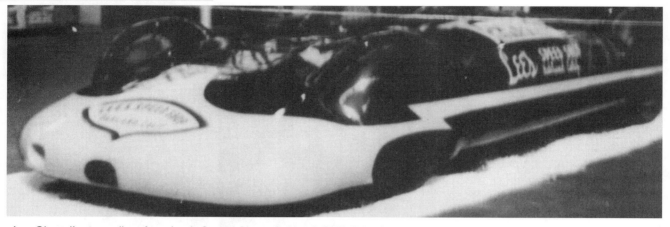

Lee Chapel's streamliner from Lee's Speed Shop, Oakland, Calif. Tube frame, torsion-bar suspension, hand-formed aluminum body. 296-CID Merc engine ran fuel injection, magneto, Tornado OHV conversion designed by Chapel. Turned 224.144 mph at 1952 Bonneville meet for Class C record.

possibility of the judges faulting him for having a stock engine—but essentially the car was ready for Oakland.

At some point the question was asked: who would like to go along? Jeez, I'd wanted to go to the Oakland show for three years! I'd been making plans to drive down with my friend Jimmy Graham, the only guy I knew who owned a car that might make it, but our plans were fantasy. I told Earl that I wanted to go. He probably looked at me, saw a skinny, 17-year-old high-school senior, absolutely broke, and decided that I might be able to change a tire on that ground-hugging Merc. Why else would he want me along?

Junk sold for travel $$

I probably didn't even contribute gas money. Two days before we left I got several old batteries and three (now valuable!) radiators from the garage, loaded them in my not-too-sharp '39 Mercury convertible and sold them to a junk dealer on Harbor Drive. I packed a bag, grabbed my old Ansco camera and with less than $20 in my pocket I skipped school for a week to go to California!

Earl drove the Merc and his chief employee, Ray, rode. Because of the high floor the backseat was almost useless for passengers and if the car had carried any extra weight the rear bumper would have been kissing the asphalt. I rode in the Chev along with Gotcher and Ron Love, a fellow Road Angel who

Then we drove through easy traffic to the Exposition Building. The weather was perfect and the cars seemed to glow with excitement.

I loved this car, a 1932 Ford roadster, channeled but full-fendered. I believe it came from Hawaii, but was owned by William Montero of San Jose, Calif. It had a 274-CID Merc engine, was painted Fairfax blue and had blue-and-white pleated Naugahyde interior.

This was a cool street coupe and although it was later featured in Hot Rod Magazine I felt it didn't get the attention it deserved. It was built and owned by Dick Marchant, a young guy who came to the show with wife and kids. 1931 Model A coupe was chopped 5-1/2 inches, frame stepped 3-1/2 inches, had '32 grille and bumpers. Paint was Sarasota green, which was white with a hint of green; interior was rolled-and-pleated cream-and-green Naugahyde. Full Merc engine ran four carbs, as I recall. It was a very clean coupe that I thought would make a swell daily driver.

Sharp '29 roadster on '32 frame, '32 grille, full Merc engine and black-lacquer paint. Unusual windshield built to fit within stock windshield posts suggests, to me, that it could originally have been built in mid-to-late 'Forties.

This was perhaps my favorite car of show. Ralph Jilek's '40 Ford convertible came from North Hollywood, and body modifications by famous Valley Custom shop. Body sectioned 4 inches, top chopped 3 inches, frame stepped, dropped axle. Custom Stewart-Warner dash, '41 Studebaker taillights. Black paint, with rolled-and-pleated blue-and-white interior. Seeing that it was being neglected, I began dusting it every day, which is one reason I love this car.

was also skipping school (and who is still deeply into cars). We left Portland early, and for reasons I never understood we drove along the crest of the Cascades rather than following old 99 down the valley. By 10 o'clock we stopped at Government Camp on the side of Mt. Hood and I regret that I did not take a photo of that moment: the air was clear, the sun was brilliant, the snow at the edges of the road was spotlessly white and the cars were gorgeous. Everything was perfect.

Klamath Falls Break

I don't remember any problems on the road—no tire troubles and the weather was fine. We stopped in Klamath Falls to have holes drilled in the Merc's windshield posts for the dual spots. In those days Klamath Falls consisted of a dozen buildings and ten were cat houses—or so we were told. A couple chicks cruised past the body shop several times, honking, and I seem to recall that Earl disappeared for a time. Or perhaps I'm imagining that. At any rate he became less certain that the Merc would be wrecked en route.

We did make it. We drove through Northern California, missing any winter storms and

To a kid from Portland, this street roadster was pure California. '25 T body had been channeled over stepped frame, had suicide front end; it was low! Full-race 296-CID Merc engine had Evans four-carb intake manifold, chrome outside headers. Paint was Monterey blue, with black-and-white interior.

There was so much neat stuff in parking lot, but this '32 Ford 3-window might be typical. I took photo of it after getting to know the young guys who drove it up from Los Angeles. Primered coupe had very peaked shell, lots of louvers (chromed or buffed aluminum), dropped headlight bar, Knuckle Busters club plaque. Just a neat driver.

arrived in Oakland in the middle of the night. Now I understood why I'd been allowed to go along. The others got a hotel room but Earl made me sleep in the Merc, just in case anyone messed with it. Until then I had never realized how cold Naugahyde could be or how uncomfortable narrow pleats could be. Next morning after breakfast we washed the cars, and Earl rubbed out the road chips with a fine-grit paper dipped in gasoline. Then we drove to a nearby paint shop—Tommy the Greek's. A striper, he was as famous in northern California as Von Dutch was in southern California. He was putting the finishing touches on a tall '21 T roadster with a full-race Model A engine. Oh lordy, with that sun dancing across a blue February sky and the Greek laying a stripe across the deck of the red T, I knew I was in heaven!

Then we drove through easy traffic to the Exposition Building. The weather was perfect and the cars seemed to glow with excitement. We were surprised at the number of really old cars being driven and found out later that this was due primarily to California's insurance and licensing laws, which favored older vehicles. We were also amazed at the number of cars of all types with 1940 Oldsmobile "spade" bumpers. And we were surprised at the paucity of hot rods—I had expected to see them everywhere—and were later told that since legalized drag racing had become popular most street rods had been converted into quarter-mile hustlers. A whole generation of rods were now driven only on Sundays at the drag strip! Even so, there were enough rods and customs on the street to keep us on our toes.

Neat machines

There was no shortage of neat machines at the show site. There was "Miss Elegance," Joe Bailon's radical '41 Chevy I'd seen the year before at a show in Portland. There were cars I'd seen in magazines, such as Lee Chapel's Bonneville streamliner, and cars I'd later see in magazines, such as Frank Rose's '27 T V-8 roadster and Dick Marchant's chopped '31 Ford coupe. In the center of the exhibit hall was Dick William's '27 T V-8, a flawless car that won the title of America's Most Beautiful Roadster and the 9-foot-tall trophy.

Flophouse room for five

We got a room for the five of us in an old hotel in Oakland. It was a flophouse—Ron Love and I looked through the keyhole of the adjoining room and saw at least 20 men sleeping there—but it was walking distance from the show and we had no transportation now. Every morning I woke in that strange room, ate breakfast in the Chinese restaurant downstairs—three big pancakes and a glass of milk for 26¢—and walked to the show. Most nights I ate a Chinese dinner in the same restaurant for 60¢. During the day I studied the cars at the show, or went into the parking lot where I found everything from street rods to a super '37 Cord convert with a flathead Merc adapted to the front-wheel drive.

Or I walked. One day I made a pilgrimage to Lee's Speed Shop. It was a dinky place and I don't recall that I talked with, or even saw, Lee Chapel, but I was in heaven. I met a rodder who'd driven his '41 Ford tudor from Salt Lake City and we threw the bull for a couple of hours.

California mystique

I was living the life I'd imagined from magazines. There was a mystique about California, and it was all coming true. For example, we somehow found a place that sold 10¢ hamburgers! Sure, they were a lot smaller than the ones we paid four bits for in Oregon, but they tasted great to us as we sat in the warming sun and watched the terrific traffic. As if proof that the myth that drove us southward was true, someone mentioned that in San Diego you could get hamburgers for a nickel!

I got to know a number of rodders—members of the Bent Eights—and we got invited to a couple parties within walking distance. The neighborhood was affluent and there were girls— California girls, tanned, dark-haired, laughing. At that moment I formed the impression that California girls were so much more mature than Oregon girls— not that I'd had much experience with them in either state!

A Zen moment

Often I sat in the sun and occasionally experienced a Zen moment: I felt a sense of pleasure that was exciting and yet peaceful and I appreciated being here, *being alive*. My view of life was that it should be one long car show, where the weather and the cars are always perfect!

Only one note of dissent broke this sense of constant pleasure. For some reason Earl couldn't register the car in his name—some trouble he'd had when he had lived in California, behind in alimony payments or he'd killed a man with a ball-peen hammer or something—and so he had to register it in another's name. That bugged him, and he was cautious about being seen around the car for the same reason. He was evasive and when I saw him he was increasingly unpleasant. Then one day he walked furtively past the car, decided that the driver's door was badly rippled and he ordered me to sit beside the door, blocking it from view. A neat strategy, which I carried out for several hours, but I was young and antsy and eventually wandered away to look at another car.

All night on the street

That evening at dinner he chewed me out. I don't recall what I said, but I know that I pouted and stayed on the street all night. It was exciting! Portland's theaters closed around midnight, but a number in Oakland were open 24 hours, and I spent most of my time in two of them. How benign those days seem now! Today Oakland is headquarters of the Black Panther Party and a trendsetter for bizarre murders. In those days it was somewhat shoddy downtown, but festive, with neon that blazed all night. There was nothing sinister about anyone I met and the nearest thing I saw to conflict was in the cafe where I was drinking coffee to stay awake around five a.m. A drunk asked a biker, "Who's Hardly Davis?" in regard to the name, Harley-Davidson, on his sweater and the biker, a clean-cut guy, grinned and said, "He's your brother."

We left Oakland late Sunday night and made it back to Portland without mishap. All during that drive, inspired by what I'd seen, I thought of what I would do to my '39 Merc during the coming year with the hope that I could enter it in the Oakland show in 1954. Well, that never happened, but there is a nice coda to the trip; *Hot Rod Magazine* ran a feature story on Frank Rose's roadster in the June 1953 issue and there on page 38, wearing our Road Angel jackets, are Ron Love and me, frozen forever in time like the memory of that journey.

The program for the 1953 Oakland Roadster Show.

The Cherry

I saw myself behind the wheel of this nifty little coupe, touring the drive-ins and cruising the main streets picking up girls.

Throughout the 'Fifties there was an abundance of cars dating from the two previous decades. A hot rodder could find just about anything he might want simply by keeping an eye on traffic—for a high percentage of 20-year-old cars were still being driven—or by checking out driveways and backyards. He had to search for an Auburn or a Cord, but just about anything else—from an Austin to a Zephyr—was available, and the more popular makes were everywhere.

But there were distinctions to be made, especially between the usual old car and the exceptional. Most old cars then were like old cars today: dents, worn upholstery, faded paint. But people then drove their cars less often and not as far; out-of-town travel, before the advent of the interstate freeway system, was more comfortably done by train or bus. In the mid-'Fifties I had a

Coupe was lowered a bit, sat at nice angle. The windshield was cranked out on this hot July 1953 day. Car had antenna but no radio!

1947 Ford that I drove every day for two and a half years. I put about ten miles a day on the car, or 70 miles a week, for a total of only 4,000 miles a year!

There were people who put even fewer miles than that on their old cars, as if they were saving them, like money in the bank. A car did represent an investment, and, if I can generalize, it seems to me that many people took awfully good care of their cars. They were finicky about such things as rotating tires every 5,000 miles and adding distilled water to the battery; they washed and waxed and lubed and did oil changes like clockwork. So it was possible to find an old car with a like-new interior and a super-straight body. The terms "one owner" and "original paint" had meaning; the latter suggested that the car had never been in an accident.

Cherry

A car like that was *cherry* (i.e., a virgin), and very desirable. There were hundreds of, say, 1936 Ford sedans, but then you'd see one with shiny original black paint, rubbed until the red primer showed on the fender crowns. Beneath that paint the metal was straight as an arrow; the doors closed with a solid thud and the car rode better than a new model, with nary a rattle.

My friend Gary loved '40 Ford coupes, and he used to find pristine examples with great regularity. He'd put on a set of wide whitewalls and dual exhausts, and drive the car until he found another. Once he deviated and bought a '40 coupe of a different sort—a LaSalle, a big black machine with a hood six feet long and a trunk almost that length, and a finish as smooth as

a baby's posterior. He gave it the same treatment, plus lowering blocks and a deck job; it was an unusual and elegant mild custom—and it was cherry!

An exceptional '37

I don't want to romanticize the good old days, and I must admit that many of the very-used cars I owned were dogs. One, however, was, if not cherry, at least exceptional.

It was a 1937 Ford coupe, a year that didn't kindle enthusiasm among rodders, and in fact I didn't like them much myself. They lacked the interesting rounded lines of the 1936 and 1939 Fords, I thought; the rear of the roof was too sharp, the split-back window ungainly, and the grille and side panels were uninteresting. I bought the coupe from a friend, Larry Deyoe, simply because I needed a car and he was considering selling this one.

The year was 1953. I had graduated high school and returned from my first National Guard camp, all in the same month, and I had my $45 Guard check in my pocket. I offered it to Larry for the '37, he accepted, and as I drove the car home I began to grow fond of it. I liked the way the car rode and handled, and, now an owner, I suddenly realized that this was a bitchin' way to begin this terrific summer. I saw myself behind the wheel of this nifty little coupe, touring the drive-ins and cruising the main streets picking up girls.

I'll admit that the car wasn't perfect. The area below the trunk had met a number of bumpers, and occasionally when the car hit a severe bump the left side panel fell off. The car's worst feature was its brakes, or lack thereof. In

1937 and 1938 Ford used mechanical brakes operated by cables—*cabledraulic*, I think they were called—and over the years those cables stretched or rusted in the housings or both. I know, I know, all I needed to do was replace the cables, rebush the pedal assembly and crossbar, and keep the brakes in adjustment, but who got around to doing things like that? I never did, and anyway, I wanted to have *fun* in my sweet '37!

A wonderful set of duals

It was a fun car. It had a new aftermarket chrome grille (rather than the painted factory grille), four-inch shackles in the rear, which gave the car a nice stance, and it was painted gray primer—racing gray! It had a wonderful set of duals; quiet at low speeds, they attained a throaty roar through the gears, and rumbled a bit on deceleration. The sheet metal was super-straight, the mohair interior was almost like new, and the car didn't have a rattle. All the little things were right—for example, the door handles didn't droop from wear as they often did. The steering didn't have any free play, and the transmission was tight as a drum. The original 21-studder—stone-stock—must have been an exceptional engine, one of those rare ones that come off the assembly line when all factors are right. Not only did it not burn oil, it was quiet and terrifically fast: I'd quickly wind it to 45 mph in low, speed shift, get rubber, and move right up to 70 mph in second.

Painting white sidewalls

Right away I began to "fix it up"—or, rather, I did what I could without funds. I cleaned the firewall and painted it; the paint

Nifty '37 Ford coupe, with painted whitewalls and various hubcaps, in the summer of '53. The fields behind it are now full of houses.

came from the remainder of three cans of house paint, and the resultant color was pink with a gritty texture. After that experiment I bought a pint of blue enamel and, using a brush, painted the dash and garnish moldings. I scraped the old paint off the ashtray and radio panel and discovered they were stainless steel. A touch that seems silly now but which made the car really distinctive was the tire treatment: I painted the sidewalls white with a "rubberized" paint made for that purpose. It was supposed to last for months but it yellowed and became checked fairly quickly, and so I sat in the driveway every other Saturday afternoon repainting them. If I rubbed against a curb the right ones had to be done more often than that!

Fortunately I had plenty of free time that summer, because painting the tires became an occupation.

Custom touches

I had a number of 16-inch accessory hubcaps in the garage, but I didn't have a set; I put a pair of Hollywood spinners on the right and a pair of full Moons on the left. The area of the rim that showed between the hubcap and the tire I painted a bright-red enamel. I put a rare 1937 DeSoto bumper on the rear, and mounted the license plate in the center. With my last two bucks I bought a pair of chrome echo cans. When I stood back to admire my handiwork, I thought that the car really looked great!

That car was a natural— naturally fast, sharp, smooth. I drove it all summer, and it was a wonderful vehicle to convey me through the rites of initiation. The season complemented the car: the weather was always warm, with clear skies and cool evenings. After dinner I'd put on a clean pair of Levi's and a short-sleeve blue shirt that matched the car's interior, run the hose over the gray primer and painted

tires, and cruise down Foster Road where I could admire the car's reflection in store windows. I'd crank the windshield open on a hot day, and the only twinge of regret I felt all summer was on those occasions when I desired a radio. Because I rarely worked, by chance rather than design, I was able to sit for hours at Merhar's Drive-In, or under the million stars that formed a panoply over Mount Scott. For that summer I learned that, yes, the sidewalks were full of girls who would talk to me and my friends and who were eager to go for a ride. And who wouldn't want a ride in an almost-cherry '37 Ford coupe?

Going downhill

That's not to say that there weren't problems. Occasionally the needle valve on the Stromberg 97 would stick, flooding the engine with gas. The brakes got worse. The battery got feeble. But, in general, the car ran well all summer and then, like some kind of metaphor, with the coming of fall, it began to fail. The engine suddenly began to burn oil. I bought a tube of a popular piston sealer and carefully squeezed the additive through the spark-plug holes, but it didn't live up to the manufacturer's claims. Then the clutch began to slip. The brakes got even worse. When the wiring developed a short, draining the battery regularly, I parked the coupe. Later, I found an interesting Ford custom—a car I called *The Beast*—and gave the owner my '37 and some cash. The rains came, the coupe was gone, and a brief but important part of my life ended. Much later, 20 or 30

years later, I would have dreams about the '37 coupe, and the feeling I had on waking was not a desire to own the car again but simply to see it once more cruising down 82nd Avenue, easily identifiable by its garish, and now slightly ghostly, pink firewall.

Finest moment

But the coupe's finest moment came in mid-July, when it was running strong. One Saturday night I was trying to get my roadster ready for the drags at Scappoose. They kept changing the rules, requiring safety equipment on open cars—things that had seemed unnecessary the

summer before, like roll bars and fire extinguishers—and I was trying to comply. I had a crude roll bar welded; I bolted it to the frame, and made a deck lid of cardboard. I made some crummy-looking but effective shock brackets, and found a fire extinguisher.

I took the roadster to Bill Cahill's muffler shop to work on it; I had four or five friends helping me, and when everything looked right, when it seemed as though we would make it to the strip the next morning, someone noticed grease oozing in a steady stream from the bell housing. I had knocked out a transmission the week before in a street race,

That's a real '37 DeSoto bumper (which I still have) and real dents above it. I have no idea where the taillight is, although I recall getting a ticket once for not having one.

and replaced it with another unit; I hadn't checked the four bolts on the bearing housing, which were loose and allowed grease to run into the clutch area. We yanked the rear end and transmission, tightened the bolts, and tried to figure out how to clean the clutch disc. I recalled that I had a big bottle of carbon tetrachloride at home that I used to clean my saddle shoes, and I figured that that would do the job.

Street racing

Eleven o'clock; the streets were almost empty. I was clipping right along, thinking that we could have that car back together in an hour if I hurried, and on Holgate a pair of headlights shot up from behind. I thought, oh hell, a cop. Then it swung alongside, the driver gunning the engine, and I saw it was a blue '49 Ford sedan owned by a friend, Jimmy Graham. I began to breathe again, and at 92nd, when we stopped, Jim waved over the head of his passenger, a pretty girl, and said: "Hey, you ready to race that heap?"

Some explanation is necessary to understand the full impact of that challenge. First, I was driving an old car and Jim's was almost new. We all envied him when he bought that 1949 Ford, even though it was a four-door sedan, for it represented the future, with its envelope body and modern suspension. Second, if Jim was proud of his car he was also defensive, because it was a dog: the car rattled, the springs were weak, the doors fit badly, the door handles flopped around. Third, about two months after he bought the car it began to depreciate rapidly. Because new cars hadn't been produced during World War II, the market

for used cars was high during the post-war years—then in 1953 the supply exceeded demand, and prices plummeted. In fact, the value of Jim's car dropped an amount equal to the monthly payment. We gave Jim a hard time about that, motivated by jealousy, I suppose. Although he hated to lose money month by month on the car, he began to spend even more money to fix it up: hubcaps, duals, a Mallory ignition, lowering blocks. It was a hot item.

So there we were at the light, me alone in my old '37, and Jim, with three other people, in his hot, new '49; it was a battle of generations, of old versus new, of egos in conflict. He had been goading me for over a month to race him; I had refused, probably because I figured that his car was faster, but tonight I was in a hurry and in no mood to be messed with.

"Okay, muther," I said, "let's run it to 103rd Street."

"Well okay, daddio," Jim yelled—he always talked like that—laughing, revving his engine.

When I tromped the gas, the little coupe leaped forward; Jim laid a patch of rubber for 30 feet, but when he got traction the sedan's front fender moved up beside the coupe's door. I wound the engine tight, felt the dual exhausts send vibrations through the floorboards, into my soles, up my legs, and I rammed a speed shift into second, the nice, tight lever moving unerringly into its slot. The coupe's rear tires chirped once and the car shot forward. The coupe was far lighter than the '49 sedan, and perhaps that weight made the difference. At 70, when I dropped the lever into high, the coupe was perhaps two lengths

ahead of the newer car and I kept my foot on the gas until I could see Jim's headlights in the mirror.

Then I saw another light, the flashing stoplight at 103rd, and I let up on the gas; when I hit the brakes they did not even slow the coupe. I pushed with all my weight against the pedal, pulling up against the steering wheel for leverage. Darkened houses whizzed past. The right front brake might have caught, jerked, just before the stoplight appeared overhead, but its effect was not noticeable. I sailed right through the intersection, swearing, glancing quickly in all directions for a cop, and then I relaxed, let up on the pedal—nor did that seem to have any effect—and told myself I had to get modern, get me a vehicle with juice brakes at least.

Eastern Auto Ad from December 1954 issue of Hot Rod Magazine.

"Off the Deep End"

STROKER McGURK

By Medley

From December 1954 issue of Hot Rod Magazine.

The Beast

One thing was certain, the car represented a lot of work.

A post-World War II phenomenon was the home-built car. No figures exist on the number of such cars built, but the car cult grew rapidly after the war, giving rise to totally new magazines like *Hot Rod Magazine,* creating new forms of racing, such as track roadsters, increasing the number of auto races and attendance at those races, creating a new industry called *speed shops*, and among all this activity was an interest in the home-built car.

During the 'Twenties and 'Thirties it was possible to buy a speedster body to mount on a stock Model T or A chassis, but that idea is similar to the kit car of today. I'm thinking of the car that is a combination of parts assembled by the owner/builder, and represents his vision. You can call such a car a *radical*

Sectioned body allowed '37 Ford hood to fit without side panels. Dual chrome air cleaners were not functional. The car was built after WW II, and can you imagine this thing coming down the street among the tall cars of the 'Thirties and early 'Forties?

"The Beast" was titled as a 1935 Ford, the year of the chassis and rear half of the body. Front half was from a 1937 Ford; top was chopped and body sectioned. The two halves were joined with sheet metal that bridged the '37 roof to the '35 deck area. Dropped axle, longer shackles in rear brought chassis down.

custom, a home-built, a special, a one-off, a gizmo or whatever. One thing is certain, and that is that the car represented a lot of work.

There were several reasons for building a home-built. New cars were expensive; old cars were cheap, abundant, and lent themselves to revision. It was possible to rebuild an old car into a customized version for a fraction of the cost of a new car. And the model lines became blurred: a car of the 'Thirties, nicely altered, could take on a timeless quality, so that it was difficult to know not only what make the car was but also what decade it was from. Another reason was that many people felt that Detroit cars could be improved upon; they handled badly, lacked sufficient power, and needed to be streamlined. Thousands of GIs returned to America having seen and been impressed by foreign cars which were less bulky and more agile than their American counterparts. And finally there was that vision—the car that the backyard builder saw in his head. After he had lowered

his '35 Plymouth, put on duals and white sidewalls, removed the running boards, blanked-out two-thirds of the grille with sheet metal, made the side panels solid, added a continental kit and later-model bumpers, he stood back and took a look and thought what if he could start all over again, beginning with the bare frame, and perhaps channel the body, adding a late-model Cadillac grille, and rear fenders from a 1942 Lincoln Zephyr, and…

Some beautiful cars were built for those reasons, and, it must be admitted, some pretty weird ones too. No doubt many builders wanted to imitate the works of the well-known body builders of the 'Thirties and 'Forties, such as Darrin, Coachcraft, Bohman and Schwartz, Judkins, Rollston, Murphy and LeBaron, and to create a car that was aesthetically pleasing. But that wasn't always the case and the difference wasn't simply a matter of taste.

Shaped like a rocket ship

An example of a home-built

car is the one pictured here. A friend came by one day in the fall of 1953 and told me about a crazy Ford he had seen; I was intrigued by his description, so we went to take a look at it. We drove a few blocks off a main street, then down a rutted dirt road, and at the last house on the block we saw it parked on the lawn. It was an old car, shaped like a rocket ship, with two chrome air cleaners on the hood. I remembered I had seen the car once, a year earlier, at a local drive-in restaurant. I looked it over, talked briefly with the owner, and came to a quick and easy agreement: I gave him a worn-out '37 Ford coupe and $50 and I was the new owner of a weird machine!

I thought it was an interesting car, but my friends thought it was awful and named it "The Beast," a name that stuck. I liked the car because it was different; I suspect the builder thought it was beautiful. There's no accounting for taste, of course; probably we'd all agree that it was a good example of American ingenuity, with enthusiasm running rampant. I like to think of the car as being someone's vision of what the car of the future might look like.

I don't know who built the car although I have tried to find out; I do know that it was built in Portland, Oregon, right after WW II. The builder started with a 1935 Ford coupe, keeping only the running gear and the rear portion of the body; the front fenders, hood, and front half of the body came from a 1937 Ford coupe. The body was sectioned and the top was chopped; the open area between the '37 roofline and the '35 deck lid was filled with sheet metal and leaded smooth to make a fastback 3-window coupe unlike anything on the road! Shades of Buck Rogers!

Dumb-looking, well-built

The car may have looked dumb but it was in fact well-built. Miles of conduit had been welded around the door openings, over the roof area, and along the body flanges to make a strong one-piece unit; the body was solid, tight, free of rattles and squeaks, and not subject to flexing.

It rode and handled well. The brakes had been updated with the addition of 1940 Ford hydraulics, and tube shocks had been added front and rear. The front axle was dropped, and the spring eyes had been reversed; side sway was controlled with sway bars front and rear.

The engine was a 1948 Merc with one-eighth-inch stroke, full cam, headers, Shanafelt dual manifold, Sharp heads, light flywheel and Auburn clutch. The 258-CID flathead pulled the car easily, yet was docile enough so it could be used in heavy traffic without snorting, loping or overheating.

Inside were a pair of bucket seats, and behind them an area large enough for two people to sleep comfortably; the seats, doors and headliner were done in medium-blue flat Naugahyde. Beyond the '39 Ford banjo wheel was a dash with 12 gauges, 20 switches, lights, knobs, etc.—it looked like an airplane cockpit. Gauges included an 8,000-rpm tachometer and a 160-mph speedometer.

Impressive details

I was impressed with the car's many details; too often a builder never got around to finishing a car in this way. It had all road equipment, including radio and heater, a spare tire mounted in the original place on the rear, windshield wipers, horn, etc. Then it had certain touches, such as the two non-functional chrome air cleaners on the hood, the dual exhaust tips that exited through the rear fenders, '39 Ford taillights, and Kelsey-Hayes wire wheels on the

Car was old when I got it in 1953; everything needed to be tidied up. Note oil cooler on left front fender, 1939 Ford taillights, odd antenna location on roof, dual electric gas caps high on each quarter panel, dual exhaust pipes exiting through rear fenders.

front. On the left front fender was an oil cooler built from a heater radiator (which, along with the oil-temperature gauge, makes me suspect that the builder had something to do with race cars). The car was practical, and suitable for long trips, which was what it might have been used for, as it had two 20-gallon gas tanks. Access to the tanks was through a pair of locking gas caps, one on each side, electrically controlled from the dash.

I enjoyed driving the car—it was tight, rattle-free, had a nice running flathead and a beautiful set of dual pipes—and the only complaint I had was that I couldn't see out the back! But I guess I didn't like it well enough to keep it intact. I always wonder what happened to old rods and customs; in this case I know, but I don't know why I was motivated to do what I did. I got the car in the fall of 1953, drove it regularly for the next seven months and then got tired of it, I guess.

One day my buddy Jon Olson came by and wanted the dropped front end from "The Beast" for his 1940 Ford four-door. It was 1954, and the "raked" look was in. The year before every car was dropped in back; suddenly the back end was up in the air and the front end was on the ground, a look influenced by drag-strip machines. Somehow Jon talked me out of that dropped front end. We unbolted it, and towed it to his house behind my '47; halfway there the rope broke and the entire front end took off, hit the curb and ended up on a lawn. It wasn't hurt, but thank God it didn't happen on Holgate Hill!

For that dropped front end I got $20 cash, a louvered '40 standard hood, a '36 hood, some odds and ends and a complete 1936 Ford four-door convertible. Well, it was almost complete—it lacked an engine, wheels and some other things. Jon was moving to California and he couldn't take it, so he gave it to me.

I hauled home the odds and ends, the '40 hood, a '36 hood with solid side panels and a tonneau cover for the convertible sedan. I recall selling the tonneau to a car dealer on Union for $12, so I suppose I came out all right. But economics aside, what could I have been thinking of? I had had a complete running car; now I had a car without a front end. I began to dismantle "The Beast," saving every upholstery tack, every bolt, nut and screw as if therein lay the car's true value. I saved the tube-shock brackets, all the Stewart-Warner instruments and a few other things. The Merc stroker I put in my roadster. The entire body I gave away to some guy who perused the neighborhood for old metal. Who knows what happened to it, or where it might be today.

What might have been

There have been a few nights over the past 45 years when I have lain awake wondering what possessed me to dismantle a perfectly good--albeit odd—hot rod. True, I had paid almost nothing for the car—$50 and a worn-out '37 coupe—but it must have been worth more than that. Of the 1936 Ford four-door convertible—a car I covet only slightly less than I do a phaeton or roadster—I have only the title. I couldn't get the body home—I lacked a trailer, I was too lazy to get it on wheels or replace what was missing, I was too busy chasing skirts, whatever. I gave the car away to two kids I met once. I don't know what hap-

pened to that car either, but on the rare nights when I lie awake I realize that that four-door convertible, even with the windshield chopped, would be worth several thousand dollars today. But it isn't the money that nags at me, it's the *idea* that I could allow such *interesting* cars to be cast aside. To remind myself that such incidents happened daily during that decade is no consolation. It's hard to look back at the lost metal that litters a lifetime.

Flathead V-8 had 1/8-inch stroked crank, which suggests it was built before '49 Mercury crank was available; also full-race cam, Sharp aluminum heads, Shanafelt dual manifold; it ran great, docile around town, lots of power, never heated up.

Dash had everything: many switches, lights and a dozen old-style Stewart-Warner gauges. Note defroster horns atop '37 dash, and banjo steering wheel. Conduit was welded along door edges and throughout entire body for strength

The Mild Custom

...a car made distinctive by minor alterations

A phenomenon of the 'Fifties was the *mild custom*. Such cars were extremely rare before 1950, and they suddenly disappeared with the advent of the 'Sixties muscle cars. A mild custom is a car made distinctive by minor alterations—nosed and decked, lowered, duals, aftermarket hubcaps, a nice interior. Generally, the owner avoided complicated sheet-metal changes. The mild custom was a daily driver and the car couldn't be laid up for more than a weekend. For the same reason, the engines were usually left stock or changes limited to bolt-on equipment.

Once the idea of owning a mild custom caught on, the streets of the town where I grew up were full of them. There were, I think, two reasons for the mild custom's sudden popularity: the post-1949 body styles were radically different from previous years, which made many owners want to update their older cars, and the availability of interesting

Coupe was not a show car—note two types of hubcaps—but I always kept it clean and it got noticed. A really good daily driver.

When I bought this 1947 Ford coupe in October, 1953 it was a solid, straight car with duals, wide whitewalls, 6-inch shackles in back. It also had Thickstun dual manifold and Columbia two-speed.

aftermarket bolt-ons.

Most cars of the 'Forties were *dull*— painted dull colors, dull interiors and dinky hubcaps. However, their lines were interesting and with little work they could be made attractive—even showy. Today, cars of the 'Forties are being restored with loving care due a Cord or Duesenberg, and at the risk of being accused of heresy, I have to admit that I think such cars look *better* as mild customs. Show me, say, a 1948 Plymouth coupe, lowered, with whitewalls and Olds Fiesta hubcaps, nosed and decked, duals, perhaps '50 Pontiac taillights, and I can get excited. This was especially true when such cars were common. In the early 'Fifties, new cars were expensive and hard to get. If you couldn't afford, or couldn't get, a new car you could make your pre-1949 car *appear* as interesting as a new car.

Eastern Auto's straight-bar grille

Aftermarket manufacturers began to offer new products weekly. Everything from box skirts to imitation Cadillac tailfins to continental kits could be found at the corner auto supply house. The first straight-bar grilles were owner-built, but within a short time Eastern Auto offered a three-piece straight bar kit that allowed the owner of a 1949-50 Ford to alter his grille in an afternoon. When the 1951 Ford came out, Eastern offered a straight bar that could be installed in an hour. That grille soon became almost as common as a stock grille, and '51 Ford owners began looking about for something different (fortunately the grille in the 1951 Meteor, the Canadian Ford, fit perfectly). With all these parts available, it became relatively easy to make your stocker into a mild custom.

I had several mild customs during the 'Fifties, but the one I liked best was a 1947 Ford coupe that I owned from 1953 until 1956. It was my first good car and although it had the older style body, it seemed like a new car to me. I had been driving my roadster every day for over a year and a half; it was getting dingy and, as the season became deep fall, I was getting cold. In late September, I got a job in a garage (at a lousy dollar an hour) and by the end of October I'd had it with the roadster. I wanted to buy a $50 beater but my mother said she'd lend me the money for a good car, so I raised my sights and began to look about for a newer model. Actually, I had a car in mind: a 1947 Ford coupe parked on a used-car lot on Foster, not far from my house. The dealer wanted $550; I mentioned cash and he came down $25. I did some walking—back home, to the bank, to the car lot—and drove that baby home like an owner!

Although I probably paid a little too much for the coupe, I knew the previous owner, and knew that he had put a rebuilt engine in the car only two months before it was repossessed. I also knew the Ford specialist who had rebuilt the engine and knew he did superior work. I drove the car for two and a half years, and the only problem I had with the engine was a dead fuel pump. Like many other Ford owners, I spent a great deal of time trying to end clutch chatter—without success, I might add. Important to me at the time was the fact that the car had a super heater and an excellent radio. It also had whitewall tires, dual pipes, dual carbs, a Columbia rear end, six-inch shackles in back, a '49 Chev license plate guard and one spotlight. Someone had removed the trunk chrome but had not filled in the holes—maybe if the hardware had been there I would have left the car alone. Maybe.

Unity spotlight

I drove it through the winter, polishing hopelessly faded blue paint, and by spring I had the car nearly paid off. About that time a flatbed truck rolled back into the hood. With the insurance money, I was able to have a body shop fix that dent, a dent in the trunk, and to nose and deck it as well. I liked the car even more! It was somewhat of a mark of prestige to have primer spots on a mild custom to show that work was in progress! When the Columbia rear end went out, I replaced it with a standard axle and housing, and put four-inch shackles on the rear—I was tired of the back bumper dragging on every driveway. I found another Unity spotlight and learned that it would fit if I bought a right-hand mount, which I did for a buck. Today, there's a demand for Appleton spots, whether real or dummy lights, but as I recall Unity lights were much more popular, especially on 1941-48 cars.

1950 Lincoln taillights

But the most interesting change was the taillight treatment. In a junkyard, I found a pair of perfect 1950 Lincoln taillights—I can't recall why I chose those lights, but I know that I had never seen a pair mounted in a 1941-48 Ford. This installation was the first done in Portland, and it looked so neat. I had a body shop remove and lead in the stock taillights and install the '50 Lincoln lights low on the body; they fit the body contour as if they were made for the car.

The stock grille was banged up a little; it would have been okay if I had left the car alone but it wouldn't suffice if I wanted a nice mild custom. The question was, should I buy a new or good used grille, which even then was fairly expensive, or should I put in a custom grille, say, a 1955 Chev grille? I solved the problem by buying a new aftermarket grille at discount from a wrecking yard; this grille, made when '46-48 Fords were more common, was a one-piece stamped grille completely chrome-plated. The stock grille is stamped sheet metal to which the chrome pot-metal top piece and the three stainless-steel strips bolt. A

Maybe if the trunk hardware had been there I would have left the car alone. Maybe.

Spring 1955: car had new grille, dual Unity spotlights, was painted 1955 Buick Baltic blue—a cool ride! Engine had dual carbs, lots of chrome, everything painted and tidy. I painted radiator shroud white, then got the idea I knew something about striping, which was new trend.

By summer, 1954 I had body shop nose and deck it, lead in old taillight holes and install '50 Lincoln taillights lower on fender. They fit fender contour perfectly, and were first ones in Portland. Red primer was mark of distinction: it indicated work-in-progress.

common trick back then was to remove the pot-metal top bar, fill in the holes, build up the center section so it met the center strip on the hood, and then paint the grille the same color as the rest of the car. This left a three-bar grille that looked neat. I avoided all that work with this aftermarket grille by simply sanding and painting the top bar, leaving the chrome areas on the front edges of the lower three bars.

Along the way, I messed with the engine a bit. I painted the block and heads red, put on chrome head-nut covers, chrome-plated the oil filter, got a slip-on chrome generator cover, and painted firewall, fender panels and radiator shroud white enamel. I somehow got the idea that I could handle a striping brush and so I did some shaky-jake striping on the shroud. I polished the radiator top tank until the brass shone, and damn

that engine looked good when I opened the hood at the service station!

When I bought the car it had a Thickstun dual manifold and beehive air cleaner. I really disliked the setup, the carbs mounted close together and the painted (red) manifold and air cleaner, and I got rid of it as fast as I could. I sold the whole setup to a kid in the neighborhood for $20. Today, a reproduction air cleaner like that sells for $150! I put on a Fenton super manifold, with the carbs sitting farther apart, and added chrome air cleaners, a Fenton fuel block and neoprene beer hose for gas lines. I don't think it improved the car's performance any, but it sure looked good!

And, like most mild customs, mine wasn't built for speed anyway.

Finally, I had the car painted. The exterior was done in 1955

Buick Baltic Blue and the interior was done in 1955 Cadillac Bahama Blue. I got a set of inexpensive seat covers with lots of blue in them. I removed the clock and speedometer from a 1946 Ford deluxe and put them in my '47; the numbers on the glass were painted red and looked a lot neater. I'd bought a set of Edelbrock heads from a friend who had ruined one by tightening it down on a battery strap, and I traded the heads for chrome pieces that replaced the dash plastic. With these simple low-buck changes—paint, different gauges and chrome trim—that dash was beautiful!

I never considered the '47 to be a show car— I didn't even have matching hubcaps on both sides!—but it was a darn nice daily driver. I loved to wash and wax the car, and spent a lot of time keeping it clean. There are any number of reasons why a person might want to own a mild custom; I know that I enjoyed working on the car, seeing it slowly change, enjoyed the way people looked at it. I loved to drive it on a date, or to simply sit in it for hours at a drive-in, knowing that I had a neat set of wheels. One reason I wanted to own a mild custom, I realized years later, was because it represents order in one's world. In those days, my world was pretty shaky—lousy job, no money, no skills—and the future was bleak. But when the '47 was clean and running well, the whitewall tires unblemished, the interior rich with the odor of wax and pine from the little green tree-shaped deodorizer that hung near the heater, I went cruising and— hey!—everything was okay!

The Mild Custom II

Not every 'Fifties custom was notable or represented an ideal machine.

To illustrate that not every 'Fifties custom was notable or represented an ideal machine, I submit the example of my '51 Chevy. I had spent two years building my 1947 Ford coupe and drove it in finished condition for several months before being hit by a stupid attack and traded it straight across for the Chevy. I have wondered about that occasionally over the past 40 years, trying to understand exactly why I made the trade. The Ford was done, it looked great, ran beautifully, attracted attention and—it was paid for!

Maybe I do know the reason, but I cannot recall how intense I felt about it. I wanted a car with the post-1948 body style, I wanted to get modern! Because car production ceased during World War II, the demand for new cars exceeded the supply until around 1953; then the price of all used cars dropped significantly. If you could afford a car with the new envelope body, why

In 1956 I traded a swell '47 Ford coupe straight across for this 1951 Chevrolet coupe because the Ford looked old, the Chev looked modern.

April, 1957: The Chev was nosed, decked, had Frenched headlights and no door handles. Spot primer on a custom was cool; it showed that work was in progress.

would you want a fat-fendered model, much less a tall 'Thirties model? The 'Fifties cars not only looked modern, they offered great potential for restyling. They were low, the early models had little chrome trim to remove and many models had great interiors.

My '51 Chevy had nice lines. Dave Hill, the previous owner, had nosed it and removed the door handles (but had not offered an alternative method of opening the doors—you reached through the vent window!). He had also Frenched the headlights, cut a coil up front and put lowering blocks on the rear. It had wide whitewalls with '53 Olds hubcaps and the seat and door panels were redone in red-and-white Naugahyde, It was powder-blue with red rims, and it looked nice.

Great potential

In fact, I felt the car had great potential. The year was 1956:

custom cars were King. Car shows were booming and at least six magazines were catering primarily to custom cars. I had been inspired by features I'd seen on Joe Mello's smooth '50 Chevy Bel Air and Don Landon's Barris-built chopped '50 Chevy coupe. Not that I would go that far, but there were so many mildly customized 'Fifties cars and taking off from the examples on the printed page I knew that I wanted to make my Chevy really distinctive.

It didn't work out that way. The Chevy got washed, but that was about all. Most of the time it served as a tow vehicle. I got my roadster out of the garage after two years, completely rebuilt it and was entering it in Northwest car shows. The Chevy was a draft horse while the roadster got all the praise. In fact, the Chevy was treated badly. I was just 21, and some nights, with a few too many beers, I thrashed the

Chevy. It seemed indestructible, requiring only a new water pump, a new rod (babbitt-poured) and a rebuilt distributor in three years.

Then one morning on the way to work a car pulled from a side street in front of me. Goodbye grille and bumper. I got some insurance money and began to have visions of gran-deur. I saw the Chevy with a '50 Merc cavity filled with a floating bar from a Kaiser or '51 Ply-mouth; Frenched '53 Buick headlights (the fenders had been buckled); '53 Lincoln taillights; Buick spear side trim; lots of scoops with little teeth, louvers and grilles.

Reality

Reality was something else. A body shop straightened the hood and fenders. I found I could buy a new 1955 Chevy truck grille for less than a used stock grille. I had the shop install it, then I removed the vertical bars and chrome-plated the three horizontal bars. It was a neat low-buck swap that gave the car a Ferrari-look, I thought. I had the shop dechrome the trunk, French the taillights low on the fenders, and build eyebrows over the headlights similar to the 1955 Chevy.

When it was time to paint, I chose gray. Why, I don't know. I like to think it was because that was the national color of the Mercedes-Benz grand prix cars, and they looked so neat! But I probably chose it because it would conceal waves and warps in the body. The car was not straight, which was why it had been painted powder-blue. There are some cars that are inherently *right*, with straight metal and solid underpinnings; others are inherently without integrity. The '47 Ford was *right* while the Chevy was something else. I doubt that Barris himself could have made it *right*.

I'd built a back seat for it because the business coupe had no rear seat and when I lifted the plywood platform I found the area below packed with mud! Had the car been in a flood? I wondered. It was looking less and less like a prize-winning custom and more and more like a second-rate car that had been messed with.

The luster of linoleum

I left the car at Gene Cargill's paint shop and went to San Francisco for a week. When I picked it up I was dismayed. The color must have been Battleship Gray—it had all the luster of opaque linoleum. Washing the car was like mopping the floor!

I had started college and didn't have time or money to redo what had been badly done. I thought perhaps I could highlight all that awful gray. So I painted the wheel rims gold, put on brass-plated license-plate holders and had Phil Shaffer stripe it in gold. Many times I thought of having scallops painted in a complementary color, and having side trim installed to break up that expanse of gray, but I never did.

I bought an almost-new sports car and a new Vespa scooter, and what happened to the Chevy is probably what happened to most of the custom cars of the 'Fifties. I drove it occasionally when I had to tow the roadster or when I went drinking. But mostly it sat, getting more and more dingy. Not only did I not take out the dent in the left rocker panel, I never even bothered to replace the molding that would cover it.

When I think about the '47 Ford coupe, I have good thoughts and envision it in pristine condition. When I think about the '51 Chevy I can again smell the mildew that came from the floor mats. I'd park it somewhere and come back for it days later, never worrying about whether someone would steal it. Perhaps I wished they would! Finally, I got tired of looking at it and in August 1958, two and a half years after I got the car, I sold it for $250 to a young woman and I don't think I ever saw it again. Or maybe I just kept my eyes closed when it went past.

By September 1957, the coupe had a 1955 Chevrolet truck grille, eyebrows over the Frenched lights and awful gray-lacquer paint job.

A '47 Chevy panel wagon, taken in front of Jeryl's Muffler on Magnolia Avenue in Riverside, California.

From May 1953 issue of Honk! Magazine.

Mild Custom '49 Merc.

Cool Threads

You could wear them for days before they showed the dirt.

The familiar image of the 'Fifties hot rodder is the young guy wearing Levis and T-shirt, leather jacket and engineer boots—maybe a stroker cap. That image developed in California, where the T-shirt was just right on a hot day and the leather jacket was needed at night. Levis were cheap, durable, fit right and you could wear them for days before they showed the dirt. The stroker cap had been worn by rodders since the 'Thirties with the bill forward to shield against the sun in those years when sunglasses were rare, and with the bill in back when racing. Used by butchers and painters, the caps were cheap, and when they got dirty they were discarded and the rodder got a new one.

Rodders in other parts of the country borrowed against that image. Levis were standard, and for the reasons listed above. A few guys wore stroker hats, but

In 1953 Dick Bell came back from Korean War, was discharged, started college and still found time to build neat '40 Ford coupe with very husky flathead. Here he's wearing his G.I. black-leather flight jacket and black shoes, a white shirt under V-neck sweater and popular blue-denim pants.

they were never as popular in the northwest in the 'Fifties as they were in California—perhaps because there was less sun. Nor were boots, although I often wore them because I had motorcycles. We wore T-shirts often, weather permitting, although I remember my friend Jimmy wore them through the winter (and he constantly complained of being cold!). The only T-shirts I can recall that had a design were my Road Angels shirts, although there may have been others that advertised a product or cited an event. Toward the end of the 'Fifties an industry was developed by Ed "Big Daddy" Roth when he began hand-painting T-shirts with zany designs and sayings. From what I later read, Roth did a tremendous mail-order business with these shirts, employing artists like Robert Williams and others; but I cannot remember anyone I knew who

had one of those shirts.

Jackets

The jacket situation was born of necessity, because it's often cold and wet in the northwest, and of convenience. During the 'Fifties there was still an abundance of surplus materials from WW II and outlets that specialized in handling the surplus. In addition to things like canteens, machetes, hammocks and even airplane engines, there were air force bomber jackets—some leather, some fabric, some with an insulated lining and furry collar. These were ideal for hot rodders, especially if you were driving a roadster. And they were ridiculously cheap. This is a good example of something a guy should have invested in, and bought several to leave in the closet. Today a genuine WW II A-1 or G-2 jacket is worth upwards of $1,000!—especially to the

Japanese who have a perverse desire to own clothing worn by the Americans who were dropping bombs on Japan.

Perhaps because those jackets were cheap, and because they were military surplus, we didn't value them as highly as we might have. And perhaps a distinction holds true: there were those clothes we wore while we were rodders—that is, working on a car or driving it to a friend's house or to the wrecking yard—and what we wore other times. I clearly remember the jackets I wore during the 'Fifties. In 1949 my mother bought me a gold-and-black satin jacket—something a jockey might wear, and I hated it. I took it off as soon as I

During the 'Fifties there was still an abundance of surplus materials from WW II.

I love this photo because of the period footwear. At left, Tex Ranger is wearing Mexican huaraches that became popular around 1948; probably dyed with oxblood or cordovan polish. Bob Lee, sitting on ground, is wearing English Brogues; they appear to have a double half-sole, a necessary touch. Marilyn Fosberry is wearing the popular saddle shoe. At right, Bill Sullivan has a pair of highly polished smooth-toed shoes dyed with cordovan polish. Too young to drive when this photo was taken, a couple of the guys later became hot rodders.

Roberta beckons movie goers from the front door of the Ames Theater where she worked in early 'Fifties. She's wearing a white cotton blouse (no polyester back then), wide white-leather (not plastic) belt, pastel gathered skirt 3 inches above the ankle and white-canvas shoes. The Joan Crawford movie poster says it all: "This Woman is Dangerous!"

was around the corner and carried it. After perhaps a month of complaining I was able to get a letterman's jacket that I cherished. It was red with cream-leather sleeves, and I would walk with my arms away from my sides so the red would not rub off on the sleeves. I wore that jacket through four years of high school. About six months after graduation I was working and bought another leather letterman's jacket; this one dark-blue with black-leather sleeves—a combination that was easier to

keep clean.

Not until 1957 did I buy a WW II jacket at a military-surplus store; I was riding a Vespa scooter every day and I was a getting wet. One morning I stopped at a surplus store and bought a knee-length coat with a snap-in alpaca liner and hood for $12 (as I remember). Although it was olive-drab, I think it was Navy issue, and while the cloth outer layer got wet instantly, that alpaca liner shed water in even a heavy rain. In the summer of 1951 I joined the Road Angels. Shortly after I bought a club jacket: red wool with white inserts at the shoulders and white knit material at the neck and cuffs. On the back was the patch with the club name, the initials C. T. A. for Columbia Timing Association, and the image of a fenderless roadster. It was the type of jacket that would soon become standard fare by 1954-55, when car clubs proliferated.

A religious experience

I've seen photos taken at car shows during that time and can clearly recognize a dozen different club jackets in the crowd. But to continue my distinction: I know I never wore my Road Angels jacket to high school. I did wear it to the drags, to local car shows and the times I went to the Oakland Roadster Show. There was also a period of time, between the two letterman jackets, when I did not have a decent sport coat. I remember being uncomfortable, perhaps even embarrassed, when I wore it on a date. I also wore the jacket when I went to church; the members saw that logo, Road Angels, and probably thought I was having a religious experience.

The times, and the fashions, change. I never thought about clothes until I graduated from eighth grade, when I got a swell robin's-egg-blue, hidden-button shirt. That summer of 1949 I went downtown almost every Saturday. After I'd hit the used bookstores, where I bought several early issues of *Hot Rod Magazine* for a dime each, and the pawn shops, where I looked at the guns, I'd go to the big department stores or the smaller men's clothing stores where, for the first time in my life, I shopped. As I was learning about cars, so was I learning about clothes. There was the Stradavari shirt, easily identifiable by its slightly slanting pockets—available in a wide variety of colors, such as chartreuse, rose, purple, strawberry—colors that would have looked great on a car.

Shoe of the year

There were snow-white cords, shiny suntan pants, narrow-collar striped dress shirts, blue-denim pants and Levis. Styles were dictated by some unseen force, and somehow we *knew* we had to have a certain style and a certain brand. The shoe of the year was the Brogue, a shoe designed like a boat turned upside down with a distinct prow. But it had to be a certain type of brogue—the one whose sides and top came to a blunt point—available only from London Bootery in Portland, and not the cheaper but similar shoe available from, say, Thom McAnn. There was also the popular saddle shoe, but again of a certain type, with creamy white sections and a light-tan middle section. These were available only from Armishaw's store in Portland, and should not be

Peggy Brendel, left, and Kathy Taylor are the top girl hot rodders on the West Coast, Peggy topped 118 mph. From Hot Rod Handbook 129, 1951.

Al Rogers was a cool cat in 1950. Here he's wearing a white terry-cloth T-shirt with the sleeves rolled up, Day's sun tan pants, a narrow belt, Argyle socks and saddle shoes. His hair, with the help of Wave Set, *was combed to a wave in front, a duck's ass (or DA) in back. He remembers, "That was when it was very important to have every hair in place. You couldn't let anyone mess it up." I'm happy to say that Al is still a cool cat!*

confused with saddle shoes covered with brown-and-white shoe polish. I had a pair of Armishaw saddle shoes, and they were lovely!

Neat colors on cars and clothes

By the mid-'Fifties the Ivy League look, long popular on the east coast, got to Portland. You had to have tan or olive-drab slacks with the belt in the back, a V-neck long-sleeve sweater and a striped shirt. I don't know how to describe the shirts of that period—striped or cross-striped, with such neat color combinations that in memory they seemed delicious enough to eat. They're the shirts worn by teenagers on TV shows from the mid- and late-'Fifties, such as "Leave It to Beaver," although those shows are in black-and-white. The shirts had the popular button-down collars with two buttons in front and a perfectly useless button on the rear of the collar. By this time pink and black were popular colors and loafers were popular footwear.

Although cars and clothes were always related, they definitely came together by the mid-'Fifties. There was something in the textures—the neat colors, trim lines, the sleekness. Looking back we can see the relationship between, say, a chartreuse Stradavari shirt and that same color which was introduced on the 1950 Ford Crestliner. Or, less obvious, the feeling of a pair of pegged suntan pants sliding across a white rolled-and-pleated Naugahyde interior. Second, and always implied here, there was the attitude between a rod or custom owner and his appearance: if a guy had a neat car, it was essential that he appear neat, with clean white cords or Levis, a button-down Dan River shirt and a sharp haircut. Such efforts were not always easy. For example, the greasy, long-hair DA (duck's ass) of the early 'Fifties gave way to the crew cut, or some variation of it by the later 'Fifties, although some guys wore their hair in a crew cut all during the decade. Only someone who has had a crew cut knows what I mean: you have to have it cut every two weeks, or it looks awful. I was never able to achieve that schedule, but I tried, because, like everyone else, I wanted to be cool.

Rockin' & Roddin'

The music we listened to in the 'Fifties wasn't all rock 'n roll!

In a perfect world this essay would neatly unify hot rods and rock 'n roll. Every movie or television program made in recent years about the 'Fifties has a sound track rich with Bill Haley, Elvis and little Richard— as if we listened to a steady diet of that music back then. Today, of course, we are all *terribly* aware of rock 'n roll and its history and with the benefit of hindsight we're able to discuss it clearly. I question, however, whether we were as aware of the importance of the music and the performers as we are today.

I love rock 'n roll, but I might be the wrong person to write about it from an historical viewpoint. During the 'Fifties I drove a couple roadsters, a funny radical custom, a dolled-up 1937 Ford, a couple motorcycles, a

CHROME, SMOKE & FIRE
A COMPILATION OF HOT ROD MUSIC BY ROBT. WILLIAMS

Chrome, Smoke & Fire, *a compilation of Hot Rod Music.*

Vespa scooter and a sports car; none had a radio. I often worked in the garage at night, the radio playing in the background, but it was tuned to radio dramas—mysteries, action programs, comedies, domestic situations—the stuff I'd grown up with that was still being played over the airwaves in those last years before television took over.

Rock 'n roll—NOT!

And if I did listen to music at home or in a car that had a radio, it wasn't rock 'n roll, not during the first half of the decade anyway. According to the experts, rock 'n roll didn't arrive until mid-1956, when Elvis Presley appeared on the Ed Sullivan Show—or some say in February 1956, when Elvis appeared on the Tommy Dorsey Show (although some note the birthdate as 1955, when Bill Haley did *Rock Around the Clock*). Of course, that event had its antecedents. Others point to more obscure musicians who, years earlier, had developed the heavy, insistent, repetitious bass beat—a blend of boogie-woogie and the blues, pounding through the night in a juke joint in east Texas or on the Delta, or an after-hours place in Detroit. Others can argue the fine points; I'm simply trying to remember what I can.

Popular, classical and hillbilly

As I recall, in 1950 there were three types of music: popular, classical and hillbilly. Almost no one I knew claimed an interest in the two latter types, one being too highbrow and the other too lowbrow. Popular music was a continuation of the music of the 'Forties, the crooners and the canaries, with some of the big-band sound. Frank Sinatra, Perry Como, Vaughn Monroe and Dick Haymes were hot, singing love songs to the ladies. I remember going to sleep with the little radio beside my bed, thinking about the girls in my grade in school, singing along with songs like *Paper Moon* and *Dream, Dream, Dream.* When I was old enough to go downtown with the kid next door we'd stop in the Woolworth store for a hot dog and root beer, and the sound system seemed to always be playing Les Paul and Mary Ford's version of *Red Sails in the Sunset*. Those dreamy songs were a background to adolescence—impossible to separate from the experience of owning a cashmere sweater or a Stradivari shirt—of looking at girls with an intense but goofy longing.

I have always been out of step, and so too with music. My main interest in the late 'Forties and early 'Fifties was hillbilly music—Jimmy Rogers, the original A. P. Carter family, Bob Wills and the Texas Playboys, and my favorites, Ernest Tubbs and Luke the Drifter. As with all types of music during the 'Forties and 'Fifties, there were regional distinctions, and in the North-

west there was a fair amount of hillbilly or cowboy music. Many radio programs lasted only 10 or 15 minutes, and there were both local and national programs. Before school I usually listened to several different programs. These included Dallas Turner, a local musician with a 5-minute program and the Sons of the Pioneers, who were national and had a 15-minute program. I started the day with that kind of music, the sounds bouncing around in my brain.

Give Me the Simple Life

In high school I never admitted that I listened to that kind of music. There it was the melodies of the Four Lads and the Four Freshmen, songs like *Moments to Remember* and *September Song*, a background to the Boomer Boys who stood at the bottom of the stairs in the main hall flirting with the girls. There was a string of Patti Page hits: *Old Cape Cod, Let Me Go, Lover, I'll Never Stop Living You*, with lyrics you could see the girls mouthing silently in study hall. Those were the songs the popular boys and girls danced to in the cafeteria, while the rest of us chewed slowly on tasteless hamburgers, watching in awe. There was the haunting *Great Pretender* by the Platters, *Give Me the Simple Life*, which was pretty much what we had, high-school *angst* aside, and the utterly innocent, *Make Love to Me.*

Johnny Ray, the singer, graduated from my high school a couple years before I arrived, and suddenly he had big hits early in 1952 with *Cry* and *The Little White Cloud that Cried*. For a time he seemed more famous than Sinatra, whose career was then in decline. When Johnny Ray visited Franklin High shortly

after those songs rose to the top of the top ten, we were excited simply by his presence. We could not have known then that Ray's gestures and gyrations, his spontaneity, his actual crying during his performances anticipated the emotional levels of Little Richard and Elvis.

Elvis on a cowboy station

So while I was pleased when Patti Page's version of *Tennessee Waltz* was a crossover hit, making it big in both the western and popular markets, I was much more interested in the darker songs of Luke the Drifter (AKA Hank Williams). Things began to come together for me in late 1955. I was working in Lee Cosart's Dodge-Plymouth agency and driving my 1947 Ford coupe, one of the few cars I owned that had a radio, and I had it tuned to a station that emphasized cowboy music. One morning while driving to work I heard Elvis Presley for the first time—at least I think it was for the first time—and I heard him only because I was listening to a cowboy station. They played *I Forgot to Remember to Forget*, a song I have always liked, and I believe it's on the flip side of *Heartbreak Hotel*, which became *the song* that introduced him to thousands of listeners.

Obviously rock 'n roll was upon us, but I can't be certain that we called it that, at that time, in our part of the north-west. My friend, Jimmy Graham, had a pair of blue-suede shoes in 1954, and I remember that he was always telling us not to step on them—probably because we

A particular song often calls up a certain moment from the past.

were trying to scuff them up—but that must have been a couple years before the Carl Perkins' song.

As with any kind of music, a particular song will often call up a certain moment from the past. I remember being in a tavern on Union Avenue in 1956 with, I think, Gary Klaus. We were both infatuated with the barmaid, a woman several years older than we were, who drove a new 1957 pink Thunderbird. She was closing up and we kept hanging around, each trying to outwait the other, while in the background Fats Domino sang *Blueberry Hill*. Eventually Klaus and I left together to get some Chinese food.

When I towed my roadster to Tacoma, Washington for the 1957 show I heard, perhaps for the first time, Harry Belafonte singing *The Banana Boat Song* on the radio of my 1951 Chevrolet, and I kept singing it as I drove through the night. That calypso number had little to do with rock 'n roll, and my point is that that song loomed larger for me than, say, *Jail House Rock*. I suspect I responded to the rhythms of rock 'n roll better than many people my age, but, being naive, I probably preferred Pat Boone's *Rootie Tootie* to Little Richard's version, assuming that we even heard Little Richard's version in the Pacific northwest. And I know I dug Boone's *Love Letters in the Sand*, a song I could apply to every girl I knew.

Fad beginning seldom clearly defined

The beginning of a fad, trend or movement is seldom clearly defined. We can look back and say that rock 'n roll was announced to the nation when Elvis appeared on the Ed Sullivan Show, but in a personal way, what did it mean? If you happened to be out in the garage working on your car or cruising around that night as Elvis sauntered up to the microphone you could easily have missed that momentous occasion. Newspapers and television seemed far less important in those days. A war could have been declared and I would not have known about it for a week. When the movie *High School Confidential* came out with Jerry Lee Lewis playing *Great Balls of Fire* on a piano on a flatbed truck, that opening was soundly condemned by the critics. But who read the reviews? We dug the song, but I suspect none of us knew that Lewis was being condemned from the pulpit and in editorials.

Parties!

By coincidence, I came of age at the same time that rock 'n roll was officially born, and that meant parties! "Party" became a buzzword, an imperative. It meant something different from, say, a birthday party, the kind of event with which we were familiar. Now a party seemed more spontaneous, the participants often strangers, and sometimes all we had in common was the music. That music was as different from the high-school melodies we had hummed as the party was from kids' parties; that music was a stranger, but its strong, insistent beat became an invitation to dance.

In high school dancing terrified me. I worried that I would have to ask someone to dance, or worse, that someone would ask me to dance! Dancing implied a set of rules of which I was ignorant: it did no good to talk about box steps or four-four rhythm, there were other things that I needed to know that did not get said. What rock 'n roll meant was a kind of happiness, a freedom, a liberation from the rules. All I had to do was observe the other dancers and I could see there were no rules! You danced without touching, so you were responsible for only your own body. You could do whatever you felt like doing, and, especially after a beer, you thought you knew exactly what you were doing. By that time you had no control, you were moving, gyrating, lifting a leg and coming down on a heel, shifting your shoulders, pumping your arms. Even if you did not know what to do, the music told you—forced you—to move. That was the secret and the joy of rock 'n roll.

Now we're told it was over in a couple years, by 1958 or 1959, with Elvis in the army, Chuck Berry in prison, Jerry Lee Lewis in disgrace and Buddy Holly and friends dead in a plane crash. It didn't end, of course; I remember doing that same dancing in the early 'Sixties, and then things evolved into other types of music. Maybe rock 'n roll didn't end then, but I clearly remember in 1959 the Burns brothers had a wild party at a house they rented and I remember a bunch of us, perhaps 30 people, gathered around the record player singing along with the Kingston Trio on *Tom Dooley*, singing that one song over and over, I don't know how many times, as if it were an anthem to the decade.

The Drive-In

The drive-in was central to the lives of teens and young adults

One thing the movie makers always seem to get right when recreating the period is the drive-in scene. The panoply of garish neon, the rows of neat cars, the cute carhops, the pleasure of a burger and Coke. I love the film *American Graffiti*, with carhops on skates balancing trays of food. Although I never saw skating carhops in the North-west, publisher Helen Fisher assures me that she had friends who were carhop skaters in Southern California.

The drive-in was central to the lives of teenagers and young adults back then for a number of reasons. They wanted to get away from home, at least for a while, and if they had a car or had a friend who had one, they were mobile. But this meant you had to go somewhere. After an

The Tik-Tok, an older drive-in close to downtown Portland, was a favorite hangout for rodders from the 'Thirties through the 'Fifties. Neat building was demolished in the 'Seventies, and place is now a parking lot. The Tik-Tok Drive-In is pictured in the cover illustration of this book.

hour of cruising, as the gas gauge began to fall, you wanted to stop. Day or night that drive-in beckoned like a mirage. It served the same purpose as the town square had for earlier generations: it was a place where you could socialize, see your friends and possibly make new friends. It was like a friendly tavern, without alcohol. You'd pull in, park, turn on your headlights for car service and talk with your pals while you ate. There always seemed to be a parking place, even on a busy weekend night. If you were broke you could park in the back row and no one seemed to mind. As I recall, drive-ins had only two rules: don't honk your horn and don't wander around the parking area. The latter rule was relaxed if you were in the back row, where the lights were dim.

You also went to a drive-in to get the kind of food you couldn't get at home. Mom made meat, potatoes, gravy and vegetables seven times a week. In those days there were no ethnic foods available, at least not in my town; no burritos, tacos, salad rolls, etc. Spaghetti, yes, but I never had pizza until 1956 when a Shakey's opened. For exotic food you had to go to a drive-in, where you could order a Coney Island and a banana or root-beer milkshake. There was nothing like those things at home. The same was true for the lowly hamburger, which was elevated to an art form. A friend who was in the service shortly after the uneasy truce in Korea told me recently that during the first long year he had two desires: "To drive my '40 Ford again, and to have a hamburger at Yaw's (Drive-in)." A hamburger is an uncomplicated sandwich, and yet there was something special

The last light of a summer day in 1951, and a pair of Road Angel cars at Bart's Drive-In. Bob Simonis' 1941 Ford was original, has trunk hardware removed but holes not filled. Al Rogers' '28 A-V8 had entire rear end chrome-plated! Building was circular, with cars parked around it, then space to cruise through, then another row for parking, with space for incidental parking behind second row.

about them that couldn't be duplicated at home.

50¢ hamburger—30¢ milk shake

And the prices were reasonable, even if you were making only a buck an hour, which most of us were. In 1958 a Yaw's Top Notch "steak size" hamburger, with all the trimmings, was only 75¢. At most drive-ins you could get a full-size hamburger for under 50¢. At the beginning of the decade a cup of coffee was a nickel, later a dime, as was a glass of milk. At Rutherford's Triple XXX Drive-in root beer or Coke was a dime, a float was 25¢ and an ice-cream soda or thick milk shake was only 30¢. Yaw's served memorable French fries with gravy for 20¢.

In my case, I was usually so broke I ordered fries and a glass of milk, which at Flanagan's, my favorite drive-in, was 25¢ total. The fries came on a plate—not in a wax paper or cardboard holder—and I'd eat them slowly, painting each fry with a stripe of catsup from the squeeze bottle. I could make that order last an hour or two. The point of being there wasn't to get something to eat, I could eat at home; the point

was to simply sit in my neat car, looking cool, being seen. It seemed like everyone came to the drive-in, or at least passed through. My friend Al Rogers has similar memories. He said recently, "I had to make my appearance at the drive-in every night. You could sit in your car for hours with just a Coke, and no one bugged you—no one asked you to order more or move on."

See and be seen

The routine changed somewhat on Saturday night when, with luck, I'd have a date. Before I left home I made certain that my car was spotless, freshly waxed, the whitewalls unblemished. I'd pick up my date and perhaps we'd go to a movie, a double-feature, but we might leave before the second film ended to get to the drive-in earlier, while there was still a good crowd. I'd pull into the parking area in low gear, the duals burbling, the car glowing, my date beside me, and cruise slowly past the double row of

Day or night the drive-in beckoned like a mirage.

At some time, perhaps in late 'Fifties, Bart's became The Speck. Note that the original fluted column can still be seen but the clean, futuristic architecture is lost in the clutter. In 'Sixties the owner built canopy and island, making it impossible to cruise through the place. It was closed when I took this photo in 1985, and was demolished soon after to make room for a new Burger King.

cars to the far end. Then I'd turn around and hope for a space in the second or third row, where I could see the cars that came in and, of course, be seen.

Saturday we had to have hamburgers and Cokes, maybe fries. We talked while we waited, the car's interior rich with the odor of wax and fir that came from the small green tree hung in front of the heater. In good weather the windows were rolled down, and the smell of fried foods drifted in, honing our appetites. When it rained we huddled together, an island of humanity, rain pounding on the hood, windshield and roof. I had to start the engine to run the wipers, and if I had enough gas I'd let the engine idle and run the heater; if the battery were up I'd turn the radio to a pop station. When the food came I'd quickly crank down the window, haul the tray inside and close the window. The tray on the seat between us, we savored the tastes, the warmth, the luxury of the mo-ment, insulated against the wet, cold world beyond.

Pull out slowly, being cool

But most Saturday nights were balmy, at least in the tricky circuitry of memory, and after we'd finished I started the engine, turned on the lights and waited for the carhop. Then I pulled out, slowly, being cool, hoping the clutch wouldn't chatter, rapping the pipes as we headed down the road. Many nights we made the rounds of other drive-ins. On 82nd I could hit Merhar's, where many of the cycle guys hung out, then cruise through Rutherford's Triple XXX and back through Flanagan's again, just in case someone hadn't seen me. On Sandy there was Jim Dandy's, a real hot-rod hangout, another Rutherford's Triple XXX, then Yaw's, a place where the rich kids from Grant hung out, then on up to the Tik-Tok, a favorite gathering place for rodders since the 'Thirties. That might be enough for one night, my date and I might have other things to do, but if we felt like driving and if I had enough gas we'd hit Bell's Drive-In at the east end of the Ross Island Bridge, or Waddle's, or a couple drive-ins back in the west hills. Portland was a good-size city, but a few runs through the drive-ins and you felt like you knew, or at least had seen, everybody who was car crazy.

The notion of eating in one's car seems strange, but it caught on as soon as drive-ins were built in the 'Thirties. There were enough people with cars, and people had a certain amount of money to spend on restaurant food. Drive-ins were popular during the 'Forties, flourished during the 'Fifties and began to decline during the 'Sixties, when the fast food places began to appear.

At most drive-ins you could get a full-size hamburger for under 50¢.

Not exactly a drive-in

In 1954 a new kind of eating place opened in Portland; called Scotty's, it was directly across the street from the Tik-Tok. Although it wasn't exactly a drive-in, it was instantly popular. You parked, walked up to the window and took your food back to the car. Its motto was "Instant service, no tipping, no waiting." Scotty's ads claimed it served "the Best Hamburgers in Town at Any Price;" the quality was debatable, but the price was right. A hamburger was 19¢, a milkshake was 15¢ and fries were 11¢—the whole meal was only 45¢, which was about what a hamburger cost elsewhere. Kids parked in the lot, ate, talked and sometimes challenged each other to a drag race on the road behind Benson High. On Friday and Saturday nights, in good weather, a disc jockey played music from a trailer and took requests from the crowd. It was a favorite place for a date, and it sucked a lot of business away from the Tik-Tok across the street. It was the beginning of the end for drive-ins, and it foreshadowed the first McDonalds in the northwest that was built in Portland in 1960.

But the drive-in owners themselves were also responsible for the demise. Kids cruised through the drive-in lots as part of the ritual, and they often parked without ordering food; those were reasons for going to a drive-in. To discourage cruising, many owners began to erect traffic barriers. Bart's Drive-In (later The Speck) was designed using standard drive-in architecture; the building was circular, with a tall, non-functional fluted spire. Cars parked in a circle around the building, then there was an open area, then two more rows for cars. In the early 'Sixties the owner put a canopy from the front door straight across the lot for car service and it became impossible to cruise through the drive-in.

Gone—a way of life

Something similar happened to Ted's Drive-In near Detroit, which may have been the largest drive-in in the nation. Guys would come from all over to cruise Ted's, and I'm told that it was full every night. First the owner required that every driver had to order food. Later he charged admission to enter the parking lot, and hired security guards to collect the money. Still not satisfied, he built barriers to discourage cruising in the parking area. Ted's was a booming place in the 'Fifties and became even busier during the 'Sixties muscle-car era. But because the owner did so much to discourage the car guys—the very guys who were bringing in the dough—the place fell on hard times during the 'Seventies. When I visited Ted's Drive-In in 1981 the building was boarded up and the owner had gone bankrupt. Also gone were the muscle cars, cheap gas and a way of life.

You went to a drive-in to get the kind of food you couldn't get at home.

Yaw's Top-Notch Drive-In during the mid-'Fifties. This classy place in a good neighborhood near Grant High had good food, and was generally packed, as seen in this photo.

Bonneville 1955

It was like a dream realized.

"I quit!" I told the boss.

I'd worked at the garage for two years and was still earning exactly what I had earned when I started: a buck an hour. But that wasn't the only reason for quitting. I wanted a week's (unpaid) vacation so I could go to Bonneville; he refused. So I quit—Bonneville was that important to me. Even as the words came out in a rush I felt a sigh of relief, as if a weight had been lifted. Now I was free. I got the flathead Merc engine I'd rebuilt at work, gathered my coveralls and tools, loaded everything into my '47 Ford coupe and drove away from the garage and that period of my life.

Bonneville, here I come!

Since 1951 I had wanted to go to Bonneville. I remember sitting on the back porch in July of that year, looking at my roadster in the driveway and

Sleek chopped-and-channeled '34 Ford coupe was the Jabo-Harvey-Aluminum entry running a new Chrysler V-8.

Bert Leithold's '29-A roadster had lengthened frame, ran 270 GMC, turned 127 mph. Car is a street roadster today.

reading the 1950 issue of *Hot Rod Magazine* that devoted ten pages to the meet. It was an important event: "Hot Rods Top 200 MPH" was the cover blurb. I pleaded with my father, and while he was interested he simply didn't have the time or money. I might as well have thought of going to China. I lacked the time and money for the next three years. Then in July I was talking to a guy in the club, Frank Hahn, who had just bought a new 1955 Buick Special; he mentioned he'd like to take a trip. I suggested Bonneville. He soon agreed. Nothing could deter my plans now that I'd quit my job. It was like a dream realized, but I was apprehensive

because I wasn't there yet.

We left Portland on Saturday morning and drove to Boise, Idaho, where we stayed with a friend of Frank's. It was another long day's drive through Idaho and Nevada, through some of the hottest, most arid country imaginable. We had to stop in places where the road was being repaired after it had been hit by a flash flood, and about every half hour when Frank insisted on checking the temperature of his tires.

Weird minerals in the water

Travel is broadening—you learn things. We stopped at a service station for gas and a

drink of water. I learned that the water contained salts and weird minerals. All during that long week under a hot sun I longed for a glass of cold, clear Oregon water.

Skimming down main street

We got to Wendover in late afternoon; it was, if memory serves me, a small group of weathered buildings strung along the highway. There were perhaps two newer motels, a newish gas station, and a sprinkling of neon. It was typical of the small desert towns seen in the 'Fifties sci-fi films, where a giant lizard is perched on the rimrock. Here the center of interest was the casino

Bill Bond brought his '27 T on a '32 chassis from Ames, Iowa to compete in C-modified class.

"Crimson Pirate" was neat '32 Ford roadster owned by LeBlanc brothers.
Their name was familiar, as I'd seen their very detailed belly tank at Portland car show in 1952.

on the Nevada side of town, presided over by a huge cowboy. Cars were everywhere, but the one that stands out in memory was Joe Mabee's Sorrel-bodied sports coupe—it was skimming down main street, and while it might have been going 35 mph it conveyed the impression of going twice that speed.

Just as I'd imagined

Then we drove to the course. Things were simpler in those days. You drove east along the two-lane highway until you came to the billboard announcing the flats, and turned off. I have the feeling that we drove only a short distance before arriving at the pit area, and the timing course was just beyond that. I'd been dreaming of being here for four years, and it was just as I'd

A joy of Bonneville was seeing a coupe slightly taller than its tires! I'm surprised it has hubcaps.

Fred Larsen's '27 T had Chrysler V-8 in the rear, turned 203 mph.

You could bring your street roadster and possibly be competitive. This '32 is the Miller Automotive entry, running against a 150-mph record set the year before.

Another tall '32 roadster that had been taken off the street, made into a race car. And it probably had to wait another 20 years to get back on the street!

imagined it to be: The immaculate white salt that stretched to the distant mountains, shimmering like a mirage. In the pit area tents and parachute canopies provided shade against the merciless sun. Under them men changed engines or gear ratios, drank beer, laughed and talked.

From far out on the course came the sound of a high-winding engine and people stopped talking to listen as it rose higher and higher and then diminished into the distance.

The immaculate white salt stretched to the distant mountains, shimmering like a mirage. In the pit area tents and parachute canopies provided shade against the merciless sun.

Part of the excitement of Bonneville was running into cars I'd seen in magazines. This was the Horne Equipment Special, built by Joel Horne, a guy with bucks who also ran cars at Indy. This roadster had a Ranger airplane engine, turned upside down and backward, according to the article I'd read a couple years earlier in Hop Up.

Tall '32 5-window ran a Merc flathead, entered as Shig's Service Special, from Hanford, California.

Art Chrisman's radical Model A coupe turned 195 mph. Nose made from two '40 Ford hoods, one upside down.

Machines defying description

All around us were the machines. That first day I probably ran from car to car, drooling. There were belly tanks and streamliners and hot roadsters, and the scene—more impressive to me than the pits at Indy or LeMans—defied description. Some cars I had seen in maga-

zines, such as the Kenz-Leslie streamliner which had topped 200 mph at the 1950 meet running two Merc flatheads. This year it had three flathead V-8s, for a total of 885 CID fed by 9 Strombergs. There was the Cortopassi brothers' "Glass Slipper," a lovely purple dragster which ran lakester class here. It had a special body made of

fiberglass, a fairly new material, and the car looked so slippery. The Yeakel brothers had a hot roadster painted orchid with intricate purple flames and Von Dutch striping. Their tow truck, a '55 Ford pickup and their '54 Cadillac sedan were painted, flamed and pinstriped in the same colors.

I had been riding a BSA Gold

Program listed this roadster from Seattle, Washington. No roll bar required.

The pits were busy, full of neat machines.

*Ruddy and Weinstein roadster was built by Chuck Porter. Roll bar is not head-high,
rule was changed mid-week after a driver was killed.*

*Dana Fuller brought his sleek D-class streamliner with a diesel engine. I don't remember the
car's speed, or whether it got to the course, but I remember he fired it up somewhere—in
town?—and there was lots of smoke. Neat tow truck, but primitive trailer!*

Beautiful Cortopossi brothers' dragster, "Glass Slipper," turned 130 mph in quarter; ran 181 mph with 276-CID flathead. Fiberglass body was purple, with orchid-and-white striping. Car was recently restored.

Yeakel brothers' truck towing the Cortopassi "Glass Slipper." Flames were almost unheard of in 1955, at least where I lived. Yeakel brothers had matching roadster, truck and new Cadillac: painted purple, with lavender-and-pink flames—gorgeous!

Star for two years and was crazy about the Bonneville bikes. A 40-inch Triumph in a fully enclosed streamlined shell turned 191 mph, which I later learned was the fastest time ever recorded by a cycle. There was a dual-engined Harley, which might have been Chet Herbert's "Beast," and a rare Vincent with a reworked Mercedes Benz blower which, unstreamlined, turned 180 mph.

Famous people

I had my little camera out and was, for me, shooting a lot of film—perhaps 30 photos! I wish I had taken ten times that many, and now, of course, I wish I had had a tape recorder. I was surrounded by people whose names I had memorized from magazines: Don Waite, Bill

The Kenz-Leslie '32 Ford roadster, from Denver. Originally, this was push car for the streamliner, as I recall. By 1955 it was competing. In the 'Sixties it was primarily a drag car. It's gone full circle, and today it's a street roadster again.

Niekamp, Bill Kenz, Tom Beatty, Doug Hartelt, Bob Higbee, Art Chrisman, Tom Fox, Ak Miller and a host of others.

All week we were on the salt. The sunburn we got the first day slowly became a tan, and by Saturday we were dark! In the evening we spread our sleeping bags on the ground just outside of town, and although we worried about scorpions and rattlesnakes we didn't see any. We probably drove them away with our body odors because we were unable to take a shower during that entire week! Only liberal applications of Sea and Ski kept us socially acceptable when we ate breakfast in the cafe. Other meals, usually sandwiches, came from the makings we bought at the grocery store. We wore shorts and tennis shoes, sometimes a T-shirt, and stopped shaving. It was a great week!

Serious business indeed

The only unhappy moments came when we heard news of two accidents, one fatal. They happened far out on the course, and in that sense they seemed distant but they touched everyone, participant or spectator, who cared about speed week. The fatality, the first in seven meets, served to remind us that in spite of all the fun and excitement, running a car at 200 mph at Bonneville was essentially a serious business.

Frank Hahn and his '55 Buick.

'27 T with Merc flathead in rear came from nearby Salt Lake City.

I'd been riding motorcycles for a couple years, and I dug this twin-engine Harley, dubbed "The Monster."

New OHV engine in a belly tank ran fuel injection, magneto.

I was nuts about this new Porsche.

Bill Scace of Chicago drove his new Mercedes 300-SL to a record 136 mph. He later removed fan, muffler and blew a piston—a scarce item in Wendover!

Bonneville 1955 Souvenir Program

Al Drake beside the old sign at the entrance to the flats.

Biker!

Bikers seemed to know who they were.

If you were a hot rodder in the early 'Fifties, it was because you wanted to go fast. And if you wanted to go *really fast* you bought a bike.

That desire for speed was all that bikers and hot rodders had in common. They were two very separate groups, and only a few guys crossed over. That's funny, because it would seem that the two groups had a lot in common.

Hot rodders were outlaws who desired respectability, which resulted in mild schizophrenia. A hot rodder really wanted to drag it out at every stoplight, but he had that NHRA decal on the

Al Drake in 1954. After a couple of ratty bikes he got this 1951 BSA Gold Star, a factory racer with TT carb, tach, big brakes and an all-alloy engine. Fast! And worth some bucks today—he wishes he still had it, or even the jacket and boots.

Earlier he owned this "suicide machine," a 1947 BSA twin.

windshield right under his nose, and he could read the motto: "Dedicated to Safety." He also had his club plaque on the back of his car and he knew that, if he got caught racing, he could be bounced from the club. So he built a full-race engine and drove 35 mph around town.

I got defensive whenever I was called a *hot rodder*. I felt obliged to say that that was a term journalists misused. I didn't know what to call myself, so I'd say that I was a "true hot rodder," which suggested that the jerks with junky cars were, at the very least, false. But I was a greasy punk kid with an over-grown crew cut and ratty clothes who had difficulty looking respectable in general, especially when driving a cut-down roadster. I had so few clothes I had to wear my Road Angels jacket to church; the congregation probably thought I was having a religious experience.

Riding to their fiery deaths

Bikers, on the other hand, seemed to know who they were. Society had deemed them outlaws and most seemed to embrace that title. They didn't try to be respectable. You couldn't ride a bike through an Oregon rain-storm wearing a suit, so they wore Levi's, leather jackets, boots and greasy caps. They hung out at taverns, drank beer, rode noisy cycles and had a chick on the pillion seat. They weren't Hell's Angels yet, but they were moving in that direction.

My father always had one or two old Harleys around, but he didn't fit the biker image. The guys I was in awe of hung out at Merhar's Drive-in. This was the only place you could get exotic food, like Coney Islands and root-beer milkshakes, so any-thing that happened there seemed mysterious to me. From the safety of the back seat of my parents' car I saw the row of chromed bikes parked near Merhar's side door. They were big Harleys and Indians, suicide machines, with an occasional Velocette, Triumph or BSA. The bikers stood by their bikes, drinking beer, saying things I couldn't hear to the passing car hops. Long after the bikers had ripped out of the parking lot I could hear the angry staccato of their exhausts as they roared up 82nd, and I was certain that they were riding to their fiery deaths.

So, naturally, when I later put my roadster on blocks after three years of using it as a daily driver, I bought a bike. The first one was a 1947 BSA twin, a real dog, a "suicide machine," but at least I knew who I was.

Long after the bikers had ripped out of the parking lot I could hear the angry staccato of their exhausts as they roared up 82nd, and I was certain that they were riding to their fiery deaths.

Al Drake and his riding buddy, Bob Kaseweter, on BSA B-33. Looks like no one smiled during the 'Fifties.

Drake cutting a trail. Until the mid-'Fifties there were many such places to crank it on. The suburbs wiped them out.

"POPULAR RUSSETTA TIMING PRESIDENT"

LOU WAS BORN IN JAMESTOWN, NEW YORK AND MOVED TO LOS ANGELES in 1934, WHERE HE FINISHED HIGH SCHOOL AT MANUAL ARTS HIGH.

STARTED RUNNING AT S.C.T.A. MEETS IN '41, SWITCHED TO RUSSETTA in '48 WHERE HE RAN A '32 COUPE 2 WAY AVERAGE OF 126.64 MPH

BANEY RUNS A SPEED SHOP and SERVICE STATION IN L.A. LOU IS 29 YRS. OLD.

HE TURNED 132.54 OFFICAL ONEWAY THIS YR. AT RUSSETTA!

BOY! THOSE RDSTR. BOYS AREN'T GONNA BELIEVE THIS!

COUPES

TOM MEDLEY

LOU BANEY

From August 1949 issue of Hot Rod Magazine.

I Remember the Day James Dean Died Like It Was Yesterday

I thought how awful to die so young.

Actually, what I remember is the Monday following James Dean's death. He died over 40 years ago, September 30, 1955, a Saturday, en route to a race in his new Porsche Spyder. In those days I almost never listened to or watched the news, so I didn't hear of his death until the following Monday morning, on my way to work, on the car radio. I was stunned and fascinated, although I knew little of Dean, and probably my reaction had more to do with the demise of the Porsche.

I worked in the parts department of Lee Cosart's Dodge-Plymouth dealership, and at noon, as I ate my lunch in the room above the jungle of tailpipes and fenders, I read that day's newspaper. I learned that Dean was only 24, four years older than I was, and that death was instantaneous when his Porsche hit a '52 Ford sedan, driven by Donald Turnipseed,

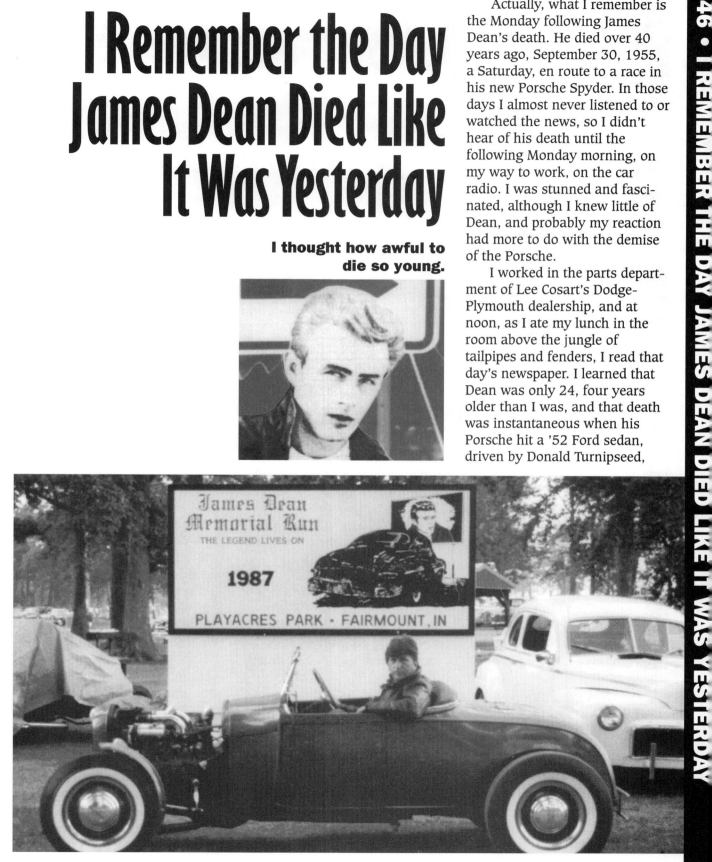

At the annual James Dean Memorial Run in Fairmount, Indiana, site of Dean's boyhood and the place where he's buried. Drake drove his '29 A-V8 to the cemetery at dawn, to commune with Dean's spirit.

Al Drake beside James Dean's grave (1988).

which turned in front of him on the rural California highway. I had a heightened sense of mortality anyway, and I thought how awful to die so young.

Defending Dean

In the afternoon I had to give a customer a ride home in the shop truck. He was a middle-aged man with strong opinions. The conversation veered toward Dean's death, and this guy voiced the opinion that anyone involved in an accident was at fault. Everyone was guilty; there was no redemption! I protested that it wasn't Dean's fault, what could he have done at that crucial moment? But this guy insisted, invoking a mixture of fate and irresponsibility, that Dean should not have been where he was.

I felt compelled to defend Dean for some reason, but how much could I have known about him? He had just finished his third film, *Giant;* his second,

Rebel Without a Cause, had not yet been released, so that left only *East of Eden*, which I feel certain I had not seen at the time of his death. But I must have known something about him— the rumors, Hollywood gossip, his interest in motorcycles and sports cars—to have established a sense of kinship with the young actor.

A month or two later I saw both *Rebel* and *East of Eden* when a downtown theater, capitalizing on Dean's death, showed them as a double billing. I drove my 1947 Ford mild custom, newly painted, and took a date. Her name was Hedy, which gave rise to numerous jokes; she was a girl with a reputation, but that's another story.

I almost forgot about her as I watched Dean move across the big screen. So much has been written about Dean in the 40 years since his death that I risk repetition, but much of what has

been written since then I knew was true that night in 1955. Here was the idol of a generation, someone who spoke for the voiceless kids in the audience. He was quirky, handsome but odd, given to surprise utterances and gestures. He was also cool, as if not much mattered, but it was a different attitude than that expressed by most actors of the 'Fifties, who had attended the school of repressed feelings. When he lost his temper, as in the fight scene in *Eden,* or when he embraced his father, Raymond Massey, in the same movie he expressed emotion in a genuine way. I've since read that the manner in which he played the scene with Massey was different from the way it was written in the script. On his own, driven perhaps by feelings he had for his real father, Dean fell to his knees, gripped Massey around the legs and began to cry. As we watch that movie today we can see the shock in Massey's face—

Porsche Spyder Replica

But most of all Dean conveyed a sense of loneliness, a feeling that every young person could identify with.

Al Drake asking for directions to the men's room. These James Dean figures are popular with car people, often used as show display props.

whoa! Things are getting too close here.

Different from his peers

Dean was truly different from his peers. Tab Hunter, Pat Boone, Robert Wagner, John Saxon, Dean Stockwell, Rory Calhoun get back! Those guys were wallpaper, hanging around. They were actors who seemed to have been taken from the same mold, all anxious to play the good-looking boy next door. Check out the hair—in the 'Fifties actors went on camera with every hair securely in place. Dean's hair was longer, and carelessly tousled. Not even Brando could do that.

Conveyed loneliness

But most of all Dean conveyed a sense of loneliness, a feeling that every young person could identify with. He was awkward, shy, introspective, often inarticulate. When he told his parents in *Rebel* to leave him alone, the audience could identify with his alienation. When he

Porsche Spyder in competition, from September 1956 issue of Sports Car Illustrated.

sat on the roof of the boxcar in *Eden,* the empty arms of his sweater wrapped around him as if someone were hugging him, in that instant, totally without dialogue, he created an image of pure isolation. This was the feeling that every young movie-goer had experienced at one time or another, and they loved Dean for showing them that they were not alone in their feelings. This was the feeling I felt as, after the movie and a hamburger, with the city's lights spread out below, Hedy and I sat in the '47 Ford's confines and hugged each other, fighting off the coldness of the world.

Ad from August 1949 issue of Hot Rod Magazine.

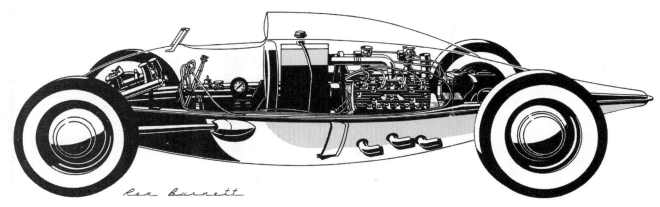

"World's Fastest Hot Rod" featured in August 1949 issue of Hot Rod Magazine.

Drive-In Theaters

A city of any size would have several such theaters.

Today it's almost impossible to find a drive-in theater, but during the 'Fifties they were a major form of entertainment. I saw a note recently that said that there were more than 4,000 drive-in theaters in the United States in 1958, which might have been when their popularity peaked. That would mean that a city of any size would have several such theaters, which indicates how popular they were.

The reasons for their popularity were similar to reasons why drive-in restaurants became extremely popular during the 'Forties and 'Fifties. America had become a more mobile society and there was extra money to spend on entertainment. There was also a baby boom during WW II and just after, and a crying baby wouldn't bother anyone, except perhaps its parents, in a drive-in setting. Money was saved because no baby sitter was needed.

Ramped parking

The first drive-in I remember was the old Amphitheater,

Only the sign remains from the 104th Street Drive-In Theater which was torn down in the mid-'Eighties. Present owner preserved history by putting a strong wire mesh around the sign (top photo).

probably the oldest drive-in in my town. It held 200 cars, parked in rows on a surface built in a series of "waves." A car parked with its front wheels on the raised section allowed the people inside to see through the windshield over the car ahead and to the screen beyond. Beside each parking space was a pole on which hung a speaker that the driver hooked on the edge of his window. All cars faced in the direction of the theater's screen, which, by today's standards, was not very large.

The Amphitheater was the only drive-in theater I can remember that was black-topped. That feature may have had something to do with the fact that a paved racetrack ran around the outside of the parking area. In fact, I think I went to the Amphitheater for the races before I went there to see a movie. They raced track roadsters—or *hot rods* as they were billed—on the track. During one race, a driver spun out and the car shot backward into the theater screen. He hit the back of his head on a metal girder with such force that it knocked his eyes from their sockets, as several people who were there have told me. Of course he died from his injuries.

This fatality stopped neither the races nor the movies.

Drive-in-theater phases

I have to break my drive-in-theater years into three phases. Phase one was when I went to the drive-in with my parents, a captive in the back seat of their sedan. Phase two was when I was old enough to go with friends my age; and phase three was when I would take a date to a drive-in. These phases are probably the same for most of the people who lived through these years, as if the drive-in-theater experience paralleled the coming-of-age process, and is part of our collective unconscious.

But first I have to puncture the romantic myth of the drive-in theater: I did not really enjoy seeing a movie from the confines of a car. I much preferred going to an enclosed theater. Every neighborhood had its own little theater and they flourished in my youth. I could easily walk from my house to the Aero Theater, see the movies—a double-feature of two full-length movies, a cartoon, newsreel, the coming attractions and, on Saturday, a serial—and walk home again. I loved the intimacy of the screen,

which allowed us to suspend all disbelief and to become involved with the story being projected, bigger than life, on a screen only feet away. The sound wasn't all that bad, either, as even a small theater had as good a sound system with as high a fidelity as could be found anywhere— usually made by Western Electric. It wasn't stereo or surround sound like we enjoy now, but mighty amplifiers powered big speakers spaced to create a "sound stage" as wide as the screen.

Distractions broke the illusion

I didn't get that same feeling in the drive-in theater—the screen seemed so distant, and the sound from the small speaker in the left front of the car was tinny and distorted. Other distractions broke the illusion of the film, things that bothered me even as I grew older. If it got cold, my father had to run the engine so the heater would work;

The drive-in solved the problem that has bothered young couples since the dawn of time: how to be alone together.

I took this photo of the 82nd Street Drive-In Theater in Portland, Oregon in 1985. A week later it was leveled, and a multiplex theater rose from the rubble.

if it rained, my father had to start the engine periodically to operate the vacuum wipers. The guy next to us would start his engine, too. Noisy mufflers and car doors closing somewhere obliterated bits of dialogue from the speaker.

But the drive-in experience became more interesting during phase two. I was old enough to drive, but lacked a car, so I'd go to the drive-in theater with some of my friends. We weren't mature enough to ask girls for a date, so we'd just go and horse around, being silly but not malicious at a time of life when stupid, trivial things create infectious laughter. Of course, we had to sneak into a drive-in. A couple guys in the front seat would pay for their admission. And two or more guys, depending on their size, would climb into the trunk. I suppose the theater owners were aware of this ploy and they probably searched the trunks on some cars, but I don't remember that any of us ever got caught. The father of a friend had a 1941 Chevrolet pickup with what must

have been one of the first canopies—I think it was corrugated aluminum, and it lacked a door or window above the tailgate. On at least one occasion several of us hid in the canopy behind some cardboard boxes. Once the truck was parked, we jumped out to see a free movie, although for the life of me I can't remember where we sat!

The third phase came when I was old enough to drive my own car to the movie and take a date. The car was cleaned and waxed, whitewall tires glowed, and I'd pick her up an hour before dusk. We'd arrive at the drive-in early, to be sure of a good location, where we could see the screen but possibly have some privacy. The drive-in or *passion pit*, as it had come to be called—solved the problem that has bothered young couples since the dawn of time: how to be alone together. It hardly mattered what film was showing, the big production was the growing darkness.

Light and sound show preceding

Then someone would impatiently honk his horn, even though it was too early to begin the movie. Another horn would sound, then another. Soon there was a cacophony of horns of all registers. Then a car's spotlight would shine on the screen. A second spotlight would appear and begin to chase the first puddle of light. Other spotlights shone on the screen, and the lights engaged in a confusing game of tag that went on until the movie began.

Actually, there was another phase, or at least a coda: when I was a new father, my wife and I would take our son to the drive-in, and for the same reasons people had gone to them 20 years earlier. I drove a 1948 Ford sedan with a huge back seat, and I could put the crib back there with the front legs dropped down. He was a good baby and he actually let us watch the movie, which was what we actually wanted to do. If he did

The last weekend for the Foster Road Drive-In Theater came in the fall of 1997.

fuss, one of us could lean over the front seat and give him a bottle without bothering our neighbors. For this reason, and others, the drive-in theater made perfect sense.

Knocked-out by television and rising land prices

By that time, the mid-'Sixties, the drive-in was on its way out, the victim of rising land prices and television, but so were the neighborhood theaters. Within a mile of the house where I grew up at the edge of Portland, there were three drive-in theaters and a neighborhood theater. Four theaters within a mile! The Aero, the neighborhood theater, closed in the early 'Sixties. One drive-in theater closed in the 'Seventies, another in the mid-'Eighties and the third, the last drive-in theater in the city closed in fall 1997 and has already been razed. I sup-pose it's safe to say that by the year 2000 no drive-in theater will exist, except in a museum.

Publisher's Note:

The idea for multi-screen theaters probably started with drive-in theaters. The Cactus Drive-In Theater (still operating in 1998 as the DeAnza Drive-In) had four screens with parking areas surrounding a centered refreshment stand and restrooms. The Rodeo Drive-In, now defunct, had two screens. Both theaters were in Tucson, Arizona. Some landowners used the theaters as a way to "bank" land while providing income as land prices rose, often substan-tially, over the years. In Tucson, where there are at least as many pick-ups as cars, the drive-in theater goers would place lawn chairs in the back of the truck, along with a cooler crammed with refreshments. They would back the truck into position so the viewers sat in the back of the truck in regal comfort to watch the movies.

The 'Fifties Lineup

The new models really were *new*.

At mid-century there was great excitement when the new car lineup was announced. This was true even for those of us who were too young to buy anything but an old jalopy, and whose parents were too poor to afford a new car. Certainly the excitement we felt then exceeds what we feel today when Detroit and Tokyo show us their offerings.

Part of the excitement was because the new models really were *new*. World War II had put automobile production on hold, and most 1948 models used pre-war shells with extra chrome. By 1949 the old pontoon fenders were gone and the new envelope body was in. This gave cars a longer, sleeker appearance, and allowed designers to create wider grilles and integrated taillights. Studebaker, for example, went from a frumpy-but-dependable

1956 Corvette

car to a sleek machine that seemed to owe something to the new jet plane. The first restyled Studebaker I saw was in 1949, and I remember the moment vividly. My father expressed an opinion that was voiced by safety experts: The car was potentially dangerous because motorists and pedestrians might have trouble knowing whether the car was coming or going.

Variety created excitement

Part of the excitement was due to the variety. In contrast with today's *uni-car*, when a Ford resembles a Toyota, cars of the 'Fifties were remarkably different. Buyers really did have a choice. No one would ever mistake a Hudson for an Oldsmobile or Chrysler product. The 1949 Plymouth station wagon was the first all-metal wagon, and it seemed light years ahead of the woodies built by the other manufacturers. In those days it was common to see a woodie wagon—or even a wooden-bodied Ford Sportsman convertible—with a splintered panel, the result of a minor collision, so a metal body, or even metal made to look like wood, seemed a step forward. In 1950 GM introduced the hardtop convertible with the Chevy Bel Air and the Olds Holiday, followed by Ford with the Victoria, and the removal of that center post made an incredible difference.

There was a car for every market or whim. If you thought big, you bought a Cadillac, Lincoln or Chrysler. Small cars, ahead of their time, included the diminutive Crosley, mid-size Henry J, Nash Rambler or Willys Aero sedan. The Henry J, named for Henry J. Kaiser, was also marketed under the name

1950 Studebaker

1954 Oldsmobile Fiesta convertible

1954 Corvette—a six cylinder!

Allstate and sold in Sears stores. One version was so low-budget it came without a glove box door or opening trunk lid. The 1950 Nash Rambler convertible was cute as a bug's ear, and the 1952 Willys Aero tudor was a car that begged to be sectioned about four inches.

Horsepower race begins

The beginning of the decade was also the beginning of the horsepower race. GM introduced its new OHV engines in the Cadillacs and Oldsmobiles of 1949, and against traffic powered by flathead V-8s and straight sixes they were hot engines. In 1951 Chrysler brought out its 180-hp "Fire Power" V-8, and it was a topic of conversation among the guys at school. I drove one a couple of years later, and while it had lots of go, the Torqueflite transmission took a full minute to shift gears. A car that won a lot of races was the Hudson Hornet, which came with the Twin-Power factory dual intake manifold on its flathead inline six engine. If Hudson had ever built a V-8, or even an OHV inline engine, it might have been a real screamer.

In the mid-'Fifties I yearned for a "modern" car. A friend and I met two young ladies with a new 1955 Ford Victoria, red and white, and I remember looking up at the perforated white headliner, thinking I should own this buggy. Later, I had my heart set on a slightly used 1956 Mercury Montclair four-door hardtop, mint green and white, which I looked at many times on the car lot. The price was $3,200, which meant all my salary for 55 weeks (plus interest), or three years of debt. I lowered my sights on a used '52 Merc hardtop with factory leather interior, then a black '50 Merc coupe, but didn't get those dreams either.

New parts for old cars

At the time I was working for a Dodge-Plymouth dealership, and was struck by the way materials on the new cars could be used on older cars. The new interiors used a fabric with either gold or silver thread running through it, and it was beautiful. The '55 Plymouth side trim would fit on older Fords or Chevrolets, and could be used as a paint divider. Chrysler had some beautiful taillights, such as those on the '55 Windsor. The textures of the new cars seemed to offer limitless opportunities to fix up older cars.

Marques disappear

By the end of the decade most models suffered from excesses—excessive chrome, excessive fins. 1958 Oldsmobiles, Buicks and Fords seemed less interesting, and the

The Torqueflite transmission took a full minute to shift gears.

1958 Buick

clouded Edsel came and went quickly. The car industry was changing, and a number of marques—even those with a long history, such as Packard, Willys, Hudson and Nash—disappeared, never to surface again.

1954 Buick

Hudson Hornet

1954 Chevrolet

1949 Ford Woodie

Girls & Rods

She loved being seen in this cool custom and, of course, boys were extremely interested in talking about the car!

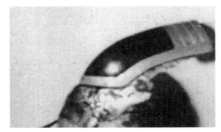

In the 'Fifties hot rodding was largely a male activity—and unmarried males at that. It's safe to say that most rodders were between 16 and 21 years old, and when a guy got married the roadster was traded for a sedan. I don't have statistics to support these generalizations—I doubt that any exist—so I have to base them on experience and observations and extrapolate from those.

I went to Franklin, a large high school in Portland, Oregon, and recently I was trying to remember the types of cars parked around the school in the early 'Fifties. There were the teachers' cars, of course, and a distinct minority, the students' cars. As I walked the side streets around the school in my mind, I realized that over half the student body would have been under age 16, which meant they could not have driven a car to school. Of the remainder, ages 16 to 18, roughly half were girls. And, unlike today, in the 'Fifties girls did not own cars. I can recall only one girl who drove a car during the time I went to

1946 Ford tudor in 1956, two years before Bonnie Peck got it. Later, car was metallic blue, with full hub caps and short lake pipes.

Bonnie Peck's 1946 Ford tudor. Photo taken about 1956, two years before she owned it.

high school. She became student body president during my senior year and it was her parents' car. There may have been others I did not see or have forgotten but it was clearly unusual for a girl in high school to be driving a car at that time.

Recently I have become friends with Roberta, a woman who was in the class ahead of me all through grade and high school, and she agrees with my conclusion about girls and cars. She did not have a car or even access to one during high school. As she recalls, "When I graduated in 1952 I was bound and determined to get a car." Her desire to own a car, and later, her husband's attitude toward her car, may be a microcosm of the gender differences about machines.

Roberta graduated, went to work, and in a few months saved enough money to buy a nearly new 1951 Chevrolet. She remembers, "When I bought that car I didn't even have a driver's license. I got my license the same week I bought the car." She met a fellow her age and they soon became engaged, She remembers that he had two different cars, both convertibles. "He had a real cute little green one when I met him, but it was in really bad shape. It kept using oil—we had to put a quart of oil in it every time we'd go any place! After that he got a red convertible, was it a Dodge? It would get a vapor lock in hot weather."

She doesn't remember whether he had customized or modified either of his cars, but he was determined to put his imprint on Roberta's car. "I got the car before we were married, that was my car, it was all paid for. And it was in beautiful condition. Then he got this hair-brained idea that he wanted to change the taillights, as my mother put it. 'A hair-brained idea—those were her words.'" Her husband removed the stock taillights and chrome trim and replaced them with a pair of 1949 Buick taillights; he ground down the sheet metal around the lights and sprayed on primer. "That was all he did to the car, the lights. They worked, but he never painted the metal. My mother was so mad! That should have been a big warning to me. If it'd been now, I'd have told him, 'Keep your lunch hooks off my taillights. No on touches my taillights without my permission.'"

My sister Bonnie had a similar experience; she did not

own a car during high school and got one shortly after graduation. In 1958 I was going to college full-time and working nearly full-time in a gas station. One of the guys I worked with was Mike—his last name escapes me—and I think he was a couple years younger, perhaps 18 or 19. He was a tall, good-looking kid with lots of black wavy hair, and he had a nice customized 1946 Ford tudor sedan that he kept in perfect condition. He'd worked at the station for a few months when he decided that he wanted to get married or he had to get married (a term no one uses anymore), and to do that he needed money. The Ford was the only thing he owned and he put it up for sale.

It was a cool car

Bonnie had graduated and needed a car. I traded a primo 1951 BSA Gold Star for a nice 1948 Chevrolet four-door sedan, which was a bad trade. Then I traded that Chevrolet for a one-

owner 1932 5-window coupe, which was a good trade. Between those deals I had intended to give the Chevrolet to my sister, as a good brother should have done. When I looked around for a car for her, my eyes fell on Mike's 1946 Ford tudor parked at the far pump island. It was a cool car and although it was his daily transportation, it could have gone into a car show, then or now. The tudor body had been nosed and decked, the headlights were frenched, the taillights were frenched 1949 Ford units that sat low in the fenders. The grille was from a 1948 Oldsmobile. The entire interior had been done in rolled-and-pleated blue-and-white Naugahyde; the headliner was white with blue piping. The original plastic sections of the dash had been replaced with aftermarket chrome pieces, and the garnish moldings were either plated or painted blue, as was the dash.

The bumpers were '49 Plymouth, and I think it had

electric doors (or at least the handles were removed). The flathead V-8 had aluminum heads, a dual intake manifold, and lots of chrome. It may have had other things, such as a cam and headers, but I'm not sure now. In general, this was a really nice example of a typical mid-'Fifties semi-custom, with duals and short chrome lakes pipes, whitewalls and full hubcaps. And it had some unusual touches, such as the four rows of louvers in the hood. The paint was dark-blue—enamel, I think—and the paint and interior had been recently done.

Her first car!

Because I was a hot rodder, and because I would've loved to own that car, I thought it would be fine for my sister. Bonnie must've thought so too, because she bought it herself—her first car! I can't remember how the deal was financed, but I think she paid $400 total—about what a nice-running semi-custom went for then. Bonnie bought it in the fall of 1958, and drove it every day to her job across town. I think the car had a dropped axle, but it wasn't extremely low and got around town fine. The dual pipes were mellow, and not loud enough for her to get in trouble with the law. She was, and is, an excellent driver, and the stick shift was not a problem. She loved being seen in this cool custom and, of course, boys were extremely interested in talking about the car! She and her girlfriends loved to cruise the drive-in restaurants, where everyone looked at them. She kept the car in pristine condition, always washing and waxing it, and although she lacked a garage, the car was never dirty. In January 1959, my car was in

Raked look, with car lower in front than in back, was popular in mid-'Fifties, as was white paint. Car had trunk chrome blacked out, stock taillights leaded in, frenched lights were from 1949 Ford. It had a '49 Plymouth rear bumper when Bonnie owned it.

the repair shop and, being a generous person, Bonnie let me take her car to Eugene, about 120 miles south of Portland, where I was going to school. I found the Ford to be a swell road car and it never missed a beat. The freeway extended only to Albany, and the rest of the trip I drove on the old Highway 99, a two-lane road. The speed limit was 75 mph, and the Ford was capable of running all day at that speed. In Eugene I had to park it on the street, and, most amazing, the car was never vandalized. Try that today!

Most custom cars went downhill

The history of most custom cars is that they went downhill, usually at a rate faster than a stocker. Some guy ran into the fender of Bonnie's custom, and it was totally his fault. Then she began having trouble starting the car, primarily because the louvers on the hood allowed rain to drip on the spark-plug wires. One night at The Speck Drive-In she smelled raw gasoline, and seconds later flames came up through the louvers after one of the Stromberg 97s had flooded. The fire was quickly extinguished, but some wiring was charred, as was the top of the hood.

Not a gender thing

This was not a gender thing—the same thing happened to cars owned by guys—in fact, it happened to me in my roadster. What went wrong had nothing to do with her abilities or that she was a girl. The blame should fall on me—if I had lived in the same town, or if I had driven to Portland and worked on the car—it might have proved trouble-free, or at least have been a good

Roberta's husband decided that her nearly new Chevrolet needed 1949 Buick taillights.

driver for years. An easy solution would have been to replace the hood with a stock hood, and to replace that dual manifold with a stock intake manifold; then the car would have been a neat semi-custom that would have been as dependable as hundreds of other fat-fendered cars of the 'Forties that filled the streets of Portland in those days.

Bonnie had the car repaired, and the Strombergs replaced with Chandler-Groves carbs. She continued to drive the car for some time—months, perhaps a year or more—and then something else happened. No one seems to remember what it was, something minor, but for some reason her husband-to-be took an ax to that beautiful Ford and whittled it into pieces. No one

even remembers what happened to the pieces, which, if one had them today, would make a spectacular swap-meet booth. But there were no swap meets then, and the parts apparently went to the dump. Another example of pieces of the past utterly lost!

Things I Don't Remember

Blue dots give taillights a purplish glow.

Recently, due to the efforts of Scott Cedergreen and his rodding buddies, the state of Washington has given the OK for the use of blue-dot taillights in vehicles 40 years and older. Although blue dots are regularly used in custom cars and street rods, they're illegal because the law in general says that cars must have only red or amber lights in back. The blue dots give taillights a pur-

plish glow, which I suppose some motorists might find confusing.

Scott called to ask whether I knew the history of blue dots, and I had to admit that I didn't. I added that when I was a hot rodder in the 'Fifties I never had blue dots, I didn't yearn for blue dots, none of my friends had blue dots in their cars and, try as I might, I can't recall ever seeing a car in the 'Fifties with blue-dot taillights. One evening recently I was visiting a friend and on his garage wall he had an original advertising display filled with blue-dot taillights. Called *Lynx Eye replacement lenses*, they were made by the Johnson Glass Company of Chicago, Illinois. The newest lens was 1939, so it's safe to assume that the display came out about that year. The friend also recalled a radio program of the early 'Fifties, "Could This Be You?"—a kind of docu-drama, where a Washington State policeman stopped a motorist for having blue-dot taillights on his car.

Blue dots—Not!

My memory gets foggy these days, so I took a look at the advertising in some 'Fifties rod and custom magazines; I could not find a single advertisement for blue dots. I looked at feature cars in those magazines and I couldn't find even one with blue dots. I began asking people who had reached the venerable age of 50 whether they had blue-dot taillights in their cars when they were growing up, and not one said he had. A couple guys who grew up in the Ohio-Tennessee area said they'd seen cars with blue dots, so maybe it was a regional fad. One guy said he'd seen cars with blue dots, but the cars were "add-on" customs, gook wagons, with mudflaps, dual antennae and fox tails, so perhaps blue dots appealed to a certain type of car owner. But I'd love to know how many people in the 50 to 60 age bracket actually had blue dots on their cars in the 'Fifties, where they lived and how else the car was altered. It seems to me that we've created a recent trend and attributed it to a tradition that never existed.

Fuzzy dice

Ditto for fuzzy dice. Approximately 75% of the custom cars, or cars of the 'Fifties seen at a car meet today, have large, colorful fuzzy dice hanging from the inside rear view mirror. They're purely ornamental, and the reason they're there, we're told, is because this was a popular trend during the 'Fifties. Again, I could be wrong, but I don't recall anyone having fuzzy dice hanging from his mirror. I checked out some old ads and could not find anyone selling fuzzy dice—not even places like Auto Discount, which sold fake continental kits and Bermuda bells. I'm certainly willing to admit that a guy could've won a pair of dice at a game of chance on the carnival midway and hung them from his mirror, but it wasn't a common practice. I remember people hanging air fresheners, necklaces, garters and even baby shoes from the rear view mirror, but not dice. On my mild custom '47 Ford in the 'Fifties I had my high-school graduation tassel hanging from the mirror, and I remember others who did the same thing; that was far more of a trend than was the non-trend of fuzzy dice.

Flamers—probably not!

Another recreation of a so-called 'Fifties trend are the "flamers" seen at custom-car meets. Some custom-car owners attach a spark plug to each echo can, wire it to an electrical source and install a switch on the dash; with a rich fuel mixture and the switch on, the result is a flame that shoots out two or three feet and lasts for seconds. "Flamers" are especially popular in the midwest and on the east coast. Until recently, when they were banned by KKOA and others, there were flame-throwing contests; contestants would converge in an area at night, pull up to the line individually, rev the engine and emit incredible flames from the back of the car. There was great variety, and the quality of the flames depended on the size of the exhaust pipe, exhaust extension and the amount of fuel available for burning. Some flames were anemic flickers while others were a minor inferno. Judging was done by the response of the crowd that gathered to watch, and they often numbered in the hundreds.

I thought the event was great fun, and although I could see the potential for disaster I have to admit most of us seem to have a fascination for fire. But when I was told that this was a reenactment of a 'Fifties activity, I had to raise an eyebrow. I had never seen a car shoot flames before 1985, although it's easy to imagine some guy, way back when, probably hooked a Model T coil to his exhaust pipe and surprised a few pedestrians. It's a trick that doesn't require sophisticated technology. But in the 'Fifties, customizers were so busy trying to get their cars closer to the pavement and then trying to get them to ride reasonably well, they didn't have time to build a flame-thrower. And they would've got strange looks if they'd drilled and tapped their exhaust extensions to accept a spark plug!

Now there might've been a couple guys who had flaming exhausts on their cars in the 'Fifties, but they weren't rodders or customizers. An article in the October 21, 1951 *Oregonian* lauds true hot rodders and condemns cars that the public might call *hot rods*.

As an example of the latter, the paper ran a photo of a car spitting flame; the headline read, "Flaming exhaust frowned on by law, true hot rodders." The car is a stock 1930 Model A Ford coupe, complete with tall wire wheels. Although the photo ran in an Oregon newspaper, the car has a California license plate; it was probably a wire-service photo. In fact, the whole deal looks like a set-up. The spark plug is held to the tailpipe by a piece of twine, which suggests that this was a one-shot deal for the photographer because after a couple flames that twine would go up in smoke. But if this photo were picked up by newspapers all over the country people might've got the idea that flame throwing was a popular fad. Perhaps from this single example came the "tradition" we celebrate today.

GIANT DICE
For the Car

BIGGEST NOVELTY SENSATION SINCE FOXTAILS

Here is the latest novelty for autos. Car dice are 2 inch cubes covered with colorful angora-type fur. Light as a feather — they swing over the dash — hang on the rear view mirror. Furnished in white or black. Blue or Green with contrasting dots.
No. 10318—White With Red Dots
No. 10319—White With Black Dots
No. 10320—Black With White Dots   Pair
No. 10329—White With Blue Dots
No. 10330—White With Green Dots   **$1.49**

From J. C. Whitney & Co. 1959 catalog.

Update on Blue Dots, Dice & Flamers

Suspicions confirmed.

A few months ago my column focused on three things that rodders today attribute to 'Fifties trends but which I can't remember being associated with cars of that time period: blue-dot taillights, fuzzy dice hanging from the rear view mirror and exhaust pipes that would shoot flames at the driver's command. That column generated a lot of mail. While no one accused me of being senile, I am aware that my memory is imperfect. I'm less concerned with being right, more concerned with confirming or denying a trend. I think it's important to set the record straight while people from the 'Fifties are still around to bear witness to what really happened.

I was curious how wide-spread these trends were, if they could be considered trends. I suggested that they could've existed in certain areas of the country and were perhaps peculiar to certain kinds of cars. The letters that came in confirmed some of my suspicions.

I said that I could not find any cars in magazines that used blue-dot taillights. Jon Rivers sent in a Xeroxed page of a car featured in *Hot Rod Magazine*, October, 1958, which had blue dots. This may well be the only magazine car with blue dots, and I should've remembered it because my old roadster was featured in the same issue. It's a strange car: a fenderless 1936 Ford roadster, channeled, dipped doors, etc. But it's true, that the '49 Chev taillights did have blue dots. That car was from Baltimore, Maryland, and ace metalman Donn Lowe, who grew up in Connecticut, said blue dots "were found on cars throughout the northeast. Illegal—but everybody had them. They were on every mild custom, mostly shoeboxes, 1949-51 Fords, Mercs and Chevs. This was in the late 'Fifties."

Chuck Klein recalled "we saw a lot of them (blue dots) in the Cincinnati area but serious rodders shunned them. Usually they were found on cars bearing Kentucky license plates that also sported mud flaps, reflectors and necker knobs." A faxed letter from Keeper of the Faith shows the writer still remembers vividly the pair of blue dots he saw one night in Beaumont, Texas in 1962. (Which suggests they were not common.) Stan Ochs and Wally Graham grew up in small Idaho towns in the late 'Fifties, and each remembered one car in their respective towns with blue dots; they were 1937 and 1938

Fords. Stan later bought the '37 and realized that a daub of black paint had been put on the backside of the blue dots; this didn't save him from getting a ticket when he got stopped for having them.

Nertz recalled that blue dots were used in Canada. He put them in a custom 1948 Ford tudor that he built in 1954. He wrote, "A number of mild customs in this area had blue dots but not all that many. About '59 or '60 John Law (began) handing out citations to anyone having blue dots so they pretty much disappeared until recent times."

James Brooks and Bob Gregor both grew up in So-Cal in the early 'Fifties and both remember a few cars with blue dots; they said the police cracked down on cars with them. Bob Gregor added an interesting note: "At that time the police motorcycles had a blue dot taillight so they didn't want civilians to copy them for safety reasons (so they said)."

Bill Aitchison lived in Saginaw, Michigan, between 1942 and 1955, and remembers a number of cars with blue dots. "They played a memorable part in the only chargeable accident I ever had. It was a warm evening in July, 1953 and I came across the Genesee Bridge with the sun at my back. I was about the third car in the stream of traffic… (when) the left-front brake hose on my 1941 Ford decided to let go and I whacked the car in front of me, a '50 Ford with blue dots… Even back then there was a public question about the legality and safety of those lenses and I tried to make that part of my defense… The judge listened, thought for a minute or two and said, 'No, this one's yours.'"

Fuzzy dice = "ticket bait"

Many people remembered fuzzy dice hanging from the rear view mirror. Bill Aitchison thought the custom came about because dice were often painted on circle-track race cars. Nertz suggested they were primarily found on "gook wagons" but others felt the dice were found in a broad range of cars. Donn Lowe said that they were "absolutely used, the standard thing for anyone into cars in the northeast in the late-'Fifties—duals, skirts and fuzzy dice. There were two kinds, regular and the real fuzzy kind."

James Brooks and Bob Gregor gave this trend a fascinating twist. They said in So-Cal in the 'Fifties the dice were made by the guy's girlfriend. Bob said, "The stores sold the Styrofoam cubes and the girls knitted the covers in colors to match or contrast the color of the car. One had to be pretty serious with a girl before she would make you a pair of dice." James added, "The dice were usually hand-knitted, with dots from angora wool. They were knitted by girlfriends, wives or someone would sell them to an individual. The really nice pairs were never made commercially. The dice went along with a pair of hand-knitted angora-wool diamond-pattern argyle socks. If the lucky guy was really cool the dice and socks would be made by different girls." James remembers that the dice were in all kinds of cars, and that they were "ticket bait" because the cops claimed the dice obstructed the driver's view.

Flamers—maybe

People were vague on flamers; it took on the qualities of an "urban myth," with the writer remembering that someone else had seen a car shooting flames. I think only one person mentioned a specific car. Steve McNicholas was waiting for a bus on East Broadway in Portland, Oregon, in the early 'Fifties when flames shot from the dual exhausts on the '40 Ford sedan that was waiting for the stop light. Bill Aitkinson recalled "sitting in Raymond's Drive-In in Saginaw on at least two occasions when cars that I didn't recognize…cut loose with a blast of flame." Nertz remembers "a number of cars that had them installed" in his area of Canada. Chuck Klein remembers "guys talking about it but I never saw one…Guys that used the stuff were called *shot rodders*."

Well, I'm glad we got all that cleared up. I enjoyed reading the letters, and I learned some interesting things. But to show we haven't solved all the world's problems, Nertz raised the lid on a couple scary subjects: "And three-cap lake pipes! I don't ever remember seeing a pair of 'em on a custom car (back then). And sun visors!!"

Blue Dot Tail Lamp LENSES

Gives the Car That Added Distinction.

A ruby red lens with a blue dot in the center that reflects a soft blue light.

Year	Car	Stk.No.	Ea.
BUICK			
1953	All	42873	1.49
1954	All	42874	1.49
CHEVROLET			
41-48	All	42110	.89
49-50	All	42112	.89
51-52	All	42116	.89
1953	Stop	42083	.89
1953	Tail	42926	.98
1954	All	42579	1.10
1955	All	42027	1.19
1956	All	42872	1.15
1957	All	42996	.89
1958	All	42-1210	.80
FORD			
42-48	All	42137	.89
49-50	All	42139	.89
1951	All	42081	1.19
1952	All	42082	1.19
1953	All	42084	2.19
1954	All	42580	1.59
1955	All	42030	2.25
1956	All	42871	2.99

Year	Car	Stk.No.	Ea.
FORD (Continued)			
1957	W/O Back Up	42995	3.29
1958	All	42-1208	2.59
MERCURY			
49-50	Rt.	42090	1.45
49-50	Lt.	42091	1.45
52-53	All	42927	.98
PLYMOUTH			
50-52	Rt.	42087	.89
50-52	All	42088	.89
1953	Late	42581	1.19
1954	All	42582	.89
PONTIAC			
49-50	All	42163	.98
51-52	All	42085	.98
53-54	All	42086	1.10
55-56	(exc. starchief) All w/o trim ring	42-1211	1.99
1957	All	42-1212	2.59
1958	All w/o trim ring	42-1213	1.99

From J. C. Whitney & Co. 1959 catalog.

The Service Station

The gas station played an important role in the commmunity.

The Arab oil embargo of years ago reminds us of, one, how dependent we are on the automobile for transportation and, two, how the big oil companies have the consumer over a barrel. Before a shot was fired, the price of gas at the pump escalated sharply. Many people, including some politicians, yelled about price gouging by the oil companies, but the price continued upward until, at this writing and in this area, it's above $1.50 a gallon, an increase of 50¢ a gallon in only three weeks. We'd all like a raise of that sort. The local station has a sign, "We're mad as hell too!" as if to say that it's the bigger folks, not the station, that you want to blame.

Some of us remember the Arab oil embargo of 1973, when gas jumped over night from around 25¢ to a buck a gallon. It never went back down. Detroit began planning smaller cars, but a million Datsuns and Toyotas arrived first. The auto industry

Bob Newcombe's Chevron station at S.E. 81st and Glisan, circa 1952. Les Connor's 1940 LaSalle convertible at the island. There were lots of hot rods at this station in the early 'Fifties. Today it's only a repair shop.

*Pat Brost built an old-time service station with restored pumps.
It matches his '29 A-V8 roadster, which has flathead and lots of 'Fifties details.*

has never been the same. A final change was the decline in the number of stations as the oil companies closed them down. They became dry-cleaning establishments, liquor stores, mini-markets and parking lots. As the number of stations declined, so did the services offered by those left. There was no competition, so no need to offer free air, paper towels, towing or even an attendant who would actually attend to your car!

In the 'Fifties the gas station played an important role in the community. Not only could you get gas there, you got your car's fluid levels checked and air put in a sagging tire; you got advice and directions; you got a map at

no charge, and a Coke for a nickel. Any station could charge your battery, fix a flat tire, do lube and oil. And there were plenty willing to rebuild your starter and generator, even your engine! The station was often open later than the stores, so it was an island of light in a dark world.

A station's reputation was based on the quality of the gas it sold—many motorists were brand-conscious, and truly believed Chevron was better than Signal, or vice versa—and the services offered. The enterprising owner of a station had a certain status in the community. Service stations were places where we hung around in the evenings, but they were also places of employ-

ment and some of us aspired to owning one. A station had a permanence, we believed, and a guy could make a good living running one. There was a future in the business, and on Career Day in high school many of the guys saw the operation of a service station as a realistic career choice.

From 1948 to 1952 my father had an Associated station in Lake Oswego, Oregon, and I spent a lot of time there. I loved the notion of the world coming to us, to get gas and oil, to shoot the breeze and to go on again. It was a small community, and my father seemed to know everyone. It was also an upper-class community, and his station was the oldest building in town. I sometimes wished he had a new, modern station but when we came in from the cold and huddled around the oil stove, with my father smoking a cigarette and his helper ringing up a two-dollar sale, I think I envisioned the station as a kind of Norman Rockwell painting: a warm and cheery place, with free suckers for the kids.

I felt a little differently about it when my father became too sick to work and I knocked off the last month of my junior year to help run the place. I pumped gas, changed tires, fixed flats, lubed and changed oil in cars full-time and took home what my father would've got: $50 a week. It seemed too little.

Regal—a new concept

I worked in several stations after that, usually part-time. Then in 1957 I got a job in a truly modern station, and saw a vision of the future. It was a Regal station, one of a chain; the station and the marketing concept were new. It sold only

gas and oil—no flats fixed, no batteries charged, no engines overhauled. It was a whole new idea in service stations and the idea looked good to me; I was tired of busting my knuckles. At Regal I wore a white shirt and pants, and a black-plastic bow tie. All I had to do was pump gas, occasionally add a quart of oil, and I could work an eight-hour shift without getting my hands dirty.

The station was on the corner of S.E. 122nd and Stark. Portland had begun to grow to the east and although there wasn't much traffic there in 1957, the planners correctly figured the city would push out into its suburbs. There were two stations on other corners, and to maintain the volume of sales Regal could always undersell the others by at least a penny a gallon. Every other week there was a gas war; gas dropped by a half-cent a gallon until it dropped to 15¢ a gallon. The other stations were forced to lower their prices but they could never

match Regal's price. Then, the point having been made, the price would shoot upward overnight to 21¢ or 22¢ a gallon and the downward spiral would begin again.

While the station didn't do any automotive work, it did sell more than gas and oil: there were stacks of Hula Hoops, plastic pails and wash tubs, pogo sticks, aluminum buckets, lawn chairs and chaise lounges. The pump islands were lined with goodies, and in a large room next to the office, called the *Premium Room*, there were chrome coffee pots, irons, toasters, gold watches, bracelets, phonograph records, you name it—all at rock-bottom prices. It was like a small department store attached to the station, and a woman worked there full-time during the day.

Quick service— real service!

People came to Regal for the same reason they go to McDonald's: low prices and quick service. In those days you got

Abandoned service station outside of Congress, Arizona.

service! Every car, regardless of the amount of the sale, got its windshield and rear window washed, its headlights and taillights wiped, its windshield wipers wiped, and the driver questioned about water and oil. I remember people driving in during a rainstorm and, without making a purchase, requesting that their tire pressure be checked.

All attendants had to wear white uniforms, be clean-shaven and have neat haircuts. The assistant manager checked the workers before each shift to make certain their appearance conveyed the kind of image that Regal stations desired. And, there were inspectors, people hired by the company to check up on the workers. They pulled into the station in the guise of an Ordinary Customer; you couldn't know who might be an inspector, and so you had to treat *every* customer the same way. You had to run to the island and be standing there when the driver got his window rolled down. "Yes, sir, fill it up, sir?" If he growled he wanted a buck's worth, you had to smile and repeat, "Yes, sir, a dollar's worth of ethyl." "Naw," he'd growl, "regular." Sometimes I wanted to hit the guy, but I was required to smile and say "Yes, sir, a dollar's worth of regular."

The intersection and the concept projected a view of the American Dream, or a *Popular Mechanics* vision of the future. The street was so new the pavement wasn't even dented, and the Regal station stood out like an advertisement for the good life. For 24 hours a day red-and-purple pennants flapped in the breeze; a line of plastic propellers spun, attracting the eye. All night long it was a clean, well-lighted place for the traveler between Portland and Gresham. At the ends of the pump islands were inexpensive and bright-colored gimmicks, a cornucopia of the Age of Plastic. The Premium Room was filled with enough appliances to outfit one of the suburban homes which were springing up on the empty countryside, that vision of growth that the city fathers espoused. In the center of all this activity was the Regal station, and above it floated the purple Regal Crown, an emblem to show that we were king, that America was king, and that gas would last forever!

I remember a terrible choice I had to make. I was offered the position of assistant manager, which meant a good salary, various benefits and a chance to move up in the company. But to do it I would have to quit college. The manager took me into his office and told me of the opportunities I'd be missing if I didn't accept the position—there was the future, the growth in the area, the company. I debated—and finally opted for college and whatever that might lead to.

I was certain that the manager was correct—how could a business concept like Regal's not succeed?

The purple crown faded

But something happened somewhere along the line. Long before the Energy Crisis, long before the price of gas shot skyward, something happened and the dream soured, the purple crown faded, the plastic propellers weathered to a dull metal color and all the glory that had been Regal was gone. When I drove into the station in the mid-'Seventies it was a shell of its former self and doing business under another name. Paint was peeling from the pumps. There were no Hula Hoops, no bounty of plastic, no joy of chrome lawn furniture—just the flat, dull business of pumping gas.

In the late 'Forties, early 'Fifties this was the D & M Associated gas station in Lake Oswego, owned by author's father. As with so many other gas stations, it has become something else—now it's a baby boutique.

Restored pumps at auction.

Company inspectors pulled into the station in the guise of an Ordinary Customer.

Momento Mori

As time moves on there are fewer and fewer of us.

There was no better time to be a hot rodder than during the Fabulous 'Fifties, but a problem inherent with having been a rodder during that decade is that as time moves on there are getting to be fewer and fewer of us. I think it was the day before yesterday that we were all young, hanging around the filling station after work, kicking a tire, and now suddenly we are older. Or gone! All those years of too many calories, too many cigarettes, too much beer and just plain hard work catch up— and something you thought would go on forever comes to an end.

The first to go was Myles Theberge. In 1951 he built a beautiful '32 3-window, stock-height, fenderless, full-race and painted pinkish-red. He ran it at the drags, often with dual tires on the rear for traction. He put it in shows and took home trophies for both go *and* show. A good-looking guy, always happy, with a crew cut and a boyish grin, he bore a remarkable resemblance to actor Bob Cummings.

I saw Myles some time in the mid-'Fifties, and I think 25 years passed before I saw him again. It was at the Happy Days Picnic, and we talked for a while. He'd never been away from rods, but

Al Drake.

247

like many 'Fifties rodders, he'd had to curtail his activities while establishing a business and raising a family. He was strokin' now; he'd just finished a full-fendered '32 roadster and was hitting all the events.

Looked like he did 25 years ago

What amazed me was the way he had not aged—he looked almost exactly the way he had 25 years before, sandy crew cut and all. Talking with him made me feel as though I were back in the 'Fifties, and that we were at a joint Road Angels and Ramblers club meeting in Ray Van Dorn's barn! A year later he was dead of cancer.

Then I heard that an old friend, Jim Davis, had cancer and it was bad. Jim was only a couple years older than me, and we had been good friends way back when. We were in the same club, the Road Angels. Although I was in high school and he was driving a chopped '40 Ford coupe when we met, we did a number of things together. We went to the Oakland Roadster Show a couple of times, and knocked around at Bonneville.

After I got out of high school I got a job driving a truck around Portland; Jim also drove a parts truck—in fact, he drove for the same company for over 30 years—and we saw each other, often on company time.

We began to have dinner about once a week. We'd meet in what was then a novel restaurant, a place that cooked hamburgers on an open pit. I can recall those meals vividly: the meat was quality lean beef, splashed with a seasoning sauce, seared on the grill and served on sesame buns. You added what you wanted—pickles, thick slices

of onions, the works. Jim and I would each eat a couple of those burgers, a pint of barbecued beans, drink cups of coffee; then he'd smoke a string of cigarettes. It was great! I was 19, skinny, able to eat more food than I could afford. Jim was about 22, husky, glowing with health. Later he'd put on too much weight, maybe 100 pounds too much, the result of years of eating, drinking and enjoying life with his car buddies.

New Old Stock (NOS) parts

When we met for dinner he began to tell me about a new weekend activity: he needed parts for his several '40 Fords, and so he had begun to hit Portland's Ford dealerships looking for whatever they might have on the shelves. The year was 1954, and it turned out that most Ford dealers had a *lot* of '40 Ford parts that they wanted *badly* to get rid of. Jim began buying up brand-new '40 Ford fenders, running boards and trim still in wrappers. Then dealers urged upon him factory wiring harnesses, gauges, knobs, all kinds of things they had not been able to move in a dozen years.

So Jim began buying everything and storing it in garages. He always wanted things perfect, and he replaced everything on his '40 Fords. There wasn't much interest in restoring '40 Fords in those days, most people were taking the trim off. Jim traded some things, and the rest—tons of it—sat in storage. Then during the 'Sixties, when swap meets became popular, he became a vendor of what became known as NOS (New Old Stock) parts. He was a popular figure at west coast meets, and an expert on

Fords from 1928-53. He even made the trip to Hershey—almost 3,000 miles—to buy and sell, and said that some of his prized personal items, such as the rare 1932 Ford dealer cuff links, were got in the Detroit area.

In the late 'Seventies he completed a gorgeous '36 Ford roadster. He opened a business, Jim's Model A and Ford V-8 Parts, but continued to drive the truck for the same company he'd worked for since the early 'Fifties. I stopped to see him in the summer of 1977. He was the same boyish, bearish guy, red-cheeked and good-natured. His crew cut had grown into a post-Beatles, over-the-ears period hair-do, and he had put on too much weight. He chain-smoked and loved beer. I arranged to interview him on tape and we twice set up appointments but he didn't show. I saw him only once again, in 1980, when we both had cars in the Portland Roadster Show. He drove out in his '36 roadster, happy as hell, a trophy on the seat beside him.

In 1984 I was back on the west coast and I heard that Jim had cancer. I called several times and, although his voice was greatly changed by chemo-therapy, we had some nice chats. I wanted to visit, but he was too tired, and later I had a cold I was afraid he'd catch. I wanted to see him, and kept saying that I'd visit next week. Well, I didn't, and a few weeks later at the Corvallis swap meet a mutual friend told me that Jim died the night before.

A month earlier, at the big Portland swap meet, some friends were manning the spaces that Jim had had for years. One guy looked familiar, and as we shook hands I heard a name I hadn't thought about for a long time: Gary Klaus. I'd known him through the 'Fifties, but hadn't seen him since 1961. He hadn't changed much in appearance—a little heavier, hair getting gray. What I couldn't see, and didn't learn until later, was that he'd had a heart attack at 48, and a second one would kill him a couple years later.

As we shook hands I thought he seemed subdued. The Klaus I remembered had been a wild man, a bruiser, a guy who was quietly menacing. He was a big guy, and he looked so tough most opponents would back down from a fight. When he didn't scare the hell out of me, we got along great, but there always seemed the potential for violence.

And no man drove a car with a heavier foot. I remember once coming back from the drags at Scappoose and Klaus shot past in his Model A sedan with the hopped-up four-barrel. He was really cooking. A few miles down the road I caught up with him. He had stopped on the shoulder, and was standing beside the car, drinking a beer. When I got out I saw the trouble: a large puddle of steaming oil collected under the engine, and when he raised the hood I saw that he'd put a rod right through the side of the block! The next week he had another A banger engine, and he was wringing it out!

In another lifetime...

That image of destruction and rebirth seemed to have happened only a year or so ago, and at the same time it seemed to have happened in another lifetime. Ditto images of Jim Davis and me one evening in 1955 at Bonneville, or cruising through the night in his 1950 Olds Holiday toward Oakland, or

Jim Davis (left) and Al Drake at Bonneville, 1955.

Jim Davis in his Model A and Ford V-8 parts business, 1977.

Al Drake's roadster in 1956, after it was rebuilt. His son, Moss, owns it now, in this same condition.

Klaus at Yaw's Top-Notch drive-in wanting to break someone's head, or Davis finding me a primo '34 Ford 5-window that lacked only an engine and helping me tow it home and we actually got it *inside* the garage before my mother ordered me to haul it back. Those images and a hundred others seem so distant and yet so close. The question that keeps rearing its ugly head is: where has time gone?

No one will know the answers

I have this feeling often when I go to a swap meet and see tons of rusty metal: there are people who know what that stuff is, who can identify the year and make of a knob or door crank or dome-light lens, but when they die no one will know the answers. In a similar vein, I can imagine an enthusiast in the year 2050 wondering about life in the 'Fifties. I want to let him know that there was lots of blue sky, good roads, little traffic and

young men who were nuts about cars and wanted only two things: to live forever, and to spend that time building hot rods.

Index

1933-34 Ford roadsters were rare, and Gary Davis, of the Road Angels, had the nicest one around. Black, with white padded top, it had full race flathead. Davis is standing beside the car at Madras, where it ran 3/4 mile strip.

Chuck Blanchard's 1949 Chevrolet coupe was one of perhaps ten (or fewer) chopped hardtop cars in Portland by 1955. His ran a big GMC six on the street and strip.

Jim Miller's '23 Dodge roadster with Ardun heads, built in 1955-56. Jim was in both Shaundos and Ramblers clubs.

Jack Lofton, of the Ramblers, built his rear-engine belly tank in 1950. Flathead V-8 had power, but linkage made for slow shifting at drags. He put the engine in his neat '29 A-V8 roadster.

Roger Cunningham's really low 1950 Ford convertible. Chopped and dropped, this was a full custom with radiused wheel wells, '53 Chevy grille, etc. Built in the mid- 'Fifties.

Don Telen's 1940 Mercury coupe was customized in 1955-56, chopped during the summer of 1956. Telen and Cunningham belonged to Portland Kustoms. Both cars were purple, and cruised together.